T0240503

Communications
in Computer and Information Science   1506

More information about this series at https://link.springer.com/bookseries/7899

Wei Lu · Yuqing Zhang ·
Weiping Wen · Hanbing Yan ·
Chao Li (Eds.)

Cyber Security

18th China Annual Conference, CNCERT 2021
Beijing, China, July 20–21, 2021
Revised Selected Papers

 Springer

Editors
Wei Lu
CNCERT
Beijing, China

Yuqing Zhang
University of Chinese Academy of Sciences
Beijing, China

Weiping Wen
Peking University
Beijing, China

Hanbing Yan
CNCERT
Beijing, China

Chao Li
CNCERT
Beijing, China

ISSN 1865-0929   ISSN 1865-0937 (electronic)
Communications in Computer and Information Science
ISBN 978-981-16-9228-4   ISBN 978-981-16-9229-1 (eBook)
https://doi.org/10.1007/978-981-16-9229-1

This Springer imprint is published by the registered company Springer Nature Singapore Pte Ltd.
The registered company address is: 152 Beach Road, #21-01/04 Gateway East, Singapore 189721, Singapore

Preface

The China Cyber Security Annual Conference is the annual event of the National Computer Network Emergency Response Technical Team/Coordination Center of China (hereinafter referred to as CNCERT/CC). Since 2004, CNCERT/CC has successfully held 17 China Cyber Security Annual Conferences. As an important bridge for technical and service exchange on cyber security affairs among industry, academics, researchers, and practitioners, the conference has played an active role in safeguarding cyber security and raising social awareness.

Founded in August 2001, CNCERT/CC is a non-governmental non-profit cyber security technical center and the key coordination team for China's cyber security emergency response community. As the national CERT of China, CNCERT/CC strives to improve the nation's cyber security posture and safeguard the security of critical information infrastructure. CNCERT/CC leads efforts to prevent, detect, alert, coordinate, and handle cyber security threats and incidents, in line with the guiding principle of "proactive prevention, timely detection, prompt response, and maximized recovery".

This year, the China Cyber Security Annual Conference was held in an online-offline hybrid manner during July 20 to 21, 2021, in Beijing on the theme of "Jointly Combating against Threats and Challenges to Data Security" as the 18th event in the series. The conference featured one main session and six sub-sessions. The mission was not only to provide a platform for sharing new emerging trends and concerns on cyber security, and discussing countermeasures or approaches to deal with them, but also for finding ways to join hands in managing threats and challenges to data security. There were over 500 attendees at our event. Please refer to the following URL for more information: http://conf.cert.org.cn.

We announced our call for papers (in Chinese) on our official website, after which 51 submissions were received by the deadline from authors with a wide range of affiliations, including NGOs, research institutions, universities, telecom operators, and companies. After receiving all submissions, we randomly assigned every reviewer with five papers, and every paper was reviewed by three reviewers. All submissions were assessed based on their credibility of innovation, contribution, reference value, significance of research, language quality, and originality. We adopted a thorough and competitive reviewing and selection process which took place in two rounds. In the first round we invited the reviewers to conduct an initial review. Based on the comments received, 28 papers passed and the authors of these 28 pre-accepted papers made modifications accordingly. In the second round the modified papers were reviewed again. Finally, 14 out of the original 51 submissions stood out and were accepted. The acceptance rate was 27.45%.

The 14 papers contained in this proceedings cover a wide range of cyber-related topics, including deep learning, API security, SMS fraud, cryptography, data traceability, security situation awareness, watermarking techniques, darknet access activity, vulnerability detection and social network security, etc.

We hereby would like to sincerely thank all the authors for their participation, and our thanks also go to the Program Committee for their considerable efforts and dedication in helping us solicit and select the papers of quality and creativity.

Finally, we humbly hope these proceedings of CNCERT 2021 will shed some light for all readers in their forthcoming research and exploration of their respective fields.

November 2021

Wei Lu
Yuqing Zhang
Weiping Wen
Hanbing Yan
Chao Li

Organization

General Chair

Wei Lu — CNCERT/CC, China

Organizing Chair

Hanbing Yan — CNCERT/CC, China

Publications Chairs

Yuqing Zhang — University of Chinese Academy of Sciences, China
Weiping Wen — Peking University, China
Chao Li — CNCERT/CC, China

Program Committee Chairs

Wei Lu — CNCERT/CC, China
Hanbing Yan — CNCERT/CC, China

Members

Yang Zhang — CISPA Helmholtz Center for Information Security, Germany
Zhenkai Liang — National University of Singapore, Singapore
Guoai Xu — Beijing University of Posts and Telecommunications, China
Purui Su — Institute of Software, Chinese Academy of Sciences, China
Xinhui Han — Peking University, China
Haixin Duan — Tsinghua University, China
Chao Zhang — Tsinghua University, China
Senlin Luo — Beijing Institute of Technology, China
Hua Zhang — Beijing University of Posts and Telecommunications, China
Jiang Ming — University of Texas at Arlington, USA
Qiaoyan Wen — Beijing University of Posts and Telecommunications, China
Min Yang — Fudan University, China
Baoxu Liu — Institute of Information Engineering, Chinese Academy of Sciences, China
Meng Xu — Georgia Institute of Technology, USA

Yongzheng Zhang	Institute of Information Engineering, Chinese Academy of Sciences, China
Huaxiong Wang	Nanyang Technological University, Singapore
Guojun Peng	Wuhan University, China
Qiang Wang	Carleton University, Canada
Xinguang Xiao	Antiy Cooperation, China
Bo Lang	Beihang University, China
Chunhua Su	University of Aizu, Japan
Xueying Li	Topsec Cooperation, China
Kui Ren	Zhejiang University, China
Yuanzhuo Wang	Institute of Computing Technology, Chinese Academy of Sciences, China
Wenling Wu	Institute of Software, Chinese Academy of Sciences, China
Feifei Li	Stanford University, USA
Stevens Le Blond	Max Planck Institute for Software Systems, Germany
Yaniv David	Technion, Israel
Siri Bromander	University of Oslo, Norway
Zoubin Ghahramani	University of Cambridge, UK
Li Ding	CNCERT/CC, China
Zhihui Li	CNCERT/CC, China
Tian Zhu	CNCERT/CC, China
Ruiguang Li	CNCERT/CC, China
Yu Zhou	CNCERT/CC, China

Contents

Data Security

A Robust and Adaptive Watermarking Technique for Relational Database

Yexing Zhang[1], Zihou Wang[4], Zhaoguo Wang[2,3(✉)], and Chuanyi Liu[2,3]

[1] School of Cyberspace Security, Beijing University of Posts
and Telecommunications, Beijing 100876, China
[2] School of Computer Science and Technology, Harbin Institute of Technology (Shenzhen),
Shenzhen 518055, China
wangzhaoguo@hit.edu.cn
[3] HIT-QIANXIN Data Security Research Institute, Shenzhen 518055, China
[4] National Computer Network Emergency Response Technical Team/Coordination Center of
China, Beijing 100029, China

Abstract. A watermarking technology is a kind of marker covertly embedded
to identify ownership of the copyright. The existing database watermarking techniques cannot automatically adapt to different types of data and have poor robustness. In this paper, we present a new robust database watermarking scheme. The
scheme can automatically adapt the watermarking algorithm and parameters according to the data characteristics for numerical and text-based data. We
have theoretically established and verified experimentally the performance of our
method in terms of robustness and less data distortion. This makes it suitable for
copyright protection, owner identification, or traitor tracing purposes.

Keywords: Relational data · Database watermarking · Copyright protection ·
Automatic adaptation · Safe and reliable

1 Introduction

In recent years, various industries have emerged with complex and diverse data, and these
data have become important production factors [1]. As the value of data is increasing,
people are more and more concerned about copyright protection, and the awareness of
copyright protection is gradually increasing. Relational data is one of the most common
types of data, therefore, the copyright protection of relational data has become one of
the hot spots of research in related fields.

In the early 1990s, digital watermarking techniques were proposed by related
researchers. As an important branch of information hiding technology, digital watermarking is an effective method to achieve copyright protection [2]. In 2002, Agrawal
and Kiernan et al. proposed the first data watermarking scheme for relational data by
combining the characteristics of relational data [3]. Since then, researchers in related
fields have started their research work on data watermarking. Data watermarking refers
to embedding the identity information of the owner who constitutes the data into the

W. Lu et al. (Eds.): CNCERT 2021, CCIS 1506, pp. 3–26, 2022.
https://doi.org/10.1007/978-981-16-9229-1_1

structured data, and the embedded information should satisfy the data with less distortion. When the original data is illegally used or maliciously copied and disseminated, the database watermarking extraction technology can be used to extract the original watermark from the embedded data, thus confirming the copyright of the data and tracing the responsibility of the leakage.

The relational data can be commonly classified into numerical data and textual data. It has the characteristics of low data redundancy and frequent data updates, so the distortion reduction and attack resistance have become a difficult problem and research hotspot in the industry. The numerical data watermarking algorithms include Least Significant Bit (LSB) algorithm [3], difference expansion algorithm [4, 5], prediction-error expansion algorithm [6, 7], and histogram shifting algorithm [8–10], etc. The text-based data watermarking algorithms mainly contain natural language-based text watermarking algorithms [11–16], invisible coding algorithms [17–20], and punctuation coding algorithms [21], etc. The current research progress that there is the lack of algorithms for multiple data types and the automatic adaptation of parameters, as well as the lack of evaluation of the effectiveness of these algorithms in terms of distortion and robustness.

In this paper, we propose for the first time a robust and adaptive relational data watermarking scheme for numeric and text-based data, which can automatically adapt the variable row embedding ratio and selected embedding column of data watermark according to the data characteristics, in addition to the data watermark embedding/extraction algorithm and parameters through data type analysis, data volume evaluation, data sensitivity analysis, automatic parameter setting, and result visualization mechanism techniques. It has better robustness against common attacks such as data watermark addition, modification, and deletion attacks. It can effectively cope with watermark erasure and attack detection. It can process numerical and text-based data simultaneously. With the distortion effect and various robustness experiments, it has been proved that the scheme has less data distortion and higher robustness, which can be used as a data watermarking scheme.

The main innovation points of this paper are as follows.

1. A robust and adaptive watermarking technique for a relational database is proposed, which can effectively solve the problem of data copyright validation and leakage traceability.
2. For common numerical and text-based data, an automatic adaptation watermarking algorithm is proposed for the first time, which combines data type adaptation, data volume evaluation, data column sensitivity judgment, parameter tuning, and result visualization to achieve intelligent adaptation of database watermarking algorithm and model parameters.
3. With the data distortion and robustness experiments, it is shown that the watermarking algorithm with automatic adaptation and parameter tuning proposed in this paper has better robustness and usability.

2 Related Work

In contrast to multimedia data, the relational database mainly stores structured data, which has the characteristics of low data redundancy and frequent data updates [22].

Therefore, on the basis of multimedia data, a series of database watermarking schemes have been proposed by researchers in related fields, combining the characteristics of structured data.

In 2002, Agrawal and Kiernan used a hash function with a key to pick specific tuples and attribute values from the data and then embed special values in the least significant bits of the attribute values [3]. These special values constitute the database watermark and it doesn't affect the normal use of the data. In 2004, a database watermarking technique based on secret sorting and grouping was proposed by R. Sion et al. to perform watermark embedding by changing the distribution of data in each grouping [23]. The algorithm reduces the effect of watermark embedding on data distortion and improves the resistance to subset modification attacks and subset addition attacks. However, it has poor robustness to subset deletion attacks. In 2003, Niu Xiamu et al. proposed a watermarking scheme capable of embedding a small number of meaningful strings in a database. This algorithm is based on parity matching for embedding the watermark, which allows the primary key hash to be paired with the least significant bit. The presence of this matching relationship is verified when detecting the watermark [24]. However, it is only possible to verify whether such matching rules are embedded in the data, but it is not possible to detect the real watermark information.

With the purpose of reducing the distortion caused by database watermarking techniques on data, a series of reversible techniques for structured data have been proposed by scholars. Currently, the common reversible database watermarking algorithms include difference expansion [4, 5], prediction-error expansion [6, 7], and histogram shifting [8–10]. (1) The difference expansion refers to picking an attribute value pair from a specific tuple and then implementing watermark embedding and data recovery by performing a specific numerical transformation on that attribute value pair [4]. In 2008, Gupta et al. proposed a scheme in which reversibility of watermarking was achieved using a difference expansion technique [4], which increased the capacity of watermark embedding and enabled more watermark information to be embedded in the original data, but the scheme was not specified for relational data. In 2013, Jawad et al. proposed a difference expansion database watermarking method based on genetic algorithm [5]. This method improves the robustness of database watermarking algorithm and reduces data distortion. (2) The prediction-error expansion technique achieves reversibility of the watermark by using a prediction algorithm which obtains the predicted value, and then selects a certain attribute value from the original data for which a numerical transformation similar to the difference expansion is performed. In contrast to difference expansion, this technique only requires modifying the value of an attribute in a tuple and it has less effect on data availability. In 2004, Thodi et al. proposed a watermark embedding process by introducing a prediction-error technique to implement image watermarking, in which the main idea is to embed the watermark into the difference between image pixel points [6]. In 2012, Farfoura et al. transformed recognizable images into bit streams embedded in the least significant bits of numerical attributes and achieved watermark reversibility by prediction-error expansion [7]. This method is mainly for floating-point type data and can be used for data tampering detection. However, it does not work for handling integer type data. (3) Histogram shifting is required to first calculate the differences of some attribute values in the data, and use the first non-zero number of these differences to construct a histogram, which is then used to change the distribution characteristics of the non-zero number according to certain rules to achieve the embedding of the watermark [8]. When data is recovered, it is sufficient to restore the data distribution characteristics of the number. This method can track the degree of data distortion, but it is difficult to resist high-intensity attacks. In 2006, Zhang et al. proposed a reversible watermarking scheme by calculating the difference of attribute values to construct a histogram, and then using histogram expansion technique to achieve reversible watermarking, which increases the watermarking capacity [8]. In 2018, Hu et al. proposed a watermarking method combining genetic algorithm and histogram shifting prediction-error techniques, which used a genetic algorithm to generate optimal watermark information, and calculated a histogram of prediction-error for candidate attributes, which was then used to embed the watermark into the peak of the histogram using histogram expansion techniques [9]. The method reduces the distortion of the data and improves the robustness against various watermarking attacks. In 2019, Li et al. proposed a low-distortion digital watermarking method for Hu's watermarking scheme, which improved the method of selecting the embedding watermark position in Hu's watermarking scheme as well as changed the histogram shifting direction, which was experimentally shown to achieve lower data distortion [10]. In 2014, a reversible watermarking scheme proposed by Iftikhar et al. used the concept of mutual information in information theory to select the embedding position of the watermark and obtained the optimal watermark by genetic algorithm to reduce the data distortion [25]. This method is highly robust and can extract the embedded watermark information and recover the original data even in the face of large-scale watermarking attacks. However, the acquisition of the optimal watermark requires a large amount of computation, which is less efficient in the face of massive data. In 2015, Tong Deyu et al. applied the database watermarking technique to GIS by embedding the interval location value and watermark together in the database, which ensures the correspondence between the watermark and the watermark location and improves the correct rate of watermark detection [26]. The embedding and extraction of this watermarking algorithm were not dependent on the primary key, which could still extract the watermark information even if the primary key was attacked. In 2019, Wang Chundong et al. classified the existing techniques mainly using whether distortion is introduced to the underlying data, focusing on the watermark generation methods and embedding methods of several typical watermarking schemes and in which they compared the attacks and application scenarios that each type of scheme can cope with [27].

In recent years, the database watermarking technique based on non-numeric data has also been further developed. In 2004, a watermark embedding by attribute value replacement method was first proposed by Sion R et al. to determine whether a watermark is embedded based on the relationship between primary key values and non-numeric attribute values [28]. In 2010, Hanyurwimfura et al. proposed a non-numeric relational database watermarking method, which first dynamically selects tuples and attributes in the watermark embedding phase, and then uses an edit distance algorithm to move the horizontal position of a word according to the watermark bit thus achieving watermark embedding [29]. In 2015, by constructing two different watermark embedding mechanisms, Melkundi S et al. were able to embed watermarks in text-based and numerical data, respectively. For text-based data, in case of embedding a binary number 1, an invisible Unicode character is added to the text data and not added if a 0 is embedded; for numerical data, the watermark is embedded through the lowest significant bit of the data [30].

Comprehensive the above watermarking schemes can be seen that only the literature [30] considered embedding watermarks into textual and numerical data separately, which did not consider the problem of automatic data type adaptation. Therefore, for this problem, a new robust and adaptive database watermarking scheme is proposed in this paper.

3 Scheme

The proposed scheme contains three parts according to data flow: (1) watermark pre-processing; (2) watermark embedding; and (3) watermark extraction. In which, the adaptive algorithm of watermark embedding contains (1) data type adaptation; (2) data volume evaluation; (3) data column sensitivity judgment; (4) automatic parameter setting; (5) result visualization mechanism in five parts. In the pre-processing stage, the processing is mainly done for copyright information. Before the embedding stage of the watermark, data type adaptation, data volume evaluation, data column sensitivity judgment, automatic setting of parameters and other operations are performed, and then by designing and using five database watermarking algorithms to embed/extract the watermark, and the final visualization results are fed back to the user, which solved the problem that the data cannot be automatically adapted in the current relational database watermarking scheme. The system architecture of the scheme is shown in Fig. 1.

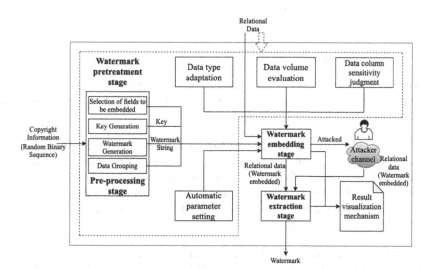

Fig. 1. System structure.

To verify the effectiveness of this scheme, theoretical analysis, and practical experiments were used, and the relevant symbols used in the scheme and their meanings are shown in Table 1.

Table 1. Symbols and meanings in the scheme.

Symbols	Meaning	Symbols	Meaning
D	Original relational dataset	D_{AW}	D_W after the attack
D_W	Relational datasets with embedded watermarks	γ	Secret Parameters Collection
K_S	Key Collection	N_g	Number of data groupings
X_{max}	Hide function maximum list	X_{min}	Hide function minimum list
r	Tuple	$r.P$	Primary key value of tuple r
W	Watermark	ξ	Minimum number of members
T^*	Threshold of the optimization algorithm	G_i	Constraint set
S_i	Single data subgroup	$text$	Text to be embedded
bit_w	Watermark Bits	$text^*$	Complete the text of the marked-up sentences
l	Watermark length	W_d	Detected watermark
$Similarity$	Watermark similarity	$message$	Copyright information of the data owner

3.1 Pre-processing Stage

The specific tasks of the pre-processing phase include (1) the selection of the fields to be embedded and the key generation, (2) the watermark generation, and (3) the data grouping.

Selection of Fields to be Embedded and Key Generation. For the selection of fields to be embedded, the selection of attribute fields to be embedded is performed in a semi-automatic manner, i.e., the user can independently select the columns in which the attributes to be embedded are located. In terms of key generation, the specified length of key is generated based on the specified range of key characters and combined with the database and data table names.

Watermark Generation. Before the watermark is embedded, it is necessary to convert the watermark information to format for embedding into the data. In this paper, Chinese and English strings containing meaning are selected as watermark information and then embedded in the format of binary sequences. Therefore, first of all, the watermark information message should be converted into a binary sequence, which is defined as shown in Eq. (1).

$$BinarySequence = Binary(message) = \{b_1, b_2, \cdots b_i, \cdots b_l | b_i \in \{0, 1\}\} \quad (1)$$

where *message* represents the watermark information, and *BinarySequence* represents the ASCII value corresponding to the *message*, i.e. the data stream in binary format, $\{b_1, b_2, \ldots, b_i, \ldots, b_l\}$ is a set of binary numbers, The length of the sequence *BinarySequence* is the sum of the binary bits occupied by all elements in the *BinarySequence*, i.e. $l_b = len(\{b_1, b_2, \ldots, b_i, \ldots, b_l\})$.

Data Grouping. Before embedding the watermark information, it is also necessary to group the data in the database. With data grouping, a number of non-intersecting subgroups can be created in the database. The database can be grouped using Eq. (2) to obtain the number of each data subgroup in the database.

$$partition_i = H(K_S || H(K_S || r_i.pk)) \, mod \, N_g \quad (2)$$

In which, $partition_i$ denotes the number of each data subgroup after grouping, $partition_i = 1, 2, 3, \ldots, N_g$, N_g is the number of data subgroups; $H(\cdot)$ is the hash function. The hash function is used for the key (K_S) and the primary key ($r_i.pk$) of the database tuple, which can ensure the grouping is more secure. The "$||$" represents the string concatenation operation and *mod* represents the remainder operation.

The detailed process of the data grouping algorithm, as shown in Fig. 2.

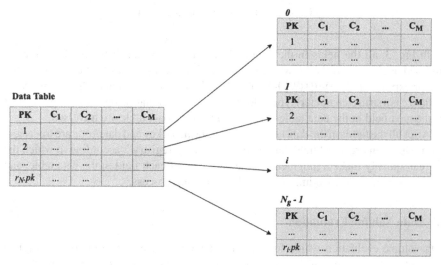

Fig. 2. Data grouping algorithm.

3.2 Data Type Adaptation

Data type adaptation, which focuses on the automatic adaptation of fields in the data table before the watermark is embedded.

In this section, the proposed data type adaptation module only considers the adaptation for numeric and string (character) type data. The detailed adaptation process is shown in Fig. 3.

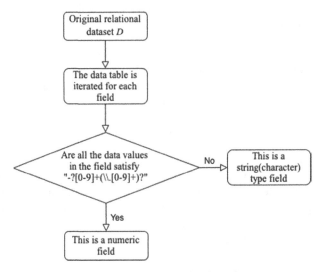

Fig. 3. Data type adaptation flow chart.

In Fig. 3, all the fields in the data table except the primary key and date/time are traversed one by one. If each row of data values of the field c in the data table satisfies the regular expression "-?[0-9]+(\\.[0-9]+)?", then the field c is a numeric field; otherwise, the field c is a string(character) type field. The same determination operation is performed for the next field in the data table until all fields in the data table are traversed.

After all the fields in the data table except the primary key and date/time are traversed, this module can create a "field data type management registry", according to which the user can quickly make a judgment on the data type of each field in the data table, and then choose the corresponding watermark embedding process.

3.3 Data Volume Evaluation

Data volume evaluation which focuses on evaluating the data volume of the original data table before watermark embedding work. For each original data table, by default the first field in the table is the primary key, and if there is no primary key in the data table, it will generate a new field for the data table as the primary key. Therefore, the last row of the tuple in the data table has the primary key value which is the total number of data volumes in the data table.

After the total amount of data in the data table is determined, the module can determine the number of data group divisions N_g for this data table based on the total number of tuples *sum* in the data table and the data grouping control parameter λ entered by the user, which is calculated as shown in Eq. (3).

$$N_g = \frac{sum}{\lambda} \tag{3}$$

With Eq. (3), the number of divisions that meet the user's expectations can be calculated.

After determining the number of data groupings N_g, the user can specify the proportion of rows embedded in the watermark μ, then the section will randomly select *fetch_count* rows of data in the data table to embed the watermark. Where *fetch_count* is the number of tuples that will be embedded in the watermark, which is calculated as shown in Eq. (4).

$$fetch\_count = sum \times \mu \tag{4}$$

When the user does not specify the specific value of μ, the proportion of rows embedded in the watermark μ defaults to 100%.

3.4 Data Column Sensitivity Judgment

Data column sensitivity judgment, which is mainly based on the sensitivity to determine whether the data column in the data table is more important before the watermark embedding, and then determine whether the data column needs to be watermarked embedded, to achieve an intelligent selection of the column to be embedded.

It is assumed that the data table contains multiple tuples, each of which has the same data schema and is all $R = (pKey, C_1, C_2, \ldots, C_n, fKey)$, where *pKey* represents the primary key, *fKey* represents the foreign key, and $C_1, C_2, \ldots, C_n$ represents the field columns. The primary key, the foreign key and the fields with unique constraints are grouped into the core field column set, denoted by *Core*; the non-sensitive numeric fields and text-based fields are grouped into the optional field column set, denoted by *Select*. In which, the non-sensitive numeric fields that is not sensitive to small changes in the value of the feeling (modifiable) fields, such as length, coordinates, weight and other fields.

In order to ensure the integrity of the data table, by default for the primary key *pKey*, the foreign key *fKey* does not perform the operation of watermark embedding.

If the number of embeddable fields in the data table is *Emb*, the relationship between *Emb* and *Core* and *Select*, as shown in Eq. (5).

$$Emb = Size(Select + Core) - 2 \tag{5}$$

When the *Emb* value is determined, the watermark is not embedded under every embeddable field, but the watermark embedding field is selected jointly based on multiple information such as user information.

The sensitivity of the embeddable fields in the data table is set to S_i, and the corresponding sensitivity list of the data table is $\{S_1, S_2, \ldots, S_{Emb}\}$. In which, the sensitivity is calculated as shown in Eq. (6).

$$S_i = \phi(\delta_1 \times \omega_1 + \delta_2 \times \omega_2 + \cdots + \delta_n \times \omega_n) \tag{6}$$

In which, δ_1 denotes the proportion of null and abnormal values in the field, δ_2 denotes the number of valid bits of data values in the field, ..., δ_n denotes the watermark content. $\{\omega_1, \omega_2, \ldots, \omega_n\}$ denotes the proportion of weights occupied by $\{\delta_1, \delta_2, \ldots, \delta_n\}$ respectively, which are automatically assigned by this module. ϕ denotes the multi-information joint selection function, and S_i is obtained by mapping the result values of the δ_i and ω_i parameters after performing the relevant operations on them.

Finally, according to the sensitivity list $\{S_1, S_2, \ldots, S_{Emb}\}$, the fields to be embedded are sorted from largest to smallest, which makes it possible to intelligently select the field columns to be embedded by this module, and then the corresponding watermark embedding process can be selected.

3.5 Automatic Parameter Setting

The automatic setting of parameters, it is mainly before the embedding of watermark, for numerical data, combined with the data type adaptation, data volume evaluation, data column sensitivity judgment, and other results information described in the previous section, and by pre-setting a number of limit parameters, so that the data value after embedding the watermark, limited to a controlled range. Thus, it can avoid excessive errors before and after embedding the watermark.

The details include (1) the control of precision, (2) the control of variation range, and (3) the control of embedded copyright information.

The control of precision, it is mainly in the watermark embedding before the user set the number of valid digits of the data value to be embedded in the watermark field. Thus, after the embedding of the watermark, it can control the degree of display of the data value. This list of specific precision control parameters is: *Precision_List* ={"10", "1", "0.1", "0.01", "0.001"}, as shown in *Precision_List*, which gradually refines the granularity of its precision control parameters.

The control of variation range, it is mainly before the embedding of the watermark, the user specified by the data value to be embedded in the watermark field of the upper and lower boundaries of the variation range (e.g. -100–100). Thus, after the watermark is embedded, it can control the approximate range where the data values are located.

The control of embedded copyright information is mainly to prove the original owner of the data by the user inputting the copyright information with actual meaning in Chinese and English, to enter the corresponding watermark embedding process (Table 2).

3.6 Watermark Embedding Stage

Table 2. The comparison of database watermarking algorithms in the watermark embedding stage

Algorithm name	Algorithm core ideas	Supported data types	Statistical distortion analysis	Robustness analysis
Optimal watermarking algorithm based on pattern search	For a given grouping S_i containing m data tuples, it is considered as an m-dimensional vector. To find an m-dimensional vector Δ_i, add it to the S_i vector to obtain the Sim vector, which can be considered as the grouped Sim after the watermark is added	Integer, floating-point	In comparison with the LSB modification algorithm, the percentage change in both mean and variance is smaller	General
LSB modification algorithm	A one-way hash function is used to make the selection of attributes and tuples to be embedded, and then their least significant bits are set to 0 or 1	Integer, floating-point	In comparison with the pattern search algorithm, the percentage change in both mean and variance is larger	Better
Space embedding algorithm	When the original watermark bit is 0, it is 2 spaces before and 2 spaces after the sentence; when the original watermark bit is 1, it is 4 spaces before and 1 space after the sentence	Text type, string type	–	General
Symbol modification algorithm	When the original text has punctuation marks, the end symbols are deleted when the specified conditions are met; when the original text does not have punctuation marks, the end symbols are appended when the specified conditions are met	Text type, string type	–	Better

(continued)

Table 2. (*continued*)

Algorithm name	Algorithm core ideas	Supported data types	Statistical distortion analysis	Robustness analysis
Lexical inverse ordinal number algorithm	If the inverse number is odd, the watermark bit after encoding is set to 1. If the inverse number is even, the watermark bit after encoding is set to 0	Text type, string type	–	Better

Numerical Database Watermarking Algorithm. (1) Optimal watermarking algorithm based on pattern search: The algorithm starts from the initial base point and implements two types of searches alternately: axial search and pattern search. The axial search is performed sequentially along the direction of the n coordinate axes, and is used to determine new iteration points and directions that favor the decrease of function values. The pattern search, on the other hand, is performed along the direction of the line connecting two adjacent iteration points in an attempt to make the function values fall faster [31]. (2) LSB modification algorithm: It is assumed that the attribute values of the tuples in the database are modified imperceptibly to the user and do not affect the availability of the data, then the least significant bit can be modified for watermark embedding. This algorithm is mainly for numerical relational databases which uses a one-way hash function to select the attributes and tuples to be embedded, and then sets the least significant bit to 0 or 1. In this way, the embedding process of the watermark is completed and does not affect the normal use of the data [3].

Text-Based Database Watermarking Algorithm. (1) Space embedding algorithm: the watermark information is hidden in the line break of text data, and the presence or absence of spaces and tabs at the end of the line or between words is visually difficult to detect, which can be decoded by the presence or absence, type and number of invisible codes during watermark extraction [20]. (2) Symbol modification algorithm: in contrast to text, people are not sensitive to punctuation marks, and therefore the possibility of embeddable watermarks exists. The substitution, deletion or addition of major punctuation marks in Chinese and English is generally unnoticeable [21]. (3) Lexical inverse ordinal number algorithm: After natural language sentences are processed by word division and lexical annotation, a lexical token sequence is obtained, which is composed of a finite number of lexical tokens. The inverse order number of the sequence is calculated by the biased order relationship defined in advance on the lexical token set, and the 1-bit information is hidden according to the parity of the inverse order number. If the current parity does not match with the hidden information bits, the lexical token sequence is modified by transformations such as swapping the positions of two symbols, adding or removing some symbols. Finally, the natural language sentence is modified according to the lexical token sequence [16].

3.7   Watermark Extraction Stage

Numeric database watermarking algorithm performs watermark extraction based on the corresponding Optimal watermarking algorithm based on pattern search and LSB modification algorithm. The text-based database watermarking algorithm performs watermark extraction on based on the corresponding space embedding algorithm, symbol modification algorithm, and lexical inverse ordinal number algorithm. The corresponding specific analysis processes, respectively, are shown in Table 3.

Table 3. The comparison of database watermarking algorithms in the watermark extraction stage

Algorithm name	Algorithm core ideas	Supported data types	Statistical distortion analysis	Robust-ness analysis
Optimal watermarking algorithm based on pattern search	According to the optimal threshold T calculated during the watermark embedding process, and using the majority voting mechanism, it is found the value of the watermarked bits embedded in this data subgroup. Then, the splicing is performed to calculate the original watermark information	Integer, floating-point	In comparison with the LSB modification algorithm, the percentage change in both mean and variance is smaller	General
LSB modification algorithm	It corresponds to the inverse process of the watermark embedding algorithm	Integer, floating-point	In comparison with the pattern search algorithm, the percentage change in both mean and variance is larger	Better
Space embedding algorithm	It corresponds to the inverse process of the watermark embedding algorithm	Text type, string type	–	General
Symbol modification algorithm	It corresponds to the inverse process of the watermark embedding algorithm	Text type, string type	–	Better
Lexical inverse ordinal number algorithm	It corresponds to the inverse process of the watermark embedding algorithm	Text type, string type	–	Better

3.8   Result Visualization Mechanism

The result visualization mechanism which is mainly for the data table after the watermark embedding/extraction, adding the result visualization mechanism. In this way, users can quickly feel the difference in accuracy control and statistical distortion of the data table before and after watermark embedding/extraction.

When the watermark embedding/extraction is complete, the specific information displayed by the module is shown in Fig. 4.

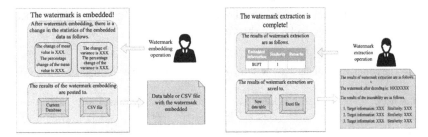

Fig. 4. Result visualization mechanism.

Finally, it will make an exhaustive evaluation of the current watermark embedding/extraction results based on the results shown in Fig. 4 and a series of pre-set thresholds, which will eventually be fed back to the user.

4   Experimental Analysis

This section focuses on the database watermarking algorithms designed and used earlier, to further analyze the characteristics of various algorithms, and to conduct data distortion analysis experiments and robustness experiments. The experimental environment is: (1) Processor: 2.6 GHz hexa-core Intel Core i7; (2) Memory: 16 GB 2667 MHz DDR4; (3) Operating system: macOS Catalina version 10.15.7. All algorithms are implemented with Java language, and the experimental data sets are as follows (1) Integer dataset: German credit risk dataset [32]; (2) Floating-point dataset: Dow Jones Industrial Average (DJIA) stock dataset [33]; (3) Text-based dataset: Reddit WorldNews Channel historical news headlines dataset [33]. In which, (1) for the integer dataset, set the number of fields to 5 and the number of tuples to 1000; (2) select and transform the floating-point dataset, set the number of fields to 8 and the number of tuples to 1000; (3) for the text-based dataset, set the number of fields to 3 and the number of tuples to 1000.

4.1   Invisibility Analysis Experiments

To check the effect of statistical distortion on the data before and after watermark embedding, the invisibility analysis experiments are designed for numerical data in this section.

In this section, the effect of watermarking on the database is analyzed by applying the Optimal watermarking algorithm based on pattern search (OPS) and LSB modification algorithm (LSB) to integer data and floating-point data, respectively, and then three fields are selected to calculate the change values of the data before and after watermark embedding, respectively. The two statistics, mean and variance, are selected in this section of the experiment to measure the effect of watermarking on the database. Finally, a comparison is made between them, and the final results are shown in Table 4. It can be seen from Table 4 that the change of the mean and variance of the data by the embedding of the watermark is relatively small and is basically invisible to the user. Therefore, it is clear from the experimental results that both algorithms have some invisibility.

Table 4. The comparison of numerical database watermarking algorithms - the statistical distortion results before and after database watermark embedding

Algorithm and data type names	Field name	The change of mean value	The change of variance	Percentage change in mean (%)	Percentage change in variance (%)
OPS (floating-point data)	C1	8.73	92.41	0.06%	0.00%
	C2	8.74	103.38	0.07%	0.00%
	C3	4.93	−205.32	**0.04%**	**0.00%**
LSB (floating-point data)	C1	−324.64	−100911.79	2.41%	1.02%
	C2	−54.53	537309.29	0.41%	5.41%
	C3	−59.57	484431.34	**0.44%**	**4.90%**
OPS (integer data)	C1	−0.14	2.42	0.39%	1.87%
	C2	4.80	−119.15	**0.15%**	**0.00%**
	C3	0.29	2.06	1.37%	1.42%
LSB (integer data)	C1	−0.89	3.21	2.50%	2.48%
	C2	−27.60	−146845.69	0.84%	1.84%
	C3	−0.15	0.50	**0.74%**	**0.34%**

4.2 Precision Control Analysis Experiment

To check the effect of watermark embedding before and after on the statistical distortion of the data, the precision control analysis experiment is designed in this section for numerical data. In which, precision is defined as the degree of accuracy and precision of data display.

In this section, it observes the changes of mean and variance of database watermark before and after embedding by using the optimal watermarking algorithm based on pattern search (OPS) and LSB modification algorithm (LSB) for integer and floating-point data, respectively, when the precision is {"10", "1", "0.1", "0.01", "0.001"}.

The results of the experiments are shown in Fig. 5. It can be seen from the left panel of Fig. 5 that for the optimal watermarking algorithm based on pattern search, the effect of mean change of integer data is slightly smaller than that of floating-point data, but the difference is not significant. For the LSB modification algorithm, the effect of the mean change of integer data is generally smaller than that of floating-point data in terms of the overall trend. It can be seen from the right panel of Fig. 5 that for the optimal watermarking algorithm based on pattern search, whether it is for integer or floating-point data, it is almost negligible in terms of variance variation. For the LSB modification algorithm, on the other hand, there is less effect of variance change for integer data compared with floating-point data from the overall trend.

In conclusion, for precision control analysis, the effect of statistical distortion of the optimal pattern search-based watermarking algorithm is slightly less than that of the LSB modification algorithm.

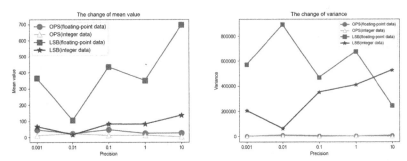

Fig. 5. The effect of different precision on statistical distortion before and after watermark embedding in databases.

4.3 Watermark Robustness Ability Comparison Experiment

In this section, it is focused on the robustness analysis of the five database watermarking algorithms designed and used earlier, and the corresponding watermarking attack simulation experiments are designed.

In this section, the watermark similarity *Similarity* is used to measure the robustness of the watermarking method [34], and the watermark similarity is defined as shown in Eq. (7).

$$Similarity = 1 - \frac{sum(W \otimes W')}{|W|} \tag{7}$$

It is obvious that higher *Similarity* indicates better robustness; on the contrary, we can see that lower *Similarity* means worse robustness.

In this section, the experiments such as subset deletion attack, subset modification attack, and subset increase attack are performed respectively, and the specific cases can be classified as the attacker attacks (deletion, modification, and addition) 0%–90% (or 100%) of the tuples. In particular, the experimental results corresponding to the numerical watermarking algorithm are shown in Fig. 6, 7 and 8, and the experimental results corresponding to the text-based watermarking algorithm are shown in Fig. 9, 10 and 11, respectively. In which, the y-axis indicates the watermark similarity *Similarity*, and the x-axis indicates the percentage (%) of the number of attacked (deleted, modified, added) tuples to the total number of tuples. For each subset of attack experiments, the experimental results are the average of 10 experiments.

Robustness Analysis of Numerical Watermarking Algorithms. The numerical data supported in this section, which includes mainly the following types, are shown in Table 5.

Table 5. The numerical types supported by the numerical watermarking algorithm

Numerical types	Support or not
TINYINT	✓
SMALLINT	✓
MEDIUMINT	✓
INT or INTEGER	✓
BIGINT	✓
FLOAT	✓
DOUBLE	✓
DECIMAL	✓

In this section, the numerical watermarking algorithm designed and used in this paper is analyzed for robustness, and a comparative experimental analysis is performed with the literature [7], literature [25], literature [26], and literature [30] concerning the resistance to attacks of the watermark.

Subset Deletion Attack Experiments. The subset deletion attack refers to the deletion of a certain percentage of tuples from the relational data containing watermarks, to reduce the number of tuples embedded with the watermark and achieve the purpose of destroying the watermark [35].

The results of the experiments are shown in Fig. 6. From Fig. 6, it can be seen that for the LSB modification algorithm, the watermark similarity of this algorithm is still 1 when 90% of the tuples in the database are randomly deleted. When the percentage of randomly deleted tuples is less than or equal to 90%, the two algorithms in the literature [7] and the literature [25] are the same as this algorithm. The algorithms in literature [26] and literature [30] can no longer extract the original watermark completely when the proportion of randomly deleted tuples is 88% and 90%, respectively. Therefore, it is clear from the experimental results that the present algorithm is more robust against subset deletion attacks.

Subset Modification Attack Experiment. The subset modification attack refers to the modification of a certain percentage of tuples in the relational data containing the watermark, which leads to an error in the watermark detection and achieves the purpose of destroying the watermark [35].

The results of the experiments are shown in Fig. 7. It can be seen from Fig. 7 that for the LSB algorithm, the watermark similarity of this algorithm remains 1 when the percentage of tuples subject to subset modification attack reaches 100% for both

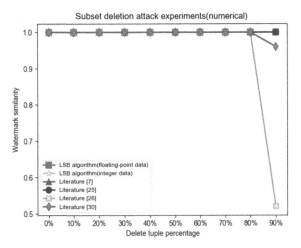

Fig. 6. Subset deletion attack experiment (numerical).

floating-point and integer data. When the percentage of modified tuples reaches 90%, the two algorithms in the literature [25] and the literature [30] are the same as this algorithm. The algorithms in literature [7] and literature [26] can no longer extract the original watermark completely when the proportion of modified tuples is 90% and 70%, respectively. Therefore, it is clear from the experimental results that the present algorithm is more robust against subset modification attacks.

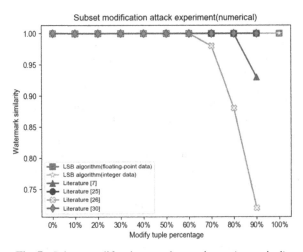

Fig. 7. Subset modification attack experiment (numerical).

Subset Addition Attack Experiment. The subset addition attack refers to adding a certain percentage of tuples to the relational data containing the watermark, which does not affect the original data but disrupts the watermark detection, leading to incorrect watermark detection [35].

The results of the experiments are shown in Fig. 8. It can be seen from Fig. 8 that for the LSB algorithm, the watermark similarity of this algorithm remains 1 when the percentage of tuples added by the attacker reaches 100%. The three algorithms in the literature [25], literature [26], and literature [30] are the same as this algorithm when the percentage of tuples added reaches 100%. The algorithm in literature [7] can extract only 80% of the watermark information when the percentage of tuples added is 60%. Therefore, it is clear from the experimental results that the present algorithm is more robust against the subset addition attack.

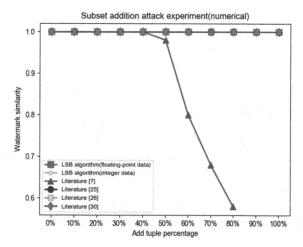

Fig. 8. Subset addition attack experiment (numerical).

Robustness Analysis of Text-Based Watermarking Algorithms. The string type data supported in this section, which includes mainly the following types, are shown in Table 6.

In this section, the text-based watermarking algorithm designed and used in this paper is analyzed for robustness, and the space embedding algorithm, the symbol modification algorithm, and the lexical inverse ordinal algorithm are compared and experimentally analyzed with respect concerning of the watermark.

Table 6. The string types supported by the text-based watermarking algorithm

String types	Support or not
CHAR	✓
VARCHAR	✓
TINYBLOB	✗
TINYTEXT	✓
BLOB	✗
TEXT	✓
MEDIUMBLOB	✗
MEDIUMTEXT	✓
LONGBLOB	✗
LONGTEXT	✓

Subset Deletion Attack Experiments. The results of the experiments are shown in Fig. 9. It can be seen from Fig. 9 that the watermark similarity of the space embedding algorithm and the symbolic modification algorithm have exactly the same change trend with the addition of the percentage of the deleted tuples. The changing trend of the lexical inverse ordinal number algorithm is more similar to the above two algorithms, and its corresponding watermark similarity is also slightly lower, but the difference is less than 5%–6%. Therefore, it is clear from the experimental results that the above three algorithms are generally robust against subset deletion attacks.

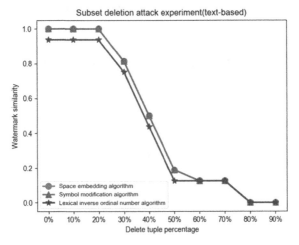

Fig. 9. Subset deletion attack experiment (text-based).

Subset Modification Attack Experiment. The results of the experiments are shown in Fig. 10. It can be seen from Fig. 10 that when the percentage of modified tuples is smaller, the difference of the three algorithms against attacks is not much, and the difference is less than 5%–6%; when the percentage of modified tuples is larger, the robustness of the lexical inverse ordinal algorithm is better than the symbolic modification algorithm in terms of the overall trend, and both of them are much better than the space embedding algorithm. Therefore, it is clear from the experimental results that the symbolic modification algorithm and the lexical inverse ordinal number algorithm are more robust against subset modification attacks, while the space embedding algorithm is generally robust.

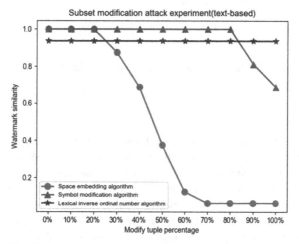

Fig. 10. Subset modification attack experiment (text-based).

Subset Addition Attack Experiment. The results of the experiments are shown in Fig. 11. It can be seen from Fig. 11 that the symbolic modification algorithm and the lexical inverse ordinal number algorithm can still maintain an extremely high watermark similarity even after adding twice the number of tuples to the database. Specifically, the symbolic modification algorithm slightly outperforms the lexical inverse ordinal number algorithm, but the difference is not significant, and the difference is less than 5% to 6%. When the percentage of added tuples exceeds 60%, the robustness of the space embedding algorithm is much worse than the above two algorithms. Therefore, it is clear from the experimental results that the space-embedding algorithm, with respect to the subset addition attack, is generally robust, while the symbolic modification algorithm and the lexical inverse ordinal number algorithm, with respect to the subset addition attack, are more robust.

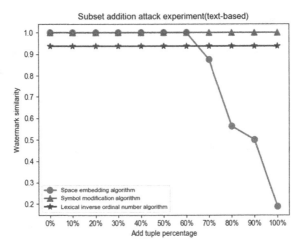

Fig. 11. Subset addition attack experiment (text-based).

5 Summary

In this paper, we have proposed a new robust database watermarking scheme the originality of which stands in a novel adaptive method. As we have shown, five database watermarking algorithms are designed and used. For numerical data, LSB modification algorithm and Optimal watermarking algorithm based on pattern search are used. For text-based data, space embedding algorithm, symbol modification algorithm and lexical inverse ordinal number-based text modification algorithm are used. The adaptive algorithm is implemented by data type analysis, data volume evaluation, data sensitivity analysis, automatic parameter setting and visualization techniques. It is robust against most common database attacks: tuple deletion and insertion as well as attributes' values modification. Our scheme is appropriate for copyright protection or traitor tracing. In addition, we have theoretically established and verified experimentally the performance of our method in terms of robustness. The proposed results allow the user to correctly select our scheme's parameters under constraints of robustness and capacity.

References

1. Naimi, A.I., Westreich, D.J.: Big data: a revolution that will transform how we live, work, and think (2014)
2. Katzenbeisser, S., Petitcolas, F.A.P.: Digital Watermarking, p. 2. Artech House, London (2000)
3. Agrawal, R., Kiernan, J.: Watermarking relational databases. In: VLDB 2002: Proceedings of the 28th International Conference on Very Large Databases, pp. 155–166. Morgan Kaufmann (2002)
4. Gupta, G., Pieprzyk, J.: Reversible and blind database watermarking using difference expansion. Int. J. Digit. Crime Forensics (IJDCF) **1**(2), 42–54 (2009)
5. Jawad, K., Khan, A.: Genetic algorithm and difference expansion based reversible watermarking for relational databases. J. Syst. Softw. **86**(11), 2742–2753 (2013)

6. Thodi, D.M., Rodriguez, J.J.: Prediction-error based reversible watermarking. In: 2004 International Conference on Image Processing, ICIP 2004, vol. 3, pp. 1549–1552. IEEE (2004)
7. Farfoura, M.E., Horng, S.J., Lai, J.L., et al.: A blind reversible method for watermarking relational databases based on a time-stamping protocol. Expert Syst. Appl. **39**(3), 3185–3196 (2012)
8. Zhang, Y., Yang, B., Niu, X.M.: Reversible watermarking for relational database authentication. J. Comput. **17**(2), 59–66 (2006)
9. Hu, D., Zhao, D., Zheng, S.: A new robust approach for reversible database watermarking with distortion control. IEEE Trans. Knowl. Data Eng. **31**(6), 1024–1037 (2018)
10. Li, Y., Wang, J., Ge, S., et al.: A reversible database watermarking method with low distortion. Math. Biosci. Eng. **16**(5), 4053–4068 (2019)
11. Kaur, M., Mahajan, K.: Performance evaluation of natural language text watermarking using encryption techniques. Int. J. Comput. Appl **129**(3), 22–28 (2015)
12. Li, G., Chen, J., Ma, H., et al.: Method for text watermarking based on subject-verb encoding. Comput. Sci. S2 (2015)
13. Lin, X., Tang, X., Wang, J.: A reversible text watermarking algorithm based on coding and synonymy substitution. J. Chin. Inf. Process. **29**(4), 151–158 (2015). (in Chinese)
14. Atallah, M.J., Raskin, V., Crogan, M., et al.: Natural language watermarking: design, analysis, and a proof-of-concept implementation. In: Moskowitz, I.S. (ed.) Information Hiding. IH 2001. Lecture Notes in Computer Science, vol. 2137, pp. 185–200. Springer, Heidelberg (2001). https://doi.org/10.1007/3-540-45496-9_14
15. Kamaruddin, N.S., Kamsin, A., Por, L.Y., et al.: A review of text watermarking: theory, methods, and applications. IEEE Access **6**, 8011–8028 (2018)
16. Dai, Z.X., Hong, F.: Text information hiding based on inverse order of part of speech symbol sequence. Jisuanji Gongcheng yu Yingyong (Comput. Eng. Appl.) **43**(14), 160–161 (2007). (in Chinese)
17. Mir, N.: Copyright for web content using invisible text watermarking. Comput. Hum. Behav. **30**, 648–653 (2014)
18. Taleby Ahvanooey, M., Dana Mazraeh, H., Tabasi, S.H.: An innovative technique for web text watermarking (AITW). Inf. Secur. J.: Glob. Perspect. **25**(4–6), 191–196 (2016)
19. Zhenyu, Z., Qianmu, L., Yong, Q.: Text watermarking design based on invisible characters. J. Nanjing Univ. Sci. Technol. (2017). (in Chinese)
20. Zhaocan, L., Liming, W., Sijiang, G., et al.: A plain text watermarking method for big data based on orthogonal coding. Comput. Sci. **46**(12), 148–154 (2019). (in Chinese)
21. Zhang, X.: Several algorithms of digital watermark based on text document. Comput. Mod. **3** (2009). (in Chinese)
22. Wang, S., Sa, S.X.: Introduction to Database System, pp. 36–69. Higher Education Press, Beijing (2011)
23. Sion, R., Atallah, M., Prabhakar, S.: Rights protection for categorical data. IEEE Trans. Knowl. Data Eng. **17**(7), 912–926 (2005)
24. Niu, X.M., Zhao, L., Huang, W., et al.: Watermarking relational databases for ownership protection. Acta Electron. Sinica A **12** (2003). (in Chinese)
25. Iftikhar, S., Kamran, M., Anwar, Z.: RRW—a robust and reversible watermarking technique for relational data. IEEE Trans. Knowl. Data Eng. **27**(4), 1132–1145 (2014)
26. Tong, D., Zhu, C., Ren, N.: A watermarking algorithm for geodatabases without relying on primary keys. Geogr. Geogr. Inf. Sci. **5** (2015). (in Chinese)
27. Wang, C., Yang, L., Wan, F., et al.: Survey on database watermarking models and algorithms. Acta Electon. Sinica **47**(4), 946 (2019). (in Chinese)
28. Sion, R.: Proving ownership over categorical data. In: Proceedings of 20th International Conference on Data Engineering, pp. 584–595. IEEE (2004)

29. Hanyurwimfura, D., Liu, Y., Liu, Z.: Text format based relational database watermarking for non-numeric data. In: 2010 International Conference on Computer Design and Applications, vol. 4, pp. V4-312–V4-316. IEEE (2010)
30. Melkundi, S., Chandankhede, C.: A robust technique for relational database watermarking and verification. In: 2015 International Conference on Communication, Information & Computing Technology (ICCICT), pp. 1–7. IEEE (2015)
31. Ma, J.: Generalized pattern search algorithm in optimization problems. Dalian University of Technology (2009). (in Chinese)
32. Blake, C.L., Merz, C.J.: UCI repository of machine learning databases (1998)
33. Sun, J.: Daily news for stock market prediction, version 1, August 2016. https://www.kaggle.com/aaron7sun/stocknews
34. Franco-Contreras, J., Coatrieux, G.: Robust watermarking of relational databases with ontology-guided distortion control. IEEE Trans. Inf. Forensics Secur. **10**(9), 1939–1952 (2015)
35. Hou, R.T., Xian, H.Q., Li, J., Di, G.D.: Graded reversible watermarking scheme for relational data. Ruan Jian Xue Bao/J. Softw. **31**(11), 3571–3587 (2020). (in Chinese)

A Privacy-Preserving Medical Data Traceability System Based on Attribute-Based Encryption on Blockchain

Yujuan Zhao[✉], Baojiang Cui, and Jie Xu

Beijing University of Posts and Telecommunications, Beijing, China
yjzhao192@bupt.edu.cn

Abstract. With the continuous development of distributed technology, blockchain has been widely applied to solve practical problems in various fields. Its advantages such as decentralization and non-tamperability perfectly meet the needs of permanent query of traceability scene information, and can solve the trust problem of multi-party participation in various links. At the same time, as data security has received more and more attention. The privacy protection and permission control of "on-chain" data need to be resolved. Medical data records are very valuable and sensitive data. Reliable storage and credible traceability are of great significance to the health of patients and the long-term development of medical undertakings. To issue the above problems, here, we propose a secure medical data traceability system that combines data desensitization and attribute-based encryption algorithms to achieve the traceability capabilities and ensure the reliable storage of medical data records on blockchain. Data desensitization provides a certain degree of security for sensitive data involving personal information in medical data. The introduction of attribute encryption has solved the problem of unauthorized access to data. Finally, we analyzed the security of the solution and Verify the efficiency of the program.

Keywords: Hyperledger Fabric · Reversible desensitization · Attribute encryption

1 Introduction

With the rapid development of information technology, medical data, as an important data asset, has received more and more attention. Research on medical data is also an important way to promote the development of the medical field. Medical data is of special importance and sensitivity, relating not only to information related to the medical treatment process, but also to personal privacy and other information, and even to industry development and national security. With the informatization of medical data, the risk of its leakage has been increasing. The methods of leakage are mainly divided into interactive leakage and non-interactive leakage. Interactive disclosure refers to the disclosure of medical information when it is released and shared among different institutions; Non-interactive disclosure refers to the disclosure of data by hospital internal systems or personnel, such as private reselling or misuse of information [1]. At present,

W. Lu et al. (Eds.): CNCERT 2021, CCIS 1506, pp. 27–36, 2022.
https://doi.org/10.1007/978-981-16-9229-1_2

most of the medical data is stored in the hospital's local database. In the daily management process, the information department of many hospitals is not very aware of prevention, and is vulnerable to attacks in the process of multi-party interaction. This will undoubtedly lead to privacy leakage and cause serious consequences.

Blockchain technology, also known as distributed ledger technology, is an Internet database technology. As shown in Fig. 1, the blockchain composes data blocks into a chain data structure in chronological order, and uses cryptographic technology to ensure that the data on the chain cannot be tampered with or forged. Each node uses the Hash algorithm and Merkle tree to encapsulate the transactions received within a period of time into a block with a timestamp, and link it to the longest main chain to form the latest block [2].

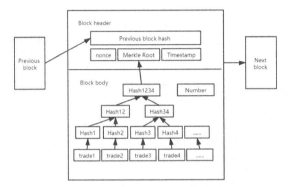

Fig. 1. The structure of blocks

Blockchain is a distributed shared ledger and database, which has the characteristics of decentralization, non-tampering, openness and transparency, traceability, and programmable. The blockchain records important data in the circulation process of blood cell extraction, transportation, processing, and use in medical scenarios, and provides traceability for the entire process. However, the data privacy issues contained in medical data are still tricky. Data desensitization can process private information such as ID card numbers closely related to patients' personal information, while ensuring the standardization and reversibility of data, and attribute encryption can provide fine-grained access control while protecting data confidentiality. This type of technology provides support for the realization of data privacy and security sharing.

Block chain fusion cryptography principle guarantees non-tampering and data confidentiality, and realizes the function of data storage and traceability [3]. Aiming at a series of practical problems such as the incomplete credibility of the current medical data and the high risk of sensitive data leakage, this paper proposes a scheme based on the combination of blockchain and reversible desensitization and attribute encryption algorithms. First, reversible desensitization was performed on ID number, mobile phone number and other private information in the patient information. Then the other on-chain data is classified and processed into fully public data and restricted privacy data. After that the restricted privacy data is encrypted and uploaded. Finally, in the traceability information query, access control through attributes is adopted to achieve hierarchical protection of data, greatly improving the security of data.

2 Related Work

2.1 Blockchain Technology

In the medical field, G. Zyshind et al. [4] proposed to store user access control permissions and data hash values in the blockchain, and encrypt the data to be hosted in a trusted third party, which did not achieve decentralization, while increasing the risk of data leakage. Azaria A [5] and others proposed to combine blockchain and public key encryption technology for access rights management, but the consensus mechanism of this scheme uses Proof of Work, which will consume a lot of computing power for data storage to ensure the authenticity of data on the chain. Wang et al. [6] proposed that the information owner distributes keys for data users and encrypts the data through the specified access rules of the Ethereum smart contract, and controls the access to the data through the attribute-based encryption mechanism.

2.2 Reversible Data Desensitization

Data desensitization technology [7] deforms sensitive data through deletion, masking, replacement and other means to achieve reliable protection of sensitive data. Data desensitization technology mainly has three types of methods: the first is a covering method, which is an irreversible solution to achieve data protection by covering the data; the second is to convert into a random sequence, using hash encryption Algorithms make data lose business attributes. This method is only suitable for scenarios with strong data protection requirements; the third is reversible desensitization, which uses reversible algorithms such as data table mapping and algorithm mapping to achieve data protection, which can guarantee the business attributes of data. It also has the characteristics of reversible reduction [8].

2.3 Attribute-Based Encryption Technology

Attribute-based encryption can refine the degree of access control to shared data to the attribute level. Li et al. [9] aimed at the centralization of existing cloud storage technologies, and proposed an attribute encryption access control based on the combination of blockchain and cryptographic accumulators to achieve privacy protection. Wang et al. [10] proposed a scheme based on Multi-Authority Attribute Based Encryption to achieve privacy protection and access control. Li et al. [11] proposed a decentralized storage solution that combines ciphertext-policy attribute-based encryption (CP-ABE), decentralized multi-authority attribute-based signatures (DMA-ABSs) and blockchain technology, but when the access policy is changed, data encryption needs to be re-encrypted and new key distribution is required.

3   System Model

3.1   Reversible Data Desensitization

Table 1 presents some of the notations used throughout the paper.

Table 1. Notations.

Notation	Description
M	Original coded data
N	Global secret integer
ID	ID of the desensitization task
g	Greatest common divisor of M and N
C	Coded data after desensitization
M'	Recovered coded data
ID'	Identification obtained by traceability
ID^{-1}	The multiplicative inverse element under N
$(M/g)^{-1}$	The multiplicative inverse element of M/g modulo N/g

The coded data reversible desensitization and traceability algorithm based on the Abelian group can generate a global security integer of the target order of magnitude according to the original coded data to be desensitized, and the size of the target order of magnitude is determined according to the data length of the data to be desensitized; The global secret integer is used to obtain the Abelian group; the desensitization task identifier is selected from the Abelian group; the original encoded data is encoded according to the desensitization task identifier and the global secret integer to obtain the desensitized encoded data:

$$C = M \cdot ID (\bmod\ N) \tag{1}$$

Restore the desensitized encoded data:

$$M' = C \cdot ID^{-1} (\bmod\ N) \tag{2}$$

Trace the source of encoded data according to the following formula:

$$ID' = C/g \cdot (M/g)^{-1} (\bmod\ N/g) \tag{3}$$

3.2   Access Control Based on Attributes

The core idea of attribute-based access control is to use attributes to express restricted information in the access control model, and generate corresponding access policies through certain logical relationships [12] (Fig. 2).

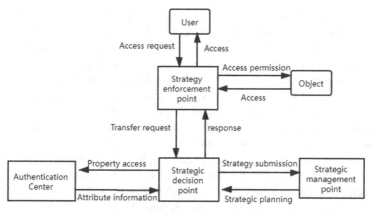

Fig. 2. Basic model architecture

An attribute-based encryption technology that can solve the problem of data access management through reasonable configuration of sharing strategies [13]. According to the different embedded objects, attribute based encryption (ABE) can be divided into Key-Policy Attribute-based encryption (KP-ABE) and Ciphertext-policy Attribute-based encryption (CP-ABE) [14].

CP-ABE uses a password mechanism to protect data [15]. The data owner specifies the strategy for accessing the ciphertext, and associates the attribute set with the access resource, and the data user can access the ciphertext information according to their authorized attributes [16].

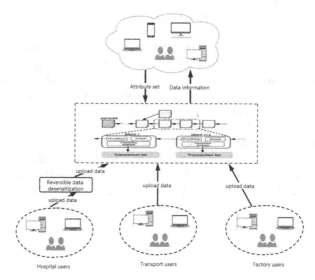

Fig. 3. System model

As shown in Fig. 3, there are three types of users in this system, namely hospital users, transportation users and factory users. Hospital users are mainly blood collection doctors, examiners, quality monitors, etc., transportation users are mainly transport managers, quality inspectors, etc., and factory users are mainly quality managers, cell processing managers, etc. The user submits the responsible part of the key information data, uploads the data to the Fabric through the smart contract for storage, and saves the personal privacy-related data submitted by the hospital user about the patient after reversible desensitization. The system process includes extracting the patient's blood cells, transporting them to the factory for Chimeric antigen receptor T (CAR-T) cell immune treatment after inspection, and transporting them back to the hospital for patient use after the treatment. Because the immunotherapy is still in clinical trials, the entire process needs to be preserved for future research and analysis. The CP-ABE strategy is used for data access, and the access authority is controlled through the attribute set and the access control tree, so as to realize the hierarchical protection of the data.

4   Scheme

We design a CP-ABE-based blockchain medical data traceability system. The scene is the whole process of CAR-T cell therapy, including information such as blood collection and testing in the hospital, cold chain transportation information of blood bags, cell separation and other processing information. The system process is as follows (Fig. 4).

The hospital collects the patient's blood and puts it into the blood bag after the collection is completed. Each blood bag corresponds to a unique QR code. The corresponding doctor submits the patient information, blood information, etc., and formulates the attribute encryption strategy and then encrypts the encrypted data. Store the blood bags on the chain, and then transport the blood bags to the factory for processing. The temperature and humidity are monitored by sensors to ensure the normal progress of the cold chain transportation process. After arriving at the factory, the corresponding factory responsible personnel will check and receive the blood bags. The processing process uses key information such as reagents and operators to be encrypted and then chained. After the preparation is completed, the blood is transported back to the hospital for patients to use. By scanning the QR code, doctors who meet the attribute policy on the hospital side can view the complete information of the blood bag, and the operators who meet the attribute policy on the factory side can view the relevant operation information of the factory and the transportation status. The personnel on the transportation side can only view the transportation-related information. A blood bag quality test must be carried out at the handover of each link, and the results and the information of the test personnel shall be recorded to ensure the quality of the blood bag.

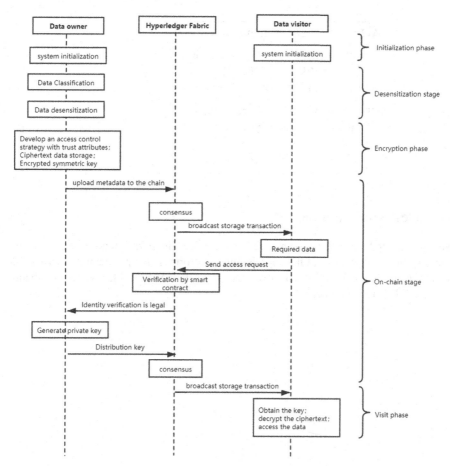

Fig. 4. System workflow

Different organizations correspond to different data collection and uploading work. First, during the upload process, the system will first perform data classification. Reversible data desensitization of ID card number, mobile phone number and other data will ensure the privacy and standardization of data. Encrypt the data through the symmetric key, and then use the attribute access control strategy to encrypt the symmetric key. When the encrypted data is on the chain, consensus, and traceability access to the data, the access application is first submitted, and then the attribute verification is performed by the smart contract. If the attribute is valid, the corresponding key will be sent, and the encrypted symmetric key can be decrypted by this key, so as to decode the ciphertext and access the data.

Algorithm : Decryption

Input: Ciphertext C. Attribute collection Ai. Decryption
Key DK. Public Key PK
Output: Invalid Signature or Unencrypted Data

1 **if** Ai **Satisfy** (Access strategy) **then**
2 | **Return** "1: Unencrypted Data "
3 **else**
4 | **Return** "0: Invalid Signature"

---

5   Performance and Safety Analysis

We implemented a prototype to analyze the feasibility and performance of the program. The specific configuration of the experimental platform and experimental environment is: Intel Core i7-8565U@1.80 GHz processor, 8 GB RAM, and the system is ubuntu 16.04LTS. Fabric version is 1.4.2.

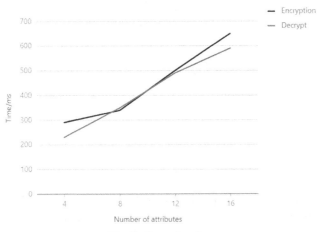

Fig. 5. Operation time

As shown in Fig. 5, the data size is set to 128B, and the number of access attributes is set to 4, 8, 12, 16. This scheme implements the Decentralized Ciphertext Policy Attribute Based Encryption schema described in [17]. The code depends on the jPBC library [18] and the Bouncy Castle library.

In terms of security, in this solution, only when the attributes of the visitor match the attributes in the access policy formulated by the data owner can the key be obtained, so that the corresponding data can be accessed. If there is no match, the key cannot be obtained. In the design of this solution, even if the visitor's identity is legal, the data can be accessed, but the private data such as the ID number is still non-real data. Therefore, this program is safe.

6 Summary

CP-ABE is a widely used solution that can achieve fine-grained access control. However, the direct use of traditional CP-ABE in medical information systems will still have certain access strategy leaks and high algorithm complexity. The solution in this article combines data reversible desensitization with the improved CP-ABE, and uses the characteristics of the blockchain to have greater advantages in function and efficiency for the actual scenarios of the actual CAR-T preparation process. In the next step, we will consider issues related to attribute revocation and make a more optimized plan.

Acknowledgements. This work is supported by CNKLSTISS and the National Natural Science Foundation of China (Grant No. 61802025).

References

1. Hu, R., He, Y., Fan, X.: Research on the security technology of medical privacy protection. J. Beijing Electron. Sci. Technol. Inst. **26**(3), 46–54 (2018)
2. Zou, J.: Blockchain Technology Guide. Machinery Industry Press, Beijing (2016)
3. Venkatesh, J., Aksanli, B., Chan, C.S., et al.: Modular and personalized smart health application design in a smart city environment. IEEE Internet of Things J. **5**(2), 614–623 (2018)
4. Zyskind, G., Nathan, O., Pentland, A.: Decentralizing privacy: using blockchain to protect personal data. In: 2015 IEEE Security and Privacy Workshops (SPW), San Jose, pp. 180–184. IEEE Computer Society (2015)
5. Azaria, A., Ekblaw, A., Vieira, T., et al.: MedRec: using blockchain for medical data access and permission management. In: 2016 2nd International Conference on Open and Big Data (OBD), Vienna, pp. 25–30. IEEE (2016)
6. Wang, S., Zhang, Y., Zhang, Y.: A blockchain-based framework for data sharing with fine-grained access control in decentralized storage systems. IEEE Access **6**(7), 38437–38450 (2018)
7. Xing, Y., Zhang, B., Mao, Y.: Application of data desensitization in massive data systems. Telecommun. Sci. **33**(S1), 8–14 (2017)
8. Hu, R., He, Y., Zeng, P., Fan, X.: Design and implementation of a medical privacy protection scheme in a big data environment. Inf. Netw. Secur. **09**, 48–54 (2018)
9. Li, X.: Research and implementation of blockchain technology in secure cloud storage. PLA Strategic Support Force Information Engineering University for the Degree of Master of Engineering, Zhengzhou (2020)
10. Wang, J., Xie, Y., Wang, G., et al.: A method of privacy preserving and access control in blockchain based on attribute-based encryption. Netinfo Secur. **20**(9), 47–51 (2020)
11. Li, G., Sato, H.: A privacy-preserving and fully decentralized storage and sharing system on blockchain. In: Proceedings of the IEEE 43rd Annual Computer Software and Applications Conference (COMPSAC), WI, USA, pp. 694–699 (2019)
12. Jemel, M., Serrhrouchni, A.: Decentralized access control mechanism with temporal dimension based on blockchain. In: Proceedings of the IEEE International Conference on e-Business Engineering, Shanghai, China, pp. 177–182 (2017)

13. Li, X.: Application research and implementation of blockchain technology in secure cloud storage. Information Engineering University of Strategic Support Forces, Zhengzhou (2020)
14. Cao, L., Liu, Y., Dong, X., Guo, X.: User privacy-preserving cloud storage scheme on CP-ABE. J. Tsinghua Univ. **58**(2), 150–156 (2018)
15. Wang, X., Jiang, X., Li, Y.: Data access control and sharing model using blockchain Type. J. Softw. **30**(6), 1661–1669 (2019)
16. Tian, Y., Yang, K., Wang, Z., et al.: Algorithm of blockchain data provenance based on ABE. J. Commun. **40**(11), 101–111 (2019)
17. Lewko, A., Waters, B.: Decentralizing attribute-based encryption. In: Paterson, K.G. (ed.) EUROCRYPT 2011. LNCS, vol. 6632, pp. 568–588. Springer, Heidelberg (2011). https://doi.org/10.1007/978-3-642-20465-4_31
18. http://gas.dia.unisa.it/projects/jpbc/

Privacy Protection

Analysis of Address Linkability in Tornado Cash on Ethereum

Yujia Tang[1], Chang Xu[2](✉), Can Zhang[2], Yan Wu[2], and Liehuang Zhu[2]

[1] School of Computer Science and Technology, Beijing Institute of Technology,
Beijing 100081, China
[2] School of Cyberspace Science and Technology, Beijing Institute of Technology,
Beijing 100081, China
xuchang@bit.edu.cn

Abstract. Tornado Cash, the most popular non-custodial coin mixer on Ethereum, is widely used to protect the privacy of addresses. However, some inappropriate transaction behaviors in Tornado Cash mixing mechanism lead to the risk of privacy leakage. More specifically, the malicious attackers can link multiple addresses of the same users according to the transaction data. Motivated by the above problem, this paper systematically analyzes the privacy issues of Tornado Cash for the first time. In this paper, we give the macroscopic analysis of Tornado Cash based on the on-chain data and formalize two types of transaction patterns. Focus on the presented transaction patterns, we propose three heuristic clustering rules to link the users' addresses, which reduce the size of users' anonymity set. Finally, we perform the experiment on real Tornado Cash transaction data to describe the effectiveness of the proposed clustering rules.

Keywords: Ethereum · Tornado Cash · Address linkability · Heuristic cluster

1 Introduction

Ethereum is the second most valuable cryptocurrency which has been widely used in various areas. In Ethereum blockchain, the transaction data is publicly stored on all Ethereum full nodes, which means any node can access the complete information from the chain. Unfortunately, malicious users can also analyze it to infer correlations between addresses and even the identity of other users with the help of background knowledge.

With the increasing attention to privacy protection, more and more users are trying to hide the association between their own addresses using privacy preservation mechanisms such as coin mixing [3,8–12,15].

Supported by the National Key Research and Development Program of China (Grant No. 2020YFB1006101), the Key-Area Research and Development Program of Guangdong Province (No. 2019B010137003) and the National Natural Science Foundation of China (Grant No. 61972037).

W. Lu et al. (Eds.): CNCERT 2021, CCIS 1506, pp. 39–50, 2022.
https://doi.org/10.1007/978-981-16-9229-1_3

Tornado Cash is one of the most popular coin mixing tools on Ethereum, which had nearly 1.6 million Ether flowing into Tornado coin mixing contracts worth over 2.4 billion in USD. And its handling fee has reached a high of $2.82 million[1]. Users on Tornado Cash only need to invoke the relevant smart contract to complete the coin mixing process. It provides huge convenience for users to enhance the privacy of address linkability. However, some inappropriate use has made it much less effective and exposed some security concerns.

This paper presents the first heuristic address correlation clustering approach based on the user's behaviour in the Tornado Cash coin mixing scenario, analyses the vulnerability of Tornado Cash, and performs experimental analysis on the transaction set.

In summary, the contributions of this paper include:

- We first formally analyze the correlation of transactions on the Tornado Cash coin mixing service and systematically summarize the behavior patterns of users in Tornado.
- We propose three heuristic clustering rules to achieve address correlation for Tornado coin mixing transactions based on the time interval features behind the proposed two types of transaction patterns.
- We perform the experimental analysis on the real-world transaction dataset in Tornado Cash. The results prove the feasibility and effectiveness of the proposed heuristic clustering rules.

The remainder of the paper is organized as follows: In Sect. 2, we briefly review the related work on Ethereum address clustering. Section 3 presents the background knowledge of the proposed approach. Section 4 gives formal definitions of transactions and summarises transaction patterns based on the analytics of data. Section 5 proposes heuristic clustering rules and discusses the experiment results. Section 6 concludes this paper and describes the future work.

2   Related Work

In recent years, researchers pay more and more attention to analyzing Ethereum privacy. However, existing analyses are still limited and mainly explore the privacy of Ethereum users in terms of address correlation.

In general, address correlation methods on Ethereum involve two major categories. One is using machine learning and node embedding methods to cluster transaction behaviour patterns or user accounts with similar characteristics. Sun et al. [13] first applied the node embedding algorithm to the clustering of Ethernet accounts. Hu et al. [7] designed a transaction-based classification detection method for Ethereum smart contracts by summarizing contract transaction behavior patterns. Bhargavi et al. [2] analyzed the Ethereum transaction information to infer the behaviour characteristics in supervised and unsupervised environments.

---

[1] https://duneanalytics.com/poma/tornado-cash_1.

Another category is to use heuristic or graph-based clustering algorithms to link addresses that participated in certain transactions. Chan et al. [4] first explored the feasibility of using graph analysis to link Ethereum addresses. Chen et al. [6] created the finding entity algorithm between tokens on graph analysis. Chen et al. [5] analyzed the contract graph to cluster multiple smart contract accounts controlled by the same entity using weakly connected components. Victor [14] proposed heuristic address clustering rules based on users' behaviors in airdrops, ICOs and exchanges.

The existing work on analyzing the vulnerability of coin mixing service on Ethereum is Béres et al. [1]. They obtained multiple ground truth sets through heuristic rules for coin mixing service to evaluate other clustering algorithms. Nevertheless, in actual transactions, the same custom-set gas prices where the last 9 digits are non-zero are generally initiated by the same addresses. Hence, their proposed rules based on gas prices are not of practical significance.

Based on the above investigation, there is no systematic study of the address clustering that takes coin mixing services on Ethereum into account.

3 Preliminaries

This section introduces the basics of Tornado Cash and outlines the coin mixing principles and processes in Tornado Cash.

3.1 Basics of Tornado Cash

Tornado Cash is a kind of smart contract in Ethereum that uses Zero-Knowledge Succinct Non-Interactive Argument of Knowledge (zk-SNARK) to achieve the unlinkability between addresses that belong to the same users, and protect their privacy in a trustless manner. This paper mainly takes ETH as an example to analyse the Ethereum transactions on Tornado Cash. To avoid address linking by unique value characteristics, Tornado deployed four smart contracts with different denominations to implement the coin mixing services of the fixed value. The detail information is shown in Table 1.

Table 1. Tornado Cash about ETH.

$N.ETH^a$	$SC_{N.ETH}{}^b$	Created time (+UTC)
0.1	12D66f87A04A9E220743712cE6d9bB1B5616B8Fc	2019-12-16 19:08:43
1	47CE0C6eD5B0Ce3d3A51fdb1C52DC66a7c3c2936	2019-12-16 22:17:53
10	910Cbd523D972eb0a6f4cAe4618aD62622b39DbF	2019-12-16 22:46:55
100	A160cdAB225685dA1d56aa342Ad8841c3b53f291	2019-12-25 18:02:56

[a] $N.ETH$ represents the denominations of the Tornado smart contract.
[b] $SC_{N.ETH}$ represents the Tornado contract addresses.

3.2   Coin Mixing Process in Tornado Cash

Users are required to complete the coin mixing in two steps: deposit and withdraw. As shown in Fig. 1, the dotted line denotes the contract invocation, and the solid line denotes the funds flow.

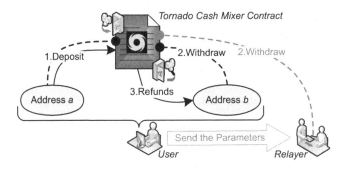

Fig. 1. The process of Tornado Cash coin mixing contract. (Color figure online)

The user uses his address a to invoke the contract $SC_{N.ETH}$ and create an $N.ETH$ deposit transaction, then he will obtain a deposit note. After a period of time, the user utilizes the previous deposit note to create an $N.ETH$ withdraw transaction, thus the contract returns the previously deposited cryptocurrency to address b. The refund address can be any address the user wants to remit funds to, or even an unused address that was originally unfunded. This kind of unused addresses does not have enough Ether to cover the gas fee, in this case, the user can send a request to relayer r with the required parameters, relayer then create a withdraw transaction upon the request as shown by the red connecting line in Fig. 2. The relayer r uses a fraction of f to pay the gas fee. When the contract validates the parameters in the withdrawal transaction successfully, it sends $(N - f)$ Ether to address b and sends f to Relayer r.

Because of the zero-knowledge property in zk-SNARK, Tornado guaranteed that the two transfers are completely independent. Furthermore, a deposit transaction corresponds to only one withdrawal transaction.

4   Analysis of Tornado Cash

The overview of our methodology architecture is shown in Fig. 2, which is divided into three steps: data acquisition, data analysis and cluster, and data presentation. Data acquisition includes the acquisition of related Ethereum transactions, the decoding of individual fields and the deletion of useless fields; data analysis includes statistical analysis of transaction data followed with the experimentation using proposed clustering rules; data presentation part presents the address clustering results.

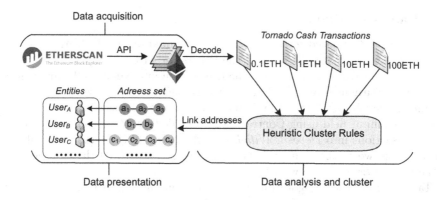

Fig. 2. Overview of our methodology architecture.

4.1   Definitions

This section describes our formal definition in Tornado Cash.

Definition 1 (Transaction). *Transaction is represented as* **tx** = {**hash, from, to, value, input, ts**}, *where:*

- **hash** *is the hash value of* **tx***;*
- **from** *is the address that creates* **tx***;*
- **to** *is the target address of the transaction* **tx***. Specially, in the smart contract invocation transaction,* **to** *is represented the address of the smart contract;*
- **value** *is the value of* **tx***;*
- **input** *is invoke parameter when* **tx** *is a smart contract invocation transaction;*
- **ts** *is the timestamp representing the time when* **tx** *was packaged on.*

The set of transactions is represented as $\mathcal{TX} = \{\mathbf{tx_1}, \mathbf{tx_2}, \ldots, \mathbf{tx_n}\}$.

Definition 2 (Deposit Transaction). *The deposit transaction set is represented as* $\mathcal{D} = \{\mathbf{d_1}, \mathbf{d_2}, \ldots, \mathbf{d_n}\} \subseteq \mathcal{TX}, \forall\ \mathbf{d_i} \in \mathcal{D}, \mathbf{d_i}.\text{input} = (\mathbf{commitment}),$ *where the* **commitment** *field is the parameter used for the zk-SNARK proof.*

Definition 3 (Withdraw Transaction). *The withdraw transaction set is represented as* $\mathcal{W} = \{\mathbf{w_1}, \mathbf{w_2}, \ldots, \mathbf{w_n}\} \subseteq \mathcal{TX}, \forall \mathbf{w_i} \in \mathcal{W}, \mathbf{w_i}.\text{input} = (\mathbf{proof},$ **nullifi- erHash, recipient, relayer, fee, refund**), *where* **proof, nullifier Hash** *are the parameters used for the zk-SNARK,* **recipient** *is the target address for receiving the withdrawal funds,* **relayer** *is the address of the relayer,* **fee** *is the transaction fee given to the relayer, and* **refund** *is the parameter related to the refund.*

- *if* **w.input.fee** $\neq$ **0** *and* **w.input.recipient** $\neq$ **w.from***, then* **w** *is a withdraw transaction using the relayer, and the true withdraw target address is* **w.input.recipient***.*
- *if* **w.input.fee** = **0** *and* **w.input.recipient** = **w.from***, then* **w** *is a withdraw transaction not using the relayer.*

4.2   Data Acquisition

Transactions data related to the four ETH denominations of the Tornado Cash coin mixer contracts are obtained by the Etherscan API[2].

We use the Error field to classify the transaction into **Success Transaction** and **Error Transaction**. The **Error Transaction** is categorized into *Out of gas* and *Reverted* according to the error type. For the **Success Transaction**, we decoded the input field using Contract ABI provided by Etherscan, and categorized transactions into *Deposit*, *Withdraw* and *Other*. On the basis of the above classification, we further removed the useless fields and stored the transactions in the form of *tx* associate with *type*.

Table 2 shows the categories and the corresponding number of transactions for each denomination of Ether in Tornado mixer after our processing since the deployment of the Tornado Cash in 2019 as of May 17, 2021. In addition to deposit and withdrawal transactions for coin mixing, there are a small number of failed transactions, as well as individual transactions related to contract creation, etc.

Table 2. Tornado Cash transactions details about ETH.

Value (ETH)	Success transaction			Error transaction		Total	Anonymity
	Deposit	*Withdraw*	*Others*	*Out of gas*	*Reverted*		set size
0.1	5122	4159	14	205	114	9613	6079
1	6299	5694	2	90	240	12325	6156
10	6988	6572	2	29	184	13775	5655
100	4288	3919	1	13	80	8301	2765
All	22697	20344	19	337	618	44014	16661

Figure 3 shows the percentage of transactions for each denomination of Tornado mixer. As is illustrated in Fig. 3, the 10ETH mixer has the largest number of transactions, while the 100ETH mixer has the least.

4.3   Transaction Patterns

From the analysis of the transaction data, we found a special phenomenon that several transactions were created within a short period of time δ (called a small transaction set $\mathcal{TX}_i$). The time interval Δ between different $\mathcal{TX}_i$ will be much larger than the time interval δ in $\mathcal{TX}_i$ internally. Besides, during the data processing, we discovered that several users in Tornado used the same addresses to deposit and withdraw. Compared their transaction time intervals, the transactions in a small set are created by the same users. In other words, a user tends to create transactions within a short period of time. This phenomenon infers that diverse addresses of transactions within the small transaction set may be controlled by the same user.

---

[2] http://api.etherscan.io/api.

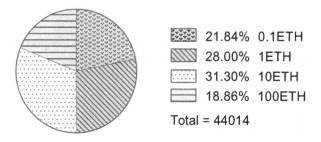

21.84%	0.1ETH
28.00%	1ETH
31.30%	10ETH
18.86%	100ETH

Total = 44014

Fig. 3. Proportion of Tornado mixer transactions by denomination.

From our analysis, we summarize two kinds of the transaction behavior patterns of users, as defined below:

Definition 4 (Single Deposit-Withdraw Coin Mixing Pattern). *The user initiates a deposit transaction* **d** *of N.ETH using address* a. *After an interval* δ, *the user creates a withdraw transaction* **w** *of N.ETH using address* b. *The above pattern is defined as* **pattern I** $: <\mathbf{d}, \mathbf{w}, \delta>$, *where* $\delta = \mathbf{w}.\mathbf{ts} - \mathbf{d}.\mathbf{ts}$, *and* **d**, **w** *satisfy the following conditions:*

- **d.from** $= a$;
- **w.input.recipient** $= b$;
- **d.to** $=$ **w.to**.

Definition 5 (Multi-Deposit and Multi-Withdraw Coin Mixing Pattern). *The user creates* n $(n \geq 2)$ *deposit transactions* $\mathcal{D} = \{\mathbf{d_1}, \mathbf{d_2}, \ldots, \mathbf{d_n}\}$ *of N.ETH using the address set* $\mathcal{A} = \{a_1, a_2, \ldots, a_n\}$. *After an interval* Δ, *the user create* n *withdraw transactions* $\mathcal{W} = \{\mathbf{w_1}, \mathbf{w_2}, \ldots, \mathbf{w_n}\}$ *of N.ETH using address set* $\mathcal{B} = \{b_1, b_2, \ldots, b_n\}$. *The above pattern is defined as* **pattern II:** $<\delta_d, \mathcal{D}, \delta_w, \mathcal{W}, \Delta, n>$, *where* $\delta_d = max\{\mathbf{d_{i+1}}.\mathbf{ts} - \mathbf{d_i}.\mathbf{ts} | \mathbf{d_i}, \mathbf{d_{i+1}} \in \mathcal{D}\}$, $\delta_w = max\{\mathbf{w_{i+1}}.\mathbf{ts} - \mathbf{w_i}.\mathbf{ts} | \mathbf{w_i}, \mathbf{w_{i+1}} \in \mathcal{W}\}$, $\Delta = \mathbf{w_1}.\mathbf{ts} - \mathbf{d_n}.\mathbf{ts}$, *and transactions in* $\mathcal{D}$, $\mathcal{W}$ *satisfy the following conditions:*

- $\forall \mathbf{d_i} \in \mathcal{D}$, $\mathbf{d_i}.\mathbf{from} \in \mathcal{A}$;
- $\forall \mathbf{w_i} \in \mathcal{W}$, $\mathbf{w_i}.\mathbf{input.recipient} \in \mathcal{B}$;
- $\forall \mathbf{tx_i}, \mathbf{tx_j} \in \mathcal{D} \cup \mathcal{W}$, *and* $i \neq j$, $\mathbf{tx_i}.\mathbf{to} = \mathbf{tx_j}.\mathbf{to}$.

Based on the above summaries of transaction patterns, and the fact that some users have the mentality of relying entirely on the tool. They think that Tornado Cash can achieve the address unlinkability without any consideration, therefore eager to withdraw immediately after deposits. We can analyze the time interval among coin mixer transactions to further link the diverse addresses owned by the same user.

5 Heuristic Cluster Rules

In this section, we perform the statistical analysis to propose the heuristic cluster rules linking the addresses belonging to the same user.

5.1 Heuristics

Figure 4 is the statistical results of the time intervals for previous identified users who used the same address to initiate coin mixing transactions based on the transaction patterns defined in Sect. 4.

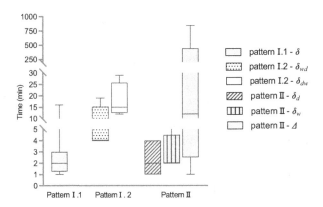

Fig. 4. The interval time statistic based on the transaction patterns.

As shown in the green block in Fig. 4, the time interval δ in ***pattern* I**, where **d** and **w** are created by the same user, is basically no more than 180s. It indicates that there is a subset of users in the Tornado mixer prefer to deposit and withdraw within a short period of time. This interval δ is much smaller than the average 2 h transaction interval that is common in the Tornado transaction set.

Heuristic 1: For ***pattern* I** $<$**d**, **w**, $\delta>$, if $\delta \leq 180s$, the addresses in the transaction pairs {**w.inpit.recipient**, **d.from**} belong to the same user.

Also, when analyzing the time interval in ***pattern* I**, it was found that the same user may create multiple tuples $<$**d**, **w**, $\delta>$ successively. Their interval distribution is shown in the yellow box in Fig. 4.

δ_{dw} denotes the maximum δ_i in the multiple transaction tuples $\{<$**d**$_1$, **w**$_1$, $\delta_1>$, $<$**d**$_2$, **w**$_2$, $\delta_2>$, ..., $<$**d**$_n$, **w**$_n$, $\delta_n>\}$, which is presented as the pure yellow block in Fig. 4; δ_{wd} denotes the maximum time interval between each $<$**d**, **w**, $\delta>$ tuples, which is presented as the dotted yellow block in Fig. 4.

It can be seen that the δ_{dw}, δ_{wd} of multiple $<$**d**, **w**, $\delta>$ tuples are larger than the time interval δ of a single $<$**d**, **w**, $\delta>$ tuple, about 20 min.

Heuristic 2: For multiple single deposit and withdraw coin mixing pairs $\{<d_1, w_1, \delta_{dw1}>, <d_2, w_2, \delta_{dw2}>, \ldots, <d_n, w_n, \delta_{dwn}>\}$, when $n \geq 2$, if $\forall \{d_i, d_{i+1}\} \subseteq \{d_1, d_2, \ldots, d_n\}, \{w_i, w_{i+1}\} \subseteq \{w_1, w_2, \ldots, w_n\}$, $\delta_{wd} = d_{i+1}.ts - w_i.ts$, satisfying one of the following conditions:

- $d_i.from = d_{i+1}.from$, and $\delta_{dwi}, \delta_{dw(i+1)} \leq 20\,min$, $\delta_{wd} > 0$.
- $w_i.input.recipient = w_{i+1}.input.recipient$, and $\delta_{dw(i+1)} > 0$, $\delta_{wd}, \delta_{dwi} \leq 20\,min$.
- $d_i.from = d_{i+1}.from$, and $w_i.input.recipient = w_{i+1}.input.recipient$, $\delta_{wd}, \delta_{dwi}, \delta_{dw(i+1)} > 0$.

The addresses $\{d_1.from, d_2.from, \ldots, d_n.from, w_1.input.recipient, w_2.input.recipient, \ldots, w_n.input.recipient\}$ in these transactions belong to the same user.

The distribution of the time intervals δ_d, δ_w and Δ, for the same user in **pattern II** $<\delta_d, \mathcal{D}, \delta_w, \mathcal{W}, \Delta, n>$ is shown in the pink blocks in Fig. 4. The pink slash blocks and vertical blocks are the maximum time interval between deposit transactions δ_d and withdraw transactions δ_w, respectively; the pure pink block is the time interval Δ. It seems that users tend to create a series of **d** in $\mathcal{D}$, and a series same amount of **w** in $\mathcal{W}$, with a small δ_d and δ_w. However, the time interval Δ between $\mathcal{D}$ and $\mathcal{W}$ is generally longer and more irregular.

Heuristic 3: For **pattern II** $<\delta_d, \mathcal{D}, \delta_w, \mathcal{W}, \Delta, n>$, if satisfying the following conditions:

- $d_1.from = d_2.from = \ldots = d_n.from$;
- $w_1.input.recipient = w_2.input.recipient = \ldots = w_n.input.recipient$;
- $\delta_d, \delta_w \leq 10\,min$ and $\Delta \leq n * 12\,h$.

The addresses $\{d_1.from, d_2.from, \ldots, d_n.from, w_1.input.recipient, w_2.input.recipient, \ldots, w_n.input.recipient\}$ in the n deposit and withdraw transactions belong to the same user.

In particular, the interval threshold Δ between $\mathcal{D}$ and $\mathcal{W}$ is related to the number of transactions n. The number of transactions n is increasing while the number of **pattern II** transactions is decreasing, then the interval threshold between $\mathcal{D}$ and $\mathcal{W}$ should be raised appropriately. In the sense that the threshold Δ is proportional to the number of transactions n.

5.2 Evaluation

We implement a proof-of-concept for the proposed three clustering rules on the Tornado coin mixer and make thorough experiments to verify the effectiveness of our rules. The program is written in the Python language and run in the

Table 3. Result of Heuristic 1–3.

Value (ETH)	Heuristic 1		Heuristic 2		Heuristic 3	
	userNum	*addrNum*	*userNum*	*addrNum*	*userNum*	*addrNum*
0.1	527	1073	61	161	119	255
1	382	840	124	334	270	600
10	310	717	106	308	353	809
100	134	371	68	246	135	373
All	1168	2734	309	953	684	1816

Python 3.6 environment based on the Windows 10 OS, with 2.5 GHz Intel Core i5-7200U CPU and 12 GB RAM.

The results of the experiment are shown in Table 3, where *userNum* and *addrNum* represents the number of clustered user entities and the number of addresses clustered in total, respectively.

As can be seen in Table 3, *Heuristic 1* has the largest number of associative clusters and clustered addresses, while the denomination 0.1ETH having the highest number, reaching 1073. After combining all the clustered results, we eventually obtain 2734 addresses related to 1168 user entities. In *Heuristic 2* and *Heuristic 3*, the highest number of associations clusters for transactions is 1ETH and 10ETH. The 100ETH mixer has the highest degree of clustering in *Heuristic 2*, with an average of 3.6 addresses per user entity.

In the experiments, we notice a particular phenomenon that the destination address **w.input.recipient** $\neq$ **w.from**, and **w.input.fee** = 0. If the relayer forwards the withdraw transaction, it is unreasonable for him to pay gas fee in advance without any forwarding fee. Thus we can infer that the two addresses are likely to be controlled by the same entity. There are a total of 95 user entities with the above case in four mixers, containing 566 related addresses.

The experiment reveals the fact that the users' behaviors hinder the achievement of their desired privacy protection. Indeed, a large proportion of users think using coin mixing tools can unconditionally protect their privacy. Unfortunately, the short time interval of deposing/withdrawing the coins exposes the users' transaction patterns that leaks the linkability of addresses they controlled. Therefore, we suggest users avoid immediately withdrawing operations after depositing their funds and prevent multiple deposits & withdrawals of the same size with one address for better privacy concerns.

6   Conclusion and Future Work

This paper presents the first systematic analysis of Tornado Cash on privacy issues. A macro analysis of the transaction in the Tornado Cash ETH coin mixer is performed. Based on the transaction time interval, two transaction patterns are formalized and three heuristic address clustering rules are proposed. The experimental results indicate that the presented methodology can reveal the address linkability in the Tornado Cash ETH coin mixer.

In future work, we can also apply the proposed methodology to other tokens with different transaction patterns.

References

1. Béres, F., Seres, I.A., Benczúr, A.A., Quintyne-Collins, M.: Blockchain is watching you: Profiling and deanonymizing ethereum users. arXiv preprint arXiv:2005.14051 (2020)
2. Bhargavi, M., Katti, S.M., Shilpa, M., Kulkarni, V.P., Prasad, S.: Transactional data analytics for inferring behavioural traits in Ethereum blockchain network. In: 2020 IEEE 16th International Conference on Intelligent Computer Communication and Processing (ICCP), pp. 485–490. IEEE (2020)
3. Bünz, B., Agrawal, S., Zamani, M., Boneh, D.: Zether: towards privacy in a smart contract world. In: Bonneau, J., Heninger, N. (eds.) FC 2020. LNCS, vol. 12059, pp. 423–443. Springer, Cham (2020). https://doi.org/10.1007/978-3-030-51280-4_23
4. Chan, W., Olmsted, A.: Ethereum transaction graph analysis. In: 2017 12th International Conference for Internet Technology and Secured Transactions (ICITST), pp. 498–500. IEEE (2017)
5. Chen, T., et al.: Understanding Ethereum via graph analysis. ACM Trans. Internet Technol. (TOIT) **20**(2), 1–32 (2020)
6. Chen, W., Zhang, T., Chen, Z., Zheng, Z., Lu, Y.: Traveling the token world: a graph analysis of Ethereum erc20 token ecosystem. In: Proceedings of The Web Conference 2020, pp. 1411–1421 (2020)
7. Hu, T., et al.: Transaction-based classification and detection approach for ethereum smart contract. Inf. Process. Manag. **58**(2), 102462 (2021)
8. Le, D.V., Gervais, A.: Amr: Autonomous coin mixer with privacy preserving reward distribution. arXiv preprint arXiv:2010.01056 (2020)
9. Meiklejohn, S., Mercer, R.: Möbius: trustless tumbling for transaction privacy. Proc. Priv. Enhanc. Technol. **2018**(2), 105–121 (2018)
10. Rondelet, A., Zajac, M.: Zeth: On integrating zerocash on ethereum. arXiv preprint arXiv:1904.00905 (2019)
11. Seres, I.A., Nagy, D.A., Buckland, C., Burcsi, P.: Mixeth: efficient, trustless coin mixing service for ethereum. In: International Conference on Blockchain Economics, Security and Protocols (Tokenomics 2019). Schloss Dagstuhl-Leibniz-Zentrum fuer Informatik (2019)
12. Shlomovits, O., Seres, I.A.: Sharelock: mixing for cryptocurrencies from multiparty ecdsa. IACR Cryptol. ePrint Arch. **2019**, 563 (2019)
13. Sun, H., Ruan, N., Liu, H.: Ethereum analysis via node clustering. In: Liu, J.K., Huang, X. (eds.) NSS 2019. LNCS, vol. 11928, pp. 114–129. Springer, Cham (2019). https://doi.org/10.1007/978-3-030-36938-5_7
14. Victor, F.: Address clustering heuristics for ethereum. In: Bonneau, J., Heninger, N. (eds.) FC 2020. LNCS, vol. 12059, pp. 617–633. Springer, Cham (2020). https://doi.org/10.1007/978-3-030-51280-4_33
15. Zhang, X.: Mixing strategies in cryptocurrencies and an alternative implementation. arXiv preprint arXiv:2010.01670 (2020)

FPFlow: Detect and Prevent Browser Fingerprinting with Dynamic Taint Analysis

Tianyi Li[1], Xiaofeng Zheng[2], Kaiwen Shen[2], and Xinhui Han[1(✉)]

[1] Peking University, Beijing, China
{litianyi,hanxinhui}@pku.edu.cn
[2] Tsinghua University, Beijing, China
{zxf19,skw17}@mails.tsinghua.edu.cn

Abstract. Browser fingerprinting is a practical user tracking technology widely adopted by many real-world websites to potentially track users' browsing behaviors. By collecting information such as screen resolution, user agent, and WebGL rendered data, the tracker can generate a unique identifier for users without their knowledge, leading to a severe violation of user privacy. Therefore, an effective detection and defense technology for browser fingerprinting is needed to protect user privacy. In this paper, we proposed FPFlow, a dynamic JavaScript taint analysis framework to detect and prevent browser fingerprinting. FPFlow monitors the whole process of browser fingerprinting, including collecting information, generating fingerprinting, and sending it to the remote server. We evaluated FPFlow on TRANCO top 10,000 websites. Our experiments showed that our framework could effectively detect browser fingerprints. We found 66.6% of the websites performing fingerprinting and revealed how browser fingerprinting is applied in real-world websites. We also showed that FPFlow could prevent browser fingerprinting with an acceptable overhead.

Keywords: Browser fingerprinting · Taint analysis · Privacy-enhancing technology

1 Introduction

Browser fingerprinting [21] is an online user tracking technique that collects a vector of browser-specific information, such as user agent, screen resolution, and installed browser fonts, etc., to uniquely identify the target browser. Previous studies [15,22] showed that the uniqueness of browser fingerprint could be as high as 89.4%. When combining hardware features by performing rendering tasks with HTML Canvas API and WebGL, browser fingerprint can even track users across browsers. Cao et al. [12] showed that they could uniquely identify more than 99% of 1,903 devices with 31 WebGL rendering tasks.

© The Author(s) 2022
W. Lu et al. (Eds.): CNCERT 2021, CCIS 1506, pp. 51–67, 2022.
https://doi.org/10.1007/978-981-16-9229-1_4

Browser fingerprinting is widely used in several scenarios, such as personalized content and targeted advertising. The widespread deployment of tracking or user analyzing scripts allows trackers to track users across websites. Since browser fingerprinting is stateless (does not rely on client-side storage of identifiers), it is hard to detect and mitigate. Moreover, even the private mode of browsers cannot prevent browser fingerprinting.

Existing fingerprinting detection and prevention methods rely on pre-defined rules or known scripts [7,8,16,17]. Yet, not all of the prevention methods actually "protect" users [14], and some may even make the browser easier to be fingerprinted [10]. Prevention methods like Tor browser [6] will sacrifice user experience(e.g., disable HTML Canvas API and fix the window size). Modern browsers like Firefox have carried out countermeasures against browser fingerprinting. However, we found that Amiunique [1], a website investigating browser fingerprinting, can still uniquely identify the latest version of browsers. It is in dire need of an approach to detect and prevent browser fingerprinting, which motivated us to conduct this research.

Our Study. In this paper, we consider a website as performing browser fingerprinting if it collects fingerprinting attributes and sends them to the remote server. We proposed FPFlow, a dynamic taint analysis approach to detect and prevent browser fingerprinting, leading to potential violation of user privacy. FPFlow marks fingerprinting related attributes as taint source. During JavaScript execution, FPFlow propagates taint between the objects. When JavaScript tries to initiate a web request that carries taint, FPFlow considers it as a fingerprinting request and can block it.

We conducted a large-scale measurement study on TRANCO top 10,000 websites, a more reliable ranking list than Alexa [27]. Our result showed that 6,661 websites transmitted fingerprinting attributes. We further analyzed the fingerprinting attributes used in real-world websites and the behaviors of the tracking scripts.

Contributions: Our main contributions are:

- We proposed a data flow-based method to detect and prevent browser fingerprinting by monitoring all potential fingerprinting data transmission.
- We implemented FPFlow, an in-browser dynamic JavaScript taint analysis framework to detect and prevent browser fingerprinting with an acceptable overhead of 9.2%.
- We performed a large-scale analysis on TRANCO top 10,000 websites. We found 66.6% of websites are sending out fingerprinting attributes, and discussed the behaviors of the related scripts.

2   Related Work

Browser Fingerprinting. Browser fingerprinting is a method to identify a web browser without a stateful identifier like Cookie. Browser fingerprint is generated with a set of browser attributes such as user agent and screen resolution.

Eckersley [15] conducted the Panopticlick experiment in 2010. He used browser properties such as user agent, cookie-enabled to generate fingerprints, and used Flash or Java applets to probe system fonts. Among 286,777 fingerprints collected, 94.2% of them are unique when Java or Flash is enabled. Other browser properties such as battery status [26], installed fonts [18], and extensions [28–30] can also be used as browser fingerprinting.

Hardware features can also be used as part of browser fingerprinting. HTML Canvas and WebGL are widely studied as browser fingerprints representing hardware features. Mowery et al. [23] and Acar et al. [7] showed that rendered data in HTML Canvas has slightly difference in different machine or browser that can be used as browser fingerprinting. Cao et al. [12] carefully designed 31 WebGL rendering tasks and can identify 99.24% of users in their experiment. Englehardt et al. [16] discovered AudioContext based browser fingerprinting when crawling Alexa top sites for online tracking behavior analysis. They tested the feasibility of AudioContext based browser fingerprinting and found 713 different fingerprints among 18,500 users.

Detection of Browser Fingerprinting. To understand browser fingerprinting prevalence in the real-world, existing work proposed different methods to detect browser fingerprinting. Nikiforakis et al. [25] discovered 0.4% of websites in Alexa top 10,000 sites performing fingerprinting by looking for three known fingerprinting scripts.

Several works studied the adoption of browser fingerprinting by monitoring JavaScript APIs. Acar et al. [8] performed a large-scale study of browser fingerprinting on Alexa top 1 million sites. They modified the rendering engine to capture access to browser properties that can be used to perform browser fingerprinting. In 2014, Acar et al. [7] performed a large-scale study on Canvas fingerprinting. They monitored the calls and returns to Canvas API to decide whether a website performs browser fingerprinting and found 5,542 out of 100,000 sites were performing Canvas fingerprinting. Englehardt et al. [16] crawled Alexa top 1 million websites by monitoring the access to JavaScript native APIs. They found 14,317 sites performing Canvas fingerprinting and 67 sites performing AudioContext fingerprinting.

Al-Fannah et al. [9] crawled Majestic 10,000 sites and checked the web requests sent out by browser. A website is defined as engaging fingerprinting if at least one of 17 properties is present in the requests. They identified 6,876 sites that were performing browser fingerprinting.

Iqbal et al. [19] used a machine learning method to detect browser fingerprinting scripts. They extracted the AST of scripts and runtime API accesses as features and found that 22.7% of Alexa top 10,000 websites were performing browser fingerprinting.

Prevention of Browser Fingerprinting. To mitigate browser fingerprinting, Torres et al. [31] introduced FPBlock, a framework to generate a new fingerprinting for each visited domain to prevent cross-domain tracking. FPRandom [20], PriVaricator [24], and Disguised Chromium [11] are frameworks that prevent fingerprinting by randomizing browser properties or Canvas data.

FaizKhademi et al. [17] proposed FPGuard. Their framework first detected browser fingerprinting with 9 metrics. If suspicious behavior is detected, FPGuard will modify the content of the fingerprint. Modern browsers have also come up with fingerprinting protection strategies these years. Firefox blocks fingerprinting related scripts with a tracking script list [2] to protect user from browser fingerprinting.

Although various prevention methods have been proposed in academic research, not all of them can actually "prevent" browser fingerprinting. Vastel et al. [32] developed FP-Scanner to explore the inconsistencies of browser fingerprinting to detect potential alters to fingerprinting attributes. Datta et al. [14] evaluated 26 anti-fingerprinting tools and showed that not all of those protection methods are equal. Azad et al. [10] showed that all tools that attempt to modify the JavaScript behavior are unique fingerprintable, which makes the browser easier to be fingerprinted.

3   Motivation

Browser fingerprinting is a complex process in the JavaScript execution context. Different fingerprinting scripts collect different properties and call different functions to generate fingerprints. We call properties or functions used in browser fingerprinting **fingerprinting attributes**. The fingerprint is generated on the client-side and sent to tracking services through network requests. We call these requests **fingerprinting requests**. To better understand browser fingerprinting, we split the process of browser fingerprinting into five stages, as shown in Fig. 1.

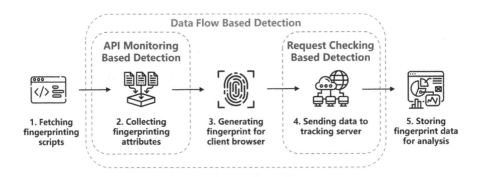

Fig. 1. The process of browser fingerprinting.

Previous studies working on Canvas-based fingerprinting detection and prevention [7,8,16,17] rely on rules defined by researchers. They monitor the access to specific APIs on stage 2, but they could not confirm that the rendered data is sent to the remote server. Their methods may lead to false-positive because Canvas and WebGL are more and more widely used in real-world websites. Besides, their methods cannot detect browser attributes based browser fingerprinting(e.g., the collection of user agent) because these attributes are likely to be accessed in benign scripts. Al-Fannah's study [9] checks whether the requests sent to remote server contains fingerprinting attributes in stage 4. However, their work relies on the value of fingerprinting attributes. As a result, their work cannot detect fingerprint encoding, which will miss some websites that performing fingerprinting. Nor can they detect Canvas based fingerprinting because the canvas data is known before rendering.

In conclusion, existing work only focuses on a single stage of browser fingerprinting. API monitoring based approaches focus on stage 2, and requests checking-based approaches focus on stage 4. These methods do not take data flow into consideration, so the accuracy and ability of fingerprint detection are limited.

To fill the gap, we first define the browser fingerprinting behavior. **We consider a website performing browser fingerprinting if the client-side JavaScript code collects fingerprinting attributes and sends them to the remote server.**

Note that websites may collect fingerprinting attributes for benign reasons like user-agent statistics and language adaption. However, these websites are still capable of tracking users with the collected data. Besides, the information needed for providing client-side functionalities like user-agent and language can be obtained in HTTP headers, which does not depend on JavaScript execution. The website does not need to extract them from JavaScript context and send them to the remote server, especially the third-party ones. As a result, we consider websites that match our definition are all potentially involving browser fingerprinting.

Based on the definition, we introduced data flow analysis to help detect and prevent browser fingerprinting. We implemented a dynamic taint analysis framework FPFlow. FPFlow is a modified Chromium browser. It marks all fingerprinting attributes as taint source and all web request related functions as taint sink. FPFlow tracks the full life cycle of fingerprinting attributes from stage 2 to stage 4, and it can detect both browser attributes based fingerprinting and Canvas based fingerprinting. Our framework can recognize fingerprinting requests and intercept them before sending them out to prevent browser fingerprinting.

4 Technique Approach

In this section, we introduce the technique approach of FPFlow. We first give an overview of FPFlow in Sect. 4.1 to help understanding how FPFlow works. The following parts of this section explain the implementation of FPFlow in detail. Section 4.2 introduces the taint source and taint sink marked by FPFlow. Section 4.3 introduces the taint table and taint name table used to store object taints. Section 4.4 introduces bytecode instrument for runtime taint propagation in FPFlow.

4.1 Overview

Figure 2 shows the abstract architecture overview of FPFlow. FPFlow extends the JavaScript engine V8 and DOM engine Blink of Chromium with taint

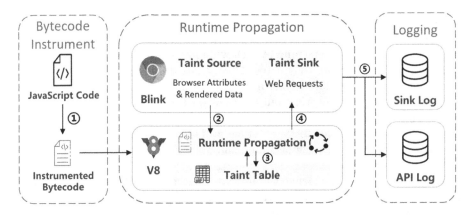

Fig. 2. Abstract architecture of FPFlow.

tracking capabilities. (1) When FPFlow visits a website, it first instruments the bytecode generated by the V8 engine to enable taint propagation. The instrumented bytecode is then executed by the V8 engine. (2) When JavaScript accesses the fingerprinting-related APIs in DOM, the V8 object is marked as tainted. (3) During the script execution, FPFlow propagates the taint between JavaScript objects and updates the taint table and taint name table. (4) When JavaScript tries to send a web request, FPFlow will check if the request carries taint before performing it. (5) If the URL or body of the request carries taint, a taint sink is triggered, and the corresponding log is generated. FPFlow will intercept such requests to prevent browser fingerprinting.

4.2   Taint Source and Taint Sink

The DOM interface of Blink is defined in WebIDL[1] files. WebIDL files define the properties and functions of DOM API. The V8-Blink binding code is generated according to WebIDL files from the code templates. FPFlow marks the taint source and sink properties or function in WebIDL files and modifies the code templates to hook the access to the taint source and sink.

FPFlow marks all fingerprinting attributes as taint sources. Fingerprinting attributes can be a property of the DOM element (e.g., `Cookie`) or the return value of a function (e.g. `toDataUrl`). When V8 tries to access the fingerprinting attributes, Blink will return an object to V8 that holds the value. If the attribute is marked as tainted, the return value is tainted with the name of the attribute.

Web tracking services need to collect user's fingerprints to identify users. Thus, the network request is a key step in browser fingerprinting that leads to privacy threats. FPFlow marks all network-related functions as taint sink. To prevent browser fingerprinting, FPFlow checks whether the request URL or body contains taint before the requests are actually processed. If the request contains

---

[1] https://heycam.github.io/webidl/.

taints, it is a fingerprinting request, and a taint sink is triggered. To prevent browser fingerprinting, FPFlow checks the taints carried by the request. If the request is recognized as an fingerprinting request, FPFlow skips the original request and returns an `undefined` object directly.

The example of marked taint source and taint sink is shown in Table 1. FPFlow marks 72 fingerprinting attributes as taint source (70 browser properties and 2 JavaScript functions) and 5 functions as taint sink. A full list of taint sources is available at https://github.com/FPFlow/FPFlow-project.

Table 1. Selected taint source and sink.

Type		DOM APIs
Source (72 in total)	Properties	`userAgent, innerHeight, colorDepth, Cookie` etc.
	Functions	`toDataUrl, getChannelData`
Sink (5 in total)		`XMLHTTPRequest, HTMLElement.src,`
		`WebSocket, Fetch, Navigator.sendBeacon`

4.3   Taint Table and Taint Name Table

To record the taint carried by JavaScript objects, FPFlow maintains a taint table, a hash table keyed on the internal addresses of V8 objects in each V8 instance. Once an object is tainted, FPFlow will add the object into the taint table along with its taint. When taint is propagated from an object to another object, the data in the object table is updated. As FPFlow uses object address as the key of taint table, there two special cases that need to be handled [13].

First, V8 garbage collection may move objects in memory. When the object is destructed or moved by V8 GC (garbage collection), FPFlow deletes or updates the corresponding entry in the taint table.

Second, Smi is a special type of JavaScript object in V8, which represents integers between -2^{30} and $2^{30} - 1$. The address allocation pattern for Smi is different from other types of objects in V8. Smi objects with the same value share one address (e.g., all Smi objects with value 0x14 shares address 0x1400000000). This feature optimizes the JavaScript runtime performance, but it causes over-taint in our system. FPFlow solves this problem with two steps. Firstly, FPFlow ensures that all values from the taint source are not Smi. If the taint source's value is a Smi value, FPFlow will convert it to HeapNumber, another number representation in V8. Secondly, FPFlow stops the conversion from any other type to Smi. Our method ensures that any object that carries taint cannot be Smi, and only introduces a slight performance overhead.

To accelerate taint propagation, the taint carried by an object is represented as a bitset. A bit in the bitset represents a certain kind of taint. If the object carries the taint, the bit in the bitset is set to 1. The taint propagation operation can be simplified to the logic or operation. We maintain a taint name table, which maps the string name of taint to the specific bit in the bitset. FPFlow maintains one object taint table and one taint name table in each V8 instance to avoid conflict.

4.4   Taint Propagation

Once Chromium receives JavaScript source code, V8 parses the source file and generates the corresponding abstract syntax tree (AST). Then V8 generates bytecode according to the AST. We implement taint propagation logic by instrument additional bytecode in the V8 bytecode generation phase. The taint propagation logic is wrapped in V8 runtime functions and called through a single bytecode `CallRuntime`. Parameters related to taint propagation are passed to the runtime function through registers. FPFlow considers direct taint propagation in the following scenarios:

- Property load: If object `a` is tainted, the properties of `a` like `a.length` carries taint.
- Basic operations: Basic operations include mathematical operations, bit operations, logic expression. If one of the operands carries taint, the result of the operation carries taint as well.
- Native function call: The native function calls in JavaScript are implemented in C++. We need to propagate the corresponding taint when these functions are called. These function includes `encodeURIComponent`, `JSON.stringify`, `toString`, etc. If the parameter passed to the native function carries taint, these functions' return value also carries taints. We extract the address of the native functions during V8 bootstrap and check if a called function is a native function by comparing the function address.

An example of taint propagation is shown in Fig. 3. On line 1, the script gets the value of `navigator.vendor`, the object that holds the value of variable x carries the taint with name "navigator.vendor". On line 2, the taint is propagated from x to y because of the call to native functions. On line 3, the taint is propagated from y to t because of binary operation add. On line 4, the script tries to initiate a web request. The URL of the request (variable t) carries taint, so a taint sink is triggered. FPFlow will log the sink event and intercept this request.

```
1. var x = navigator.vendor;            // Visit Taint Source
2. var y = encodeURIComponent(x);       // Propagate for native function
3. var t = "https://tracker.com/?v="+y; // Propagate for binary operator ADD
4. (new Image).src = t;                 // Trigger taint sink
```

Fig. 3. Example of taint propagation.

4.5 Logging

FPFlow monitors all taint sinks and accesses to DOM API. For a taint sink, FPFlow records its request method, target URL, the taint carried by the request and the stack trace of the request. Each entry in the stack trace contains the function name, the JavaScript file it belongs to and the line number. For API access, FPFlow records the name of the accessed API and the access time.

5 Evaluation

In this section, we describe the experimental setup and present the result of applying FPFlow on TRANCO top 10,000 websites. We did not use Alexa list because previous research showed that Alexa rank is not stable and it changes daily up to 20%, which makes comparability of results difficult [27]. We were able to analyze the adoption of browser fingerprinting in those websites with FPFlow. We found 66.6% of the websites transmitting browser fingerprinting, which leads to potential browser fingerprinting based tracking. We also measured the effectiveness of FPFlow in preventing browser fingerprinting.

5.1 Experimental Setup

We crawled the homepage of TRANCO top 10,000 sites and gathered their behavior with FPFlow. FPFlow was driven by puppeteer [5] for automatically testing. To avoid the interference between websites caused by cookies or browsing history, we used a new browser instance for each website during the crawling process.

We captured all the script data during the crawling process. We used mitmproxy [4] to intercept all requests to JavaScript files and stored them for further analysis. In addition, we also used js-beautify [3] to format all JavaScript files captured by mitmproxy so that FPFlow could get a clear stack trace when the taint sink is triggered.

We waited for 120 s on each website during crawling to capture as many requests as possible. Meanwhile, we need to leave enough time for JavaScript code formatting since the size of loaded JavaScript code could be very large in modern web applications.

5.2 Large Scale Experiment Result

The crawling process took 30 h to complete. The detailed result is available at https://github.com/FPFlow/FPFlow-project. During the experiment, 40 websites (0.4%) did not work properly (e.g., did not respond or returned an HTTP error). In 9,960 successful crawled websites, 6,661 sites collected fingerprinting attributes from user browsers and sent them to remote servers. We refer to such websites as **fingerprinting websites**. Among the 6,661 fingerprinting websites, 6043 sent user data to the third-party domain, while 2,094 sent data to both first-party and third-party domains.

Table 2. Usage of tracking services.

Tracker domain	Sites
doubleclick.net	5,208
google-analytics.com	4,333
google.com	2,006
googlesyndication.com	1,370
rubiconproject.com	1,354
facebook.com	1,274
adnxs.com	754
rlcdn.com	596
casalemedia.com	581
criteo.com	493

Table 3. Usage of attributes.

Attribute	Used sites
UserAgent	6,397
Cookie	6,346
AppVersion	4,512
History:Length	4,473
Resolution	3,072
Platform	3,010
NavigatorLanguage	2,952
CookieEnabled	2,948
Screen:ColorDepth	2,319
Navigator:NavigatorPlugins	2,204

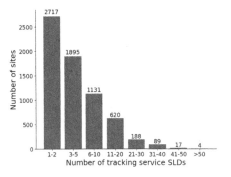

Fig. 4. Number of tracking services.   **Fig. 5.** Number of attributes collected.

We analyzed the tracking services that fingerprinting requests are sent to. Table 2 shows the most frequently used tracking services. We found that the most commonly used browser fingerprinting service providers are Google. We found 4,900 websites sending data to Google related domains[2].

We find that 5,363 websites send user data to more than one fingerprinting service. Figure 4 shows the number of tracking services used by TRANCO websites. Among 6,661 fingerprinting websites, the fingerprinting attributes were sent to an average of 5.59 domains. The maximum number of domains the fingerprinting attributes were sent to is 74.

Fingerprinting Attributes Collected by Tracking Services. The most used fingerprinting attributes are shown in Table 3. The widely used attributes are widely discussed in previous researches [15,25].

---

[2] google-analytics.com, doubleclick.net, google.com, googlesyndication.com.

We found that `document.cookie` is widely used in browser fingerprinting. This is because those tracking scripts are likely to store user fingerprint data in cookie data. The tracking service provider can track fingerprint changes in the client browser caused by software, operating system, and hardware update.

For rendering-based fingerprinting, we found 713 websites performing Canvas fingerprinting (including WebGL fingerprinting). Although previous research showed that Canvas fingerprinting could achieve high accuracy, it is not widely used in real-world websites, probably due to compatibility or performance reasons. We extract the initiator script of requests carry Canvas data. By manually inspecting the scripts, we found that Canvas fingerprinting scripts deployed to real-world websites mainly based on two open-source projects *fingerprintjs*[3] and *Picasso based canvas fingerprinting*[4]. By matching the keyword `fingerprintjs` and `picasso-like-canvas`, we found 334 websites use *the fingerprintjs* library, and 192 websites use *the Picasso* library.

We also find an obfuscated canvas fingerprinting script[5] is used by 88 websites. Our experiment found 49 websites performing AudioContext based fingerprinting.

We use the API trace recorded by FPFlow and filter rules from previous research to find Canvas-based font probing. More specifically, a website is performing Canvas-based font probing if it sets the `font` property on a Canvas to more than 20 different fonts and calls `measureText` over 20 times. We found 331 sites use Canvas-based font probing. We also found scripts using CCS-based font probing. This method is a part of *fingerprintjs* library. It first creates a `span` element, fills in some text, and sets a default font for text in span. To check if a font F is supported, the script creates another `span` element, fills in the same text, and sets the font to F. If the width and height of the two `span` elements are different, font F is supported in the browser.

The number of fingerprinting attributes collected by each website is shown in Fig. 5. A website collects 13.74 attributes on average, and the maximum number of collected taints is 55.

Request Methods. Table 4 shows the fingerprinting request methods used by TRANCO websites. We found that the most used request method is GET request with `src` attribute and POST request with `XMLHTTPRequest`. We also found that `Fetch`, `SendBeacon`, and `WebSocket` are also widely used in fingerprinting scripts, which is not mentioned in previous browser fingerprinting research.

Fingerprinting Initiator Scripts. We extract the initiator scripts of fingerprinting requests by analyzing the stack trace when the taint sink is triggered and comparing the initiator script with the target of the requests. Our result shows that the most used scripts are from the top user tracking services. We analyzed the number of different domains that a tracking script sends requests to. Most of these scripts initiate requests to a single domain. Some scripts will

---

[3] https://github.com/fingerprintjs/fingerprintjs.

[4] https://github.com/antoinevastel/picasso-like-canvas-fingerprinting.

[5] https://www.zalando.de/akam/11/2a40e12f.

Table 4. Fingerprinting request methods.

Request method	Used sites
XMLHTTPRequest	5,999
Element.src	4,795
Fetch	1,600
sendBeacon	1,319
WebSocket	128

send user data to several related domains. For example, scripts from google will send data to `google-analytics.com`, `google.com`, `googlesyndication.com` and `doubleclick.net`. We also find that some scripts try to load many different tracking scripts. We refer to these scripts as **tracker loader**. For example, we found 78 websites use tracking service from `cdn.krxd.net`. Each website using this tracking service has a configuration script indicating what third-party tracking service needs to be loaded.

Figure 6 is an example of the configuration script from `cdn.krxd.net`. The loader script from `cdn.krxd.net` will load all third-party trackers into the web page. Besides, the third-party trackers loaded by `cdn.krxd.net` use an id generated by the loader script, and the id is shared with those third-party services. This means the third-party services can also track the user with the help of the tracking service provided by `cdn.krxd.net`.

```
[{
    "id": 6,
    "name": "Google User Match",
    "content": "var kuid = Krux('get', 'user'); ... new Image().src = \
     'https://cm.g.doubleclick.net/pixel?google_nid=krux_digital&google_hm='+baseEncodedKuid"
}, {
    "id": 21,
    "name": "Acxiom",
    "content": "var kuid = Krux('get', 'user'); ... \
     var liveramp_url = 'https://idsync.rlcdn.com/379708.gif?partner_uid=' + kuid;"
}, {
    "id": 153,
    "name": "Datonics User Match",
    "content": "var kuid = Krux('get', 'user'); ... \
     var datonics_url = 'https://fei.pro-market.net/engine?mimetype=img&du=88&csync=' + kuid;"
},]
```

Fig. 6. A example of fingerprinting configuration script with shared user ID.

Fingerprinting Beacon. Our experiment shows that many sites sent user data to a URL many times. These requests contain the same or different parameters. We call a website sending **fingerprinting beacon** if it sends more than 5 requests to a single URL. We found 860 websites are sending fingerprint beacons, and 674 sites are sending out fingerprint beacons with different parameters each time.

We analyzed the stack trace of the beacon requests and extracted the function names in the stack. We searched for keywords `event` and `interval` in function names and found matched function names in fingerprinting beacon from 57 sites. The matched function names includes `postEvent`, `trackAnalyticsEvent`, `GoogleAnalyticsEventTracking` and `setInterval`. By manually analyze the web page, we found that these requests are triggered at regular intervals or when a specific event is triggered. For example, we found the script from `jd.com` add fingerprinting events to the logo of the page. The fingerprinting request is triggered when the user moves the mouse over the logo. This indicates that the tracking service is tracking the user's visit history and recording the user's detailed browsing behavior.

5.3   Evaluate the Accuracy of Taint Analysis

The lack of standard reference for browser fingerprint usage and the huge volume of front-end code make it difficult to analyze them all. Therefore, we evaluated the FPFlow detection results mainly by random sampling and manual verification.

We randomly selected 50 websites that use browser fingerprinting. These 50 sites contain 400 requests containing tainted requests. We analyzed these browser fingerprint requests manually. We determined whether the requests were false positives by analyzing the information carried in the requests and the logic of the script code that initiated the requests. In our manual analysis, we found 39 requests to be FPFlow false positives. The estimated false positive rate of FPFlow is 9.75%.

5.4   Fingerprinting Prevention

Collection of only a few fingerprinting attributes is not enough to generate a precise fingerprint for client user. As prevention method, we consider a request as fingerprinting request if (1) it is using Canvas based fingerprinting or Audio-Context based fingerprinting, or (2) it carries more than 10 taints.

To test the usability, we tested the extended FPFlow by manually browsing the top 50 sites in the TRANCO list. We stopped for 1 min to perform basic operations for each site, like click the link and log in. The fingerprinting requests were successfully blocked, and we did not observe any abnormalities during the test.

Previous research [19] discussed the page breakage caused by request blocking. They stated that URL blocking-based protection could affect the user experience because request blocking will block the content loading. FPFlow won't block the resource loading request (e.g., loading content from a tracker or advertising domain). Instead, FPFlow only intercepts data transmission requests. We found that these requests seldom return data. For example, many fingerprinting requests using `src` attributes requests for a zero-size GIF image. Such requests are only used for collecting client data, and they do not load anything. As a result, blocking such requests will not cause breakage to the web page.

We also evaluated the overhead of FPFlow by comparing it with the original Chromium browser. Since the API access monitoring feature of FPFlow is only used to compare the result with previous work and introduces relatively large IO overhead, we disabled the API access monitoring feature in the performance testing. We selected the TRANCO top 100 sites and loaded them with FPFlow and original Chromium. We recorded the time from the start of the two browsers to the end of the page loading. The performance overhead ranges from 6% to 13%, with an average of 9.2%.

6   Discussion

Our Improvements to Previous Approaches. Comparing with API monitoring based detection and prevention [7,8,16,17], FPFlow can reduce false positives. We found radio garden[6], an online FM website using Canvas and WebGL to generate the background of the page. The API access trace of this website contains many operations related to WebGL, and the generated image data is retrieved through API toDataURL. It is likely for previous work to mistake this website as performing Canvas fingerprinting. However, FPFlow showed that the rendered data is not sent to the remote server.

```
getLocation: function() {
    return fingerprint.util.MD5.hex_md5(location.href.split("?")[0])
},
getUserAgent: function() {
    return fingerprint.util.MD5.hex_md5(navigator.userAgent)
}
.....
t.push("canvas fp:" + fingerprint.util.MD5.hex_md5(r.toDataURL())),
```

Fig. 7. Fingerprinting encoding script.

We found that encoding or hashing browser fingerprints is a common practice. The encoded fingerprinting is transmitted through the web or stored in Cookie as a user identifier. Comparing with request checking based detection [9], FPFlow is not limited by fingerprint encoding since encoding or hashing does not cut off taint propagation. Figure 7 is a formatted code snippet from https://wl.jd. com/wl.js. The fingerprinting data (including location, user agent, and rendered Canvas data) is hashed with the MD5 algorithm.

Limitations. Although FPFlow can detect fingerprinting attributes transmission, it has several limitations. First, FPFlow propagates taint only with explicit data flow, and it is not able to propagate with implicit data flow, which results in false negative. As a result, our experiment revealed the lower bound of the

---

[6] http://radio.garden/.

current deployment of potential browser fingerprinting. Second, FPFlow cannot detect WebRTC fingerprinting and JavaScript font probing because these techniques do not rely on the return value of certain API. These fingerprinting methods can be detected with the API accessing pattern, as mentioned in previous researches.

7   Conclusion

In this paper, we introduced FPFlow, a pure dynamic taint analysis framework upon Chromium to detect and prevent browser fingerprinting. FPFlow monitors the data flow from retrieving fingerprinting attributes to sending them to tracking service. Based on FPFlow, we conducted a large-scale browser fingerprinting detection on TRANCO top 10,000 sites and found that 66.6% of the websites are transmitting fingerprinting data, leading to potential fingerprinting based tracking. Meanwhile, our experiments revealed the behavior of fingerprinting scripts such as tracker loader and fingerprinting beacon. We also showed that FPFlow could prevent browser fingerprinting with no sacrifice to user experience. Our work introduces data flow analysis to have a better understanding of how browser fingerprinting is adopted in the real world.

References

1. Amiunique. https://amiunique.org/fp
2. Firefox's protection against fingerprinting. https://support.mozilla.org/en-US/kb/firefox-protection-against-fingerprinting
3. JS-beautify. https://github.com/beautify-web/js-beautify
4. mitmproxy. https://mitmproxy.org/
5. Puppeteer. https://pptr.dev/
6. Tor project. https://www.torproject.org/
7. Acar, G., Eubank, C., Englehardt, S., Juarez, M., Narayanan, A., Diaz, C.: The web never forgets: persistent tracking mechanisms in the wild. In: Proceedings of the 2014 ACM SIGSAC Conference on Computer and Communications Security, pp. 674–689 (2014)
8. Acar, G., Juarez, M., Nikiforakis, N., Diaz, C., Gürses, S., Piessens, F., Preneel, B.: FPDetective: dusting the web for fingerprinters. In: Proceedings of the 2013 ACM SIGSAC Conference on Computer & Communications Security, pp. 1129–1140 (2013)
9. Al-Fannah, N.M., Li, W., Mitchell, C.J.: Beyond cookie monster amnesia: real world persistent online tracking. In: Chen, L., Manulis, M., Schneider, S. (eds.) ISC 2018. LNCS, vol. 11060, pp. 481–501. Springer, Cham (2018). https://doi.org/10.1007/978-3-319-99136-8_26
10. Amin Azad, B., Starov, O., Laperdrix, P., Nikiforakis, N.: Short paper - taming the shape shifter: detecting anti-fingerprinting browsers. In: Maurice, C., Bilge, L., Stringhini, G., Neves, N. (eds.) DIMVA 2020. LNCS, vol. 12223, pp. 160–170. Springer, Cham (2020). https://doi.org/10.1007/978-3-030-52683-2_8

11. Baumann, P., Katzenbeisser, S., Stopczynski, M., Tews, E.: Disguised chromium browser: robust browser, flash and canvas fingerprinting protection. In: Proceedings of the 2016 ACM on Workshop on Privacy in the Electronic Society, pp. 37–46 (2016)

12. Cao, Y., Li, S., Wijmans, E., et al.: (cross-) browser fingerprinting via OS and hardware level features. In: NDSS (2017)

13. Chen, Q., Kapravelos, A.: Mystique: uncovering information leakage from browser extensions. In: Proceedings of the 2018 ACM SIGSAC Conference on Computer and Communications Security, pp. 1687–1700 (2018)

14. Datta, A., Lu, J., Tschantz, M.C.: Evaluating anti-fingerprinting privacy enhancing technologies. In: The World Wide Web Conference, pp. 351–362 (2019)

15. Eckersley, P.: How unique is your web browser? In: Atallah, M.J., Hopper, N.J. (eds.) PETS 2010. LNCS, vol. 6205, pp. 1–18. Springer, Heidelberg (2010). https://doi.org/10.1007/978-3-642-14527-8_1

16. Englehardt, S., Narayanan, A.: Online tracking: a 1-million-site measurement and analysis. In: Proceedings of the 2016 ACM SIGSAC Conference on Computer and Communications Security, pp. 1388–1401 (2016)

17. FaizKhademi, A., Zulkernine, M., Weldemariam, K.: FPGuard: detection and prevention of browser fingerprinting. In: Samarati, P. (ed.) DBSec 2015. LNCS, vol. 9149, pp. 293–308. Springer, Cham (2015). https://doi.org/10.1007/978-3-319-20810-7_21

18. Fifield, D., Egelman, S.: Fingerprinting web users through font metrics. In: Böhme, R., Okamoto, T. (eds.) FC 2015. LNCS, vol. 8975, pp. 107–124. Springer, Heidelberg (2015). https://doi.org/10.1007/978-3-662-47854-7_7

19. Iqbal, U., Englehardt, S., Shafiq, Z.: Fingerprinting the fingerprinters: learning to detect browser fingerprinting behaviors. arXiv preprint arXiv:2008.04480 (2020)

20. Laperdrix, P., Baudry, B., Mishra, V.: FPRandom: randomizing core browser objects to break advanced device fingerprinting techniques. In: Bodden, E., Payer, M., Athanasopoulos, E. (eds.) ESSoS 2017. LNCS, vol. 10379, pp. 97–114. Springer, Cham (2017). https://doi.org/10.1007/978-3-319-62105-0_7

21. Laperdrix, P., Bielova, N., Baudry, B., Avoine, G.: Browser fingerprinting: a survey. ACM Trans. Web (TWEB) 14(2), 1–33 (2020)

22. Laperdrix, P., Rudametkin, W., Baudry, B.: Beauty and the beast: diverting modern web browsers to build unique browser fingerprints. In: 2016 IEEE Symposium on Security and Privacy (SP), pp. 878–894. IEEE (2016)

23. Mowery, K., Shacham, H.: Pixel perfect: fingerprinting canvas in HTML5. In: Proceedings of W2SP, pp. 1–12 (2012)

24. Nikiforakis, N., Joosen, W., Livshits, B.: PriVaricator: deceiving fingerprinters with little white lies. In: Proceedings of the 24th International Conference on World Wide Web, pp. 820–830 (2015)

25. Nikiforakis, N., Kapravelos, A., Joosen, W., Kruegel, C., Piessens, F., Vigna, G.: Cookieless monster: exploring the ecosystem of web-based device fingerprinting. In: 2013 IEEE Symposium on Security and Privacy, pp. 541–555. IEEE (2013)

26. Olejnik, Ł, Acar, G., Castelluccia, C., Diaz, C.: The leaking battery. In: Garcia-Alfaro, J., Navarro-Arribas, G., Aldini, A., Martinelli, F., Suri, N. (eds.) DPM/QASA -2015. LNCS, vol. 9481, pp. 254–263. Springer, Cham (2016). https://doi.org/10.1007/978-3-319-29883-2_18

27. Pochat, V.L., Van Goethem, T., Tajalizadehkhoob, S., Korczyński, M., Joosen, W.: Tranco: a research-oriented top sites ranking hardened against manipulation. arXiv preprint arXiv:1806.01156 (2018)

28. Sjösten, A., Van Acker, S., Sabelfeld, A.: Discovering browser extensions via web accessible resources. In: Proceedings of the Seventh ACM on Conference on Data and Application Security and Privacy, pp. 329–336 (2017)

29. Starov, O., Laperdrix, P., Kapravelos, A., Nikiforakis, N.: Unnecessarily identifiable: quantifying the fingerprintability of browser extensions due to bloat. In: The World Wide Web Conference, pp. 3244–3250 (2019)

30. Starov, O., Nikiforakis, N.: XHOUND: quantifying the fingerprintability of browser extensions. In: 2017 IEEE Symposium on Security and Privacy (SP), pp. 941–956. IEEE (2017)

31. Torres, C.F., Jonker, H., Mauw, S.: *FP-Block*: usable web privacy by controlling browser fingerprinting. In: Pernul, G., Ryan, P.Y.A., Weippl, E. (eds.) ESORICS 2015. LNCS, vol. 9327, pp. 3–19. Springer, Cham (2015). https://doi.org/10.1007/978-3-319-24177-7_1

32. Vastel, A., Laperdrix, P., Rudametkin, W., Rouvoy, R.: FP-scanner: the privacy implications of browser fingerprint inconsistencies. In: 27th {USENIX} Security Symposium ({USENIX} Security 18), pp. 135–150 (2018)

Anomaly Detection

Deep Learning Based Anomaly Detection for Muti-dimensional Time Series: A Survey

Zhipeng Chen[1], Zhang Peng[2,3], Xueqiang Zou[1(✉)], and Haoqi Sun[2,3]

[1] National Internet Emergency Center, CNCERT/CC, Beijing 100029, China
zouxueqiang@cert.org.cn
[2] School of Cyber Security, University of Chinese Academy of Sciences, Beijing 100864, China
[3] Institute of Information Engineering, Chinese Academy of Sciences, Beijing 100093, China

Abstract. Multi-dimensional time series are multiple sets of variables collected in chronological order, which are the results of observing a certain potential process according to a given sampling rate. It also has the ability to describe space and time and is widely used in many fields such as system state anomaly detection. However, multi-dimensional time series have problems such as dimensional explosion and data sparseness, as well as complex pattern features such as periods and trends. Such characteristics lead to rule-based anomaly detection methods suffer from poor detection effects. In the big data scenario, deep learning method begins to be applied to anomaly detection tasks for multi-dimensional time series due to its wide coverage and strong learning ability. This work first summarizes the definitions of anomaly detection for multi-dimensional time series and the challenges it faces. Related methods are sorted out, and then the deep learning-based method is emphasized. The existing work and its advantages and disadvantages are summarized. Finally, the shortcomings of the existing algorithms are clarified and the future research direction is explored.

Keywords: Anomaly detection · Muti-dimensional time series · Machine learning · Deep learning

1 Introduction

With the rapid development of the information age, the amount of data has exponentially increased. In the environment of big data, how to mine the hidden information from the massive data is a new topic and challenge for the development of information technology. At the same time, there are a lot of abnormal patterns in these data, which also contain a lot of important information. Anomaly detection actually refers to finding the data that does not match the normal pattern in the data [1]. Such mismatched data is called anomaly or outlier. Abnormal patterns and outliers are two types of detected entities in anomaly detection task. As shown in Fig. 1, the types of abnormalities mainly include abnormal points and abnormal sequences. In anomaly detection, traditional heuristic rules set thresholds based on historical data. If the value of a point exceeds or falls below the threshold, the point is classified as a "point anomaly". At present, most of the existing work is aimed at the detection of abnormal points.

© The Author(s) 2022
W. Lu et al. (Eds.): CNCERT 2021, CCIS 1506, pp. 71–92, 2022.
https://doi.org/10.1007/978-981-16-9229-1_5

An abnormal sequence refers to a continuous abnormal pattern in data points within a continuous period of time. For example, a time series has the same trend every day from 7 am to 9 am, indicating that the series has a certain periodicity. If the trend changes on a certain day, it is more likely that there will be an anomaly on that day. The anomaly detection method for sequence is more complex than anomaly points, and the real-time effect of the algorithm is poor.

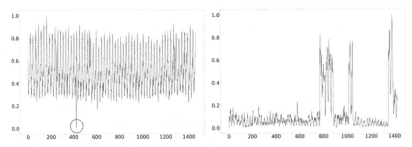

Fig. 1. Two types of anomalies (points and sequence).

An abnormal sequence refers to a continuous abnormal pattern in data points within a continuous period of time. For example, a time series has the same trend every day from 7 am to 9 am, indicating that the series has a certain periodicity. If the trend changes on a certain day, it is more likely that there will be an anomaly on that day. The anomaly detection method for sequence is more complex than anomaly points, and the real-time effect of the algorithm is poor.

There are many reasons for the abnormal pattern of the data. Firstly, there may be an error in the system, causing some noise and missing values in the data; secondly, there may be that an unknown or deviated data from the normal pattern is generated in the system, which means that there is an abnormality. When analyzing the real data set in the real world, it is necessary to identify the abnormal pattern, that is, to distinguish the data points in the data sample set that deviate from the normal pattern, and to dig out the relevant information hidden in the abnormal data. At present, anomaly detection is applied in many fields, such as fraud detection, network intrusion detection, medical anomaly detection, log anomaly detection, video surveillance anomaly detection, and industrial IoT big data anomaly detection. At the same time, the data entities in most of the above fields are typical time series data.

Time series data are recorded periodically in the form of series for the data describing the system behavior at each moment. System behavior may change due to some external events or changes in the internal state of the system. Therefore, for time series data, a large amount of system-related information can be mined from factors such as data trends, peaks, valleys, and periodicity.

Multi-dimensional time series are groups of ordered variables collected according to time sequence and a given sampling frequency. They are the result of observing a certain potential process and have the ability to describe space and time at the same time. Broadly speaking, a multi-dimensional time series is composed of multiple single-dimensional time series. For example, the CPU utilization rate collected from a server is a single-dimensional time series, while a multi-dimensional time series records multiple system indicators at the same time. In the system operation and maintenance monitoring scenario, the monitoring of the real-time status of the database includes multiple indicators such as the number of transactions per second, the number of active sessions, and the number of connected sessions and other indicators. That is, the real-time status of the database will be determined by multiple indicators.

Time series data is strongly correlated with time. The longer the time period, the more data generated, and the greater the amount of time series data in the time dimension. Existing work mostly uses sliding windows to cut the time series and divide them into multiple sub-sequences with smaller dimensions before analysis. As shown in Fig. 2, assuming that the window size of the sliding window is 4 and the step size is 2, a sequence with a length of 12 is divided into 5 sub-sequences, and there is overlap between the sub-sequences. The window and step length parameters should be analyzed in detail according to the specific algorithm.

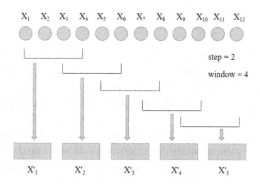

Fig. 2. Use sliding window to segment spatio-temporal series.

In addition, the multi-dimensional time series contains complex periodic components, trend components, and high-frequency residual components. As shown in Fig. 3, concept drift, periodic change and other phenomena may occur in different time periods of a time series, and there is certain noise. The particularity of multi-dimensional sequence data makes it difficult to directly model time series and apply them to downstream anomaly detection tasks.

In this context, methods such as heuristic rules based on the establishment of alarm thresholds are no longer suitable for anomaly detection in big data scenarios. The industry expects to learn the internal correlation and essence of massive data through the idea of deep learning, and detect the possible anomalies in the system through artificial intelligence. At present, how to apply deep learning and other algorithms to anomaly detection tasks oriented to multi-dimensional time series is also one of the research hotspots in the industry and academia in recent years.

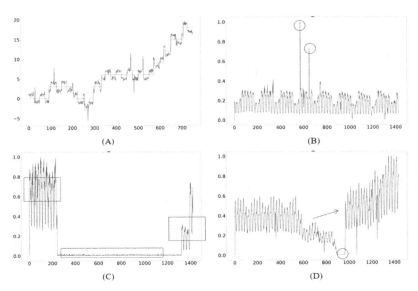

Fig. 3. Complex pattern in time series.

In this paper, the multi-dimensional time series-oriented anomaly detection technology and methods are described and summarized. The main arrangements of the paper are as follows: the first part of the introduction mainly introduces related definitions and research background, and the second part summarizes the challenges and difficulties faced by the multi-dimensional time series-oriented anomaly detection task. The third to fifth parts mainly organize and analyze different anomaly detection methods. Which focuses on summarizing the anomaly detection methods based on deep learning. Finally, the sixth part summarizes the shortcomings of anomaly detection methods based on deep learning, and looks forward to the future research direction.

2   Challenge

Multi-dimensional time series data is strongly related to time. The data at a certain moment records the real-time status information of the system at that moment, which has the characteristics of dimension explosion and data imbalance, and most of the application fields require high real-time performance for anomaly detection. At the same time, the time series contains a large number of complex temporal and spatial semantic features such as cycles and trends, which brings challenges to anomaly detection tasks for multi-dimensional time series.

2.1   Dimensional Explosion

The time series is strongly correlated with time. The longer the time period, the higher the time dimension of the collected data. Since the monitoring of the system is 7 * 24 uninterrupted, the amount of monitoring data will continue to grow as time goes by. At the same time, in the process of collecting data, some data may be lost due to sensor failure and other reasons; noise data may also be collected due to system failure and other reasons. For this kind of data, it is necessary to preprocess the noise and missing values in the time series to reduce the dimensionality of the data before performing anomaly detection.

2.2 Concept Drift

In the real world, time series are generally a non-stationary series, that is, the mean and variance of the time series do not obey a certain distribution, so there are very large limitations in the feature representation. For example, the difference integrated moving average autoregressive model (ARIMA) [2] has poor prediction effect for non-stationary series. In the process of time series anomaly detection, as time changes, both the abnormal mode and the normal mode of the sequence may change, that is, the phenomenon of concept drift occurs. At the same time, change points may also occur in the time series. These factors will affect the accuracy of anomaly detection results.

2.3 Complex Semantics

Time series data has natural time semantics, that is, the system state at time $t + 1$ may be related to the system state from time 1 to t. In addition, time series may have characteristics such as periodicity and periodicity. For example, a company draws and analyzes the historical data of system monitoring indicators, and finds that the data line chart shows some similar trends at a specific time of each day, from which some system related information can be diged out.

There are not only temporal semantics but also spatial semantics in multi-dimensional time series data. The concept of spatial semantics is mainly derived from the spatial dimensions of multi-dimensional time series data. When monitoring the state of a system, there may be multiple monitoring indicators, and there is a certain correlation between data of different dimensions and jointly determine the current system status. Therefore, for multi-dimensional time series data, it is necessary to mine spatial semantics in spatial dimensions.

When analyzing time series data, there may also be external semantic features in the data. For example, the UAH-DriveSet [3] dataset collects driving behavior data during six driving sessions, and records the speed and direction of the car at each moment. At the same time, the data set additionally records the type of road (highway, urban road, village lane, etc.) that is driven each time. The characteristics of this dimension have nothing to do with temporal and spatial semantics, but it has a key impact on the accuracy of anomaly detection results.

It can be seen that there are temporal semantics, spatial semantics and external semantics in multi-dimensional time series. The heuristic rule method based on threshold setting cannot mine rich and complex semantic features, which further affects the accuracy of anomaly detection.

2.4 Data Sparse

In a period of time, abnormal patterns only account for a small part, and most of the sequences are normal patterns. Similarly, in most public data sets related to time series, the number of abnormal patterns in the sample set is very small, and the imbalanced data sets cause certain classifiers in machine learning to have a certain bias. At the same time, there are very few public data sets for time series. The public data sets available are Yahoo Benchmark [4] and Numenta Anomaly Benchmark [5]. Since deep learning methods require a large amount of training data, the data volume of existing public data sets cannot meet the requirements. Existing works mostly use private data sets to expand the data volume, and the private data sets are generally unlabeled. On the one hand, because anomaly detection is a typical two-class or multi-classification task, it is difficult to use unsupervised learning algorithm directly because of its high dependence on data labels; on the other hand, if the algorithm adopts supervised and semi-supervised learning methods, It is necessary to label time series data, which requires strong professional knowledge and it is very labor intensive.

2.5 Poor Scalability

Anomaly detection is roughly divided into offline detection and online detection. Offline detection refers to the analysis of historical data to extract abnormal patterns; while online detection is the real-time analysis and monitoring of the system status. In an industrial environment, the version of the system will continue to change with the update of requirements and the improvement of the architecture, resulting in frequent changes in the data entities in the online inspection process, and the dimensionality of the collected time series data continues to increase. However, existing algorithms generally only analyze historical data, and the model has poor scalability, so it can not be applied to industrial production environments. In addition, the online detection method needs to control the calculation time delay of the algorithm to a lower range. If the abnormality can be detected earlier, the more the loss caused by the abnormality of the system can be recovered, but this puts higher requirements on the calculation time of the algorithm.

2.6 Summary

The challenges of anomaly detection algorithms for multi-dimensional time series are summarized in Table 1. The anomaly detection task is generally divided into four steps: data collection, data preprocessing, feature representation learning, and anomaly detection. In the above process, there may be problems such as data sparseness, noise and missing values, complex semantic information, and poor real-time performance of algorithms.

Table 1. Summary of challenges during multi-dimensional time series-oriented anomaly detection process.

Process	Challenge	Description
Data source	Lack of public dataset	Data points in existing public dataset [4, 5] are far from enough
	Unbalanced dataset	The proportion of abnormal points too low causes the Classifier to be biased
Data preprocess	Noise and missing value	Noise and missing value in real world data interfere with model performance
Feature learning	Complex contextual information	Temporal-spatial and external semantics are included in real world data which makes it too hard to extract them all
	Seasonal shift	Real world data contains seasonal component
	Trend change	Real world data contains trend component
	Concept drift	Real world data suffer from concept drift which makes the performance of trained model drop
Anomaly detection	High computational cost	Online mode calls for low latency which makes many existing expensive computa-tional cost model not applicable

In recent years, there have been more related works based on heuristic rule methods to detect abnormal patterns in single-dimensional time series, and there have also been more mature applications in industrial system monitoring. However, with the increasing complexity of the system architecture, the anomaly detection entities have evolved from a simple single-dimensional time series to a multi-dimensional time series, resulting in a significant decline in the detection accuracy based on heuristic rule methods. In view of the above difficulties, the following chapters will sort out and analyze the rule-based anomaly detection methods, and discuss their limitations and deficiencies in detail.

3   Rule-Based Anomaly Detection Algorithm

The method based on heuristic rules has been applied more maturely in the task of anomaly detection for single-dimensional time series, and the detection effect is better. However, due to the increasing complexity of the system and the explosive growth of data volume, anomaly detection entities have evolved from a single-dimensional time series to a multi-dimensional time series, resulting in rule-based methods no longer suitable for anomaly detection in a big data environment. This section will sort out the rule-based method and summarize its shortcomings.

The method based on heuristic rules is very simple and intuitive. By observing historical data, a maximum threshold and a minimum threshold are set manually. Once the value of a certain point exceeds a given range, it will be judged as an abnormal point. However, setting the threshold requires very strong prior knowledge and a large amount of historical data, which will consume a lot of manpower and material resources. At the same time, there may be phenomena such as conceptual drift in the time series. For example, when the system is upgraded, the distribution of the whole time series data will change, so that the previously set threshold may no longer be applicable, and the method's universality is poor.

An improvement to the heuristic rule is to introduce the concept of statistics, that is to calculate the mean and variance according to the historical data, and set the threshold automatically according to these indicators. Another similar statistical method is the box plot method. The box plot method divides the data into several "boxes" through the minimum non abnormal observation, lower quartile Q1, median, upper quartile Q3 and maximum non abnormal observation, and any data not in the box is classified as abnormal [6]. The box plot method is often used in the detection of abnormal points in the medical field.

The advantage of this type of method is that the algorithm has high real-time performance and can meet the requirements of real-time detection in terms of computing speed. It is suitable for the concept of real-time monitoring and alarm generation of machines and equipment in an industrial environment. However, the shortcomings of statistical methods lie in the inability to capture the spatial and temporal semantic characteristics of time series data, and the time series data in the real world are generally non-stationary, with periodicity, concept drift and other phenomena. There are some limitations in using the method of fitting distribution to divide the data. At the same time, for multi-dimensional time series, it is necessary to set a threshold for each dimension separately, which leads to the reduction of the usability and universality of the heuristic rule method. Therefore, the false negative rate and false positive rate are relatively high in the process of anomaly detection.

In recent years, machine learning algorithms have developed rapidly, and their theories and methods have been widely used to solve complex problems in engineering applications and scientific fields. Machine learning methods have good interpretability and strong generalization ability, and they are also widely used in anomaly detection tasks. The following will sort out and summarize the related work using machine learning methods.

4   Anomaly Detection Algorithm Based on Machine Learning

As a research hotspot in the field of pattern recognition and artificial intelligence, machine learning has been used to solve some complex problems in the industry and academia, including anomaly detection. In recent years, Yahoo has developed a time series anomaly detection framework EGADS [7], which belongs to the state-of-art method in KPI anomaly detection. Broadly speaking, anomaly detection can be divided into three major categories, namely supervised methods, semi-supervised methods and unsupervised methods. The supervised methods require data sets to be labeled. However, most data sets in the industry are unlabelled, because data labeling consumes a lot of manpower and material resources. Therefore, it is relatively difficult to implement supervised methods. In recent years, some work tends to use semi supervised or unsupervised methods to detect anomalies in time series.

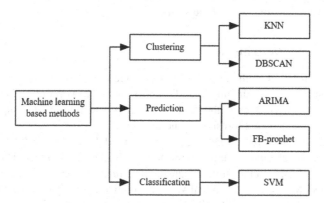

Fig. 4. Anomaly detection algorithms based on machine learning.

According to the principle of the method, the anomaly detection method based on machine learning can be divided into three parts: clustering based method, classification-based method and prediction method, as shown in Fig. 4. These three parts will be introduced in detail below.

4.1   Clustering-Based Method

Clustering is an unsupervised machine learning algorithm, which has a wide range of applications in the engineering field because the clustering algorithm does not require the data set to be labeled. The algorithm uses the idea of the distribution difference between normal points and abnormal points in the vector space to project them into the vector space. At present, some mainstream clustering algorithms mainly include the K-means algorithm (K-means), the nearest neighbor algorithm (KNN), the density-based clustering algorithm (DBSCAN), and the maximum expectation (EM) clustering using Gaussian Mixture Model (GMM).

Among them, Ramaswamy et al. [8] used the KNN algorithm [9] to detect anomalies in the data using a distance-based method, calculating the K proximity distance for each point in the data set. Then using a threshold method, once the distance exceeds the threshold, the point is judged to be abnormal. However, this algorithm requires manual determination of some parameters and abnormal thresholds, and is very sensitive to data changes. Li et al. [10] proposed a KPI clustering framework ROCKA to solve the problem of too many training models caused by too many KPIs in industry. The framework first preprocessed KPIs and extracted KPI baselines, then using density aggregation DBSCAN [11] to cluster KPIs, and divides similar KPIs into the same category. According to the above ideas, bu et al. [12] extracted 14 dimensional features such as SVD [13], Holt winters [14], wavelet [15] for each KPI baseline to train anomaly detection model, which greatly reduced the number of models to be trained. In general, clustering methods are widely used in the field of anomaly detection. However, because clustering methods divide data points by distance, density or distribution, they still cannot capture the temporal and spatial semantics of time series.

4.2 Classification-Based Method

The classification-based method uses the given data label in the training set or a custom anomaly threshold to train the model and classify the data. At present, the commonly used classification algorithms in the field of anomaly detection include support vector machine SVM [16], isolated forest and random forest.

Chen et al. [17] used the ARIMA [2] model to model the network traffic, extracted the multi-dimensional related features in the network traffic, and subtracted the real value from the predicted value of the multi-dimensional feature to construct the residual vector, and used OC-SVM to classify residual vector to realize anomaly detection of network traffic. Min et al. [18] first used the PCA algorithm to reduce the dimensionality of the time series, then used a sliding window to divide the time series and extract relevant features, finally used 1-SVM to detect anomalies in the sliced time series fragments.

In addition, decision tree algorithms are also widely used in anomaly detection. Zhou et al. [19] proposed an isolation forest algorithm for anomaly detection, which established multiple decision trees for multi-dimensional features to detect global outliers. Aryal et al. [20] improved the isolation forest algorithm to make it suitable for local anomaly detection. Liu [21] used the idea of random forest to extract hundreds of features from the labeled KPI data set, and trained the classifier through integrated learning. In response to the problem of data labeling, Zhao et al. [22] proposed a KPI sequence labeling framework Label-Less. Firstly, all candidate abnormal subsequences in KPI were screened by using isolated forest algorithm and setting an abnormal threshold, and then the similarity between all candidate sequences and manually selected abnormal sequences was calculated by using similarity alignment algorithm dynamic time warping (DTW), The candidate sequences with the highest similarity are marked as exceptions. The time of manual annotation can be reduced by 90%.

4.3 Method-Based Prediction

The method based on prediction mainly obtains the deviation degree by making the difference between the real value and the predicted value, and determines whether the data point is abnormal by the size of the deviation degree. The common prediction algorithms in time series include differential integrated moving average autoregressive model (ARIMA), Holt-Winters method (Holt-Winters) and prophet proposed by Facebook [23].

The ARIMA model is mainly used to predict short time series, and is only suitable for stationary series. However, the real sequence is generally a non-stationary sequence, so this model has certain limitations. The Holt-Winters algorithm is suitable for non-stationary series with linear trends and periodic fluctuations. The exponential smoothing method is used to fit the time series and make predictions. Similar to ARIMA, Holt-Winters can only predict short-term time series. The prophetic algorithm proposed by Facebook can automatically process outliers and missing values, and decompose the time series into trend, seasonal and holiday components, and fit the above components separately to predict the future trend of the time series.

To a certain extent, machine learning algorithms can make up for the shortcomings of heuristic rule-based methods in usability and universality. However, machine learning algorithms need to manually extract time series features, and the accuracy of anomaly detection directly depends on feature engineering. The high dimensionality of multi-dimensional time series brings greater challenges to extracting and constructing representative sequence features. In recent years, the academic community has proposed to apply the idea of deep learning to time series-oriented anomaly detection tasks, using models to learn the internal correlations of massive data, and automatically construct features to solve the limitations and limitations of the above-mentioned traditional methods insufficient.

5 Anomaly Detection Algorithm Based on Deep Learning

Deep learning is an extension of the field of machine learning. By learning the sample rules and internal representations in the data set, it has solved many pattern recognition problems. It has been applied to search recommendation, data mining, natural language processing and other researches field. At the same time, due to the high dimensionality and large amount of data in time series data, traditional outlier detection algorithms are no longer suitable for large-scale time series data sets. Chalapathy et al. [24] proposed the concept of deep anomaly detection through the idea of deep learning, the discriminative features in time series are represented and learned, and the features are automatically selected by using the model, which saves the step of manual feature selection by domain experts. However, the distinction between normal points and abnormal points in a data set is often relatively vague in most fields and may change. This kind of unclear boundary also brings challenges to deep anomaly detection methods, which often need to be analyzed for specific business.

At present, according to the principle of the method, deep anomaly detection can be divided into regression-based methods and dimensionality reduction methods. The following will focus on these two methods (Fig. 5).

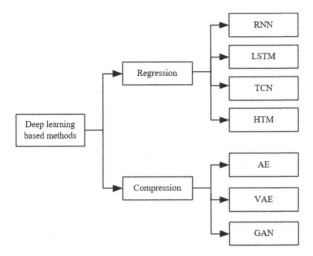

Fig. 5. Anomaly detection algorithms based on deep learning.

5.1 Method-Based Regression

One of the mainstream methods in the current time series anomaly detection task is to use the idea of regression and use a certain sequence prediction model to predict the value at t + 1 based on the observation value at the previous t time, and make the difference with the real value at that time to evaluate whether the time series at that moment is abnormal.

At present, several mainstream series prediction models based on deep learning mainly include recurrent neural network (RNN) [25], long-term and short-term memory artificial neural network (LSTM) [26], gated cyclic unit (Gru) [27], and time convolution network (TCN) proposed by Bai et al. [28] in 2018.

RNN is a type of recursive neural network that takes sequence data as input, recursively in accordance with the advancement direction of the sequence, and all cyclic unit nodes are connected in a chain. RNN can capture the temporal and spatial semantics in the time series, but it is easy to produce phenomena such as gradient disappearance during the training process, and the recursive training process cannot be parallelized, and the model convergence speed is slow. In order to solve problems such as the gradient disappearance of RNN, LSTM improves RNN by adding input gates, output gates, forget gates and memory units to the network, which can learn long-term dependencies in time series and record time series Important events with long intervals and delays. GRU is a variant of LSTM, which simplifies the network structure of LSTM, introduces update gates and reset gates, saves important features in the time series through the gate function, and ensures that the gradient is not lost during the training process. Compared with LSTM, GRU has reduced the number of parameters, which can accelerate model convergence. TCN is a newly proposed time series prediction model based on Convolutional Neural Network (CNN) [29] in recent years. It uses causal convolution to capture short-term sequence semantics, expanded convolution to capture long-term dependent semantics, and finally passes through a layer of residual the difference network solves the problem of the disappearance of the gradient, and predicts the time series through the above ideas. As a variant of CNN, TCN is different from models such as RNN in that it can support parallel computing, so it can accelerate model training. The following will introduce in detail the related work applied to the above models in anomaly detection tasks.

Among them, in the RNN-based model, Thi et al. [30] and Bontemps et al. [31] regard the network intrusion detection task as a binary classification problem, and use RNN to model the sum of deviations of an entire time series to detect abnormal patterns in the data set. Banjanovic mehmedovic et al. [32] constructed a data-driven model based on neural network for real-time monitoring of thermal power plant system, and used MLP [33], RNN and probability and statistics models for comparison. Saurav et al. [34] analyzed the shortcomings of modeling historical data in offline environments for anomaly detection tasks. Due to the dynamic changes of real-time data in the real environment, the normal mode in the time series may change, which greatly reduces the accuracy of model detection. This paper improves RNN with the idea of incremental learning, integrates new data in the real production environment, detects abnormal points and change points in the time series according to the difference between the predicted value and the real value, and updates the RNN network parameters at the same time, So that the model can monitor the anomalies in the online environment in real time. Guo et al. [35] proposed an adaptive gradient learning method based on RNN for time series prediction tasks, which modeled the local features in the time series, and automatically weighted the loss gradient of new observations generated in real time to the existing historical data, so as to achieve the purpose of adaptive learning. Experiments are carried out on artificial data sets and real data sets, and the effect of the model is evaluated. Qin et al. [36] proposed an RNN autoencoder based on the attention mechanism, which can more accurately predict the long-term dependence in the time series.

As a variant of RNN, LSTM also has a very wide range of applications in time series anomaly detection tasks. Malhotra et al. [37] used the normal points in the data set to train the LSTM, and modeled the error between the predicted value and the true value of multiple points in a period of time as a multivariate Gaussian distribution, which was used to evaluate the possibility of abnormality at each time point. Sucheta et al. [38] applied similar ideas to the task of ECG signal detection. Donghyun et al. [39] introduced the concept of edge computing to the anomaly detection model based on LSTM, which can accelerate calculations and reduce network resource consumption. The proposed system LiReD has been applied to real-time monitoring of industrial environments and achieved good performance. Hundman et al. [40] applied LSTM to the spacecraft anomaly monitoring task. In this paper, the time series data generated by each sensor are modeled separately, and an unsupervised and parameterless anomaly threshold calculation method is proposed to set the anomaly limits. LSTM is also widely used in automobile control network [41], industrial Internet of things monitoring [37], network traffic monitoring [42] and other fields.

In addition, Fu et al. [43] used LSTM and GRU to predict traffic flow, and proved that deep learning can achieve better results than ARIMA and other traditional statistical models through experiments. Mohsin et al. [44] proposed an anomaly detection framework DeepAnT, the DeepAnT is divided into two parts, namely the prediction component and the anomaly detection component. The prediction component refers to the idea of the TCN convolutional network, the output prediction value is input to the detection component, and the Euclidean distance [45] between the prediction value and the true value is used to determine whether an abnormality occurs at this moment. In the past two years, Cui et al. [46] proposed a new sequence prediction model-Hierarchical Time Memory Network (HTM), which is based on a bionic design and was subsequently used in time series anomaly detection tasks [47–49].

5.2 Method-Based Dimension Reduction

When a system is jointly monitored by multiple sensors, a large number of monitoring KPIs will be generated during the monitoring process. These KPIs not only have a very long time dimension, but may also influence each other internally, and have very complex correlation characteristics. These factors bring difficulties to the process of data mining, which jointly restricts the accuracy of anomaly detection algorithm.

In view of the above problems, it is easy to think of using the idea of dimension reduction to solve the problem of high data dimension. Among them, Principal Component Analysis (PCA) [50], a typical algorithm of dimensionality reduction, extracts the linear uncorrelated components of a set of variables through orthogonal transformation to achieve the purpose of dimensionality reduction. Based on this idea, deep learning can be used to learn the dimensionality reduction representation method of the normal pattern in the time series, and the dimensionality reduction feature vector can be reconstructed to restore to the original dimension, which is defined according to the reconstruction error of the input and output sequences Whether the sequence is abnormal. Since data labels are not required, the method based on dimensionality reduction is actually an unsupervised method. A prerequisite of this method is that there are structural differences between the normal sequence and the abnormal sequence, that is, the normal sequence can be restored by the model, and the abnormal sequence will produce larger reconstruction error. Anomaly detection algorithms that use the idea of reconstruction error mainly include Autoencoder (AE) [51] and its variant Variational Autoencoder (VAE) [52] and Generative Adversarial Network (GAN) [53].

The autoencoder uses the input information as the learning target to perform characterization learning on the input information [54]. In terms of structure, the autoencoder is divided into two parts: an encoder and a decoder. The encoder encodes the input, and the output dimension is generally much smaller than the input dimension; The decoder decodes it and restores it to the same dimension as the input. VAE is a variant of autoencoder, which is a generation model like GAN. The goal is to build a model that generates target data X from latent variable Z and learn the transformation between distributions. GAN is divided into generator and discriminator in structure, and learns the feature representation through mutual games and joint training between the two. The related work applied to the above model will be described in detail below.

Sakurada et al. [55] used the idea of dimensionality reduction to apply the autoencoder to the field of anomaly detection for the first time, and compared it with traditional dimensionality reduction methods such as PCA and kernel-PCA through experiments. The experiments proved that the autoencoder can improve the accuracy of the anomaly detection model. Kieu et al. [56] divided the time series into multiple sliding windows, extracted eight-dimensional features for each time window, and spliced them with external semantic information, and the reconstruction error is trained to the minimum by inputting to LSTM-AE and CNN-AE. Meng et al. [57] expanded on the work of [56] and combined time convolutional networks with autoencoders to detect abnormal points in the time series of the Cyber Physical Social System (CPSS). Zhang et al. [58] proposed a multi-angle convolutional recursive autoencoder (MSCRED), which first calculates the feature matrix for the multi-dimensional features of each moment in the time dimension, and then uses CNN-AE and ConvLSTM to learn the spatial semantics of the time series. Features and temporal semantic features, the model can locate anomalies based on anomalous point detection, and classify anomalies. Kieu et al. [59] used the idea of ensemble learning and proposed an autoencoder based on sparse RNN, which trains multiple AE models by changing the RNN network structure, and finally uses the median of the reconstruction error of each model output as the classification result. This method can solve the over-fitting problem in the deep neural network training process. Luo et al. [60] introduced the concept of cloud computing on the basis of AE, which can efficiently detect anomalies in wireless sensor networks in a distributed environment. At the same time, the anomaly detection algorithms based on autoencoders also have been applied in the fields of energy consumption monitoring [61–63], aircraft monitoring [64], and network intrusion detection [65].

For the generative model, Kim et al. [66] used CNN-VAE to detect the timing anomalies of edge devices in industry IOT big data environment. Guo et al. [67] proposed a GRU-based Gaussian Mixture Variational Autoencoder (GGM-VAE), by learning the temporal and spatial semantic features in multi-dimensional time series, and setting a reconstruction error threshold to define whether an abnormality occurs at that moment. Park et al. [68] used similar ideas to apply LSTM-VAE to robots in behavioral anomaly detection. Xu et al. [69] proposed a VAE-based anomaly detection framework DONUT, which uses evidence lower bounds, missing value injection, and Markov Chain Monte Carlo method MCMC to improve model detection accuracy, it is mainly used in Internet company's Abnormal detection of monitoring indicators KPI.

Similar to VAE, GAN is also a generative model. Zenati et al. [70] applied GAN to the field of sequence anomaly detection for the first time, and evaluated the effect of the model on images and network intrusion detection data sets. Li et al. [71] considered the potential interaction of time series data generated by multi-sensor in industrial environment, used LSTM-RNN as the generator in GAN to learn the common distribution of multi-dimensional time series, and detected outliers according to the results of discriminator and reconstruction error of generator. Lim et al. [72] aimed at the imbalance problem of anomaly detection data set, and used GAN to generate artificial samples to expand the data set and improve the detection effect of anomaly algorithms.

Relying on the advantages of strong learning ability, wide coverage and strong adaptability, the deep learning method automatically learns the intrinsic correlation and essence of massive data through the model, and automatically constructs representative excellent features as the decision basis of the classifier. It avoids the time-consuming and labor-consuming human feature engineering link, and further improves the accuracy of the algorithm, and effectively makes up for the shortcomings of traditional methods, and has been applied to multi-dimensional time series oriented anomaly detection task. However, the current anomaly detection algorithms based on deep learning are still immature, and many algorithms and models are still in the offline detection stage. When facing the actual production environment, there are still shortcomings such as high delay of anomaly detection methods and poor model adaptation.

6 Summary

This paper summarizes the anomaly detection methods of multi-dimensional time series, and the anomaly detection algorithms are summarized in Table 2. With the rapid development of science and technology, the complexity of industrial system architecture is also increasing. At the same time, various system monitoring indicators can be collected in real time through software, sensors and other media, thus forming a large-scale multi-dimensional time series data. Through these monitoring indicators, the real-time operating status of the system can be analyzed and evaluated, and real-time response can be achieved when abnormalities are found, and economic losses can be reduced as much as possible.

In the task of time series anomaly detection, the method of setting thresholds and box plot statistics is simple and intuitive, and can achieve better results on small sample data. When the data sample is further expanded and the time series dimension rises, the method cannot capture the spatiotemporal semantics in the sequence, which leads to the relatively high false alarm rate and missing alarm rate of traditional methods. Deep learning methods use data normalization and sliding windows to perform data normalization and sliding windows on the original time series by learning the internal connections and laws of the data, constructs regression model and classification model to predict the data value of the future time series, and captures the time semantics in the series. At the same time, learn the feature representation of the sequence through the autoencoder network, and capture the spatial semantics in the sequence, which greatly improves the accuracy of the algorithm.

However, this also puts forward higher requirements for anomaly detection algorithms, the existing algorithms still have some shortcomings that need to be improved.

The Algorithm Training Time is Long. In most fields, especially in the industrial IOT environment, the data dimension of time series is very high. At the same time, the number of parameters in the deep learning model is also very large, resulting in a large amount of network resource consumption in the training process and a long training time of the model.

Table 2. Summary of anomaly detection algorithms for multi-dimensional time series.

Type	Idea	Reference	Algorithm
Rule based	Thresholding	Ref [6]	Box Plot
Machine learning based	Clustering	Ref [8–12]	KNN
		Ref [10–12]	DBSCAN
	Classification	Ref [16–18]	OC-SVM,MC-SVM
		Ref [19–22]	Isolation Forest
	Prediction	Ref [2, 17]	ARIMA
		Ref [23]	FB-Prophet
		Ref [14]	Holt-Winters
Deep learning based	Regression	Ref [25, 30–36]	RNN, S-RNN,Attention-RNN
		Ref [28, 44]	TCN
		Ref [26, 37–42]	LSTM,Attention-LSTM,GRU-LSTM
		Ref [46–49]	HTM
	Compression	Ref [51, 55–65]	AE, CNN-AE, LSTM-AE, RNN-AE
		Ref [52, 66–69]	VAE, CNN-VAE, GGM-VAE, LSTM-VAE
		Ref [53, 70–72]	GAN

The Adaptability of Model is Poor. The data volume of the monitoring indicators increases with time, the abnormal patterns in the time series may change with the upgrade of the system architecture and the number of server clusters. If the algorithm model is only trained based on historical data, the model may no longer be applicable and the detection accuracy rate will be greatly reduced when the above situation occurs. In view of the above problems, the concept of incremental learning should be introduced, however, there is relatively little work based on incremental learning in the field of anomaly detection.

The Universality of Algorithm is Low. At present, the anomaly detection algorithms proposed by existing work often perform well in specific scenarios or for a certain data set. There is no algorithm or model that can be applied to multiple fields. The algorithms in each field cannot be universal, and the universality and scalability of the model are poor.

Generally speaking, the rule-based method has been more mature and used in industrial production environments. However, their false positive rate and false negative rate are relatively high, which brings a lot of human workload to operation and maintenance personnel. Machine learning algorithm needs to construct features manually, and the data collection and annotation is time-consuming and labor-consuming, all of these factors will cause certain influence and deviation to the anomaly detection results. At the same time, the newly proposed methods based on deep learning in recent years can be used in Improve the accuracy of the algorithm to a certain extent, but there are still difficulties in the actual implementation of the algorithm. Therefore, the future research on anomaly detection algorithms should be combined with the actual industrial production environment, and the real-time data collected in the production environment should be used as the standard to test the feasibility of the algorithm, so as to improve the practical application value of the model algorithm.

Acknowledgment. The research work is supported by National Key R&D Program of China (No. 2018YFB0804204).

References

1. Chandola, V., Banerjee, A., Kumar, V.: Anomaly detection: a survey. ACM Comput. Surv. **41**(3), 1–58 (2009)
2. Box, G.E.P., Jenkins, G.M., Reinsel, G.C.: Time series analysis forecasting and control. J. Time **31**(2), 238–242 (1976). Rev. edn.
3. Romera, E., Bergasa, L.M., Arroyo, R.: Need data for driver behaviour analysis? Presenting the public UAH-DriveSet. In: ITSC 2016, pp. 387–392 (2016)
4. Aggarwal, C.C.: An introduction to outlier analysis. In: Aggarwal, C.C. (ed.) Outlier Analysis, pp. 1–34. Springer, Cham (2013). https://doi.org/10.1007/978-3-319-47578-3_1
5. Grubbs, F.E.: Procedure for detecting outlying observations in samples. Technometrics **11**(1), 53 (1974)
6. Laurikkala, J., Juhola, M., Kentala, E., Lavrac, N., Miksch, S., Kavsek, B.: Informal identification of outliers in medical data. In: Fifth International Workshop on Intelligent Data Analysis in Medicine and Pharmacology, vol. 1, pp. 20–24 (2000)
7. Laptev, N., Amizadeh, S., Flint, I.: Generic and scalable framework for automated time-series anomaly detection (2015)
8. Ramaswamy, S., Rastogi, R., Shim, K.: Efficient algorithms for mining outliers from large data sets. ACM SIGMOD Rec. **29**(2), 427–438 (2000)
9. Hautamaki, V., Karkkainen, I., Franti, P.: Outlier detection using k-nearest neighbour graph. In: ICPR, pp. 430–433 (2004)
10. Li, Z., Zhao, Y., Liu, R., et al.: Robust and rapid clustering of KPIs for large-scale anomaly detection. In: 2018 IEEE/ACM 26th International Symposium on Quality of Service (IWQoS). ACM (2018)
11. Ester, M., Kriegel, H.-P., Sander, J., Xu, X., et al.: A density-based algorithm for discovering clusters in large spatial databases with noise. In: KDD, vol. 96, no. 34, pp. 226–231 (1996)
12. Bu, J., Liu, Y., Zhang, S., et al.: Rapid deployment of anomaly detection models for large number of emerging KPI streams. In: 2018 IEEE 37th International Performance Computing and Communications Conference (IPCCC). IEEE (2018)
13. Mahimkar, A., et al.: Rapid detection of maintenance induced changes in service performance. In: Proceedings of the Seventh Conference on Emerging Networking EXperiments and Technologies, ser. CoNEXT 2011, pp. 13:1–13:12. ACM, New York (2011). http://doi.acm.org/10.1145/2079296.2079309
14. Barford, P., Kline, J., Plonka, D., Ron, A.: A signal analysis of network traffic anomalies. In: Proceedings of the 2nd ACM SIGCOMM Workshop on Internet Measurement, pp. 71–82. ACM (2002)

15. Yan, H., et al.: Argus: end-to-end service anomaly detection and localization from an ISP's point of view. In: 2012 Proceedings IEEE INFOCOM, pp. 2756–2760. IEEE (2012)
16. Manevitz, L.M., Yousef, M.: One-Class SVMs for document classification. JMLR **2**, 139–154 (2001)
17. Chen, X., Jiang, T., et al.: Network anomaly detector based on multiple time series analysis. J. Sichuan Univ. (Eng. Sci. Edn.) **49**(001), 144–150 (2017)
18. Min, H., Zhiwei, J., Ke, Y., et al.: Detecting anomalies in time series data via a meta-feature based approach. IEEE Access 1 (2018)
19. Liu, F.T., Ting, K.M., Zhou, Z.-H.: Isolation forest. In: ICDM. IEEE (2008)
20. Aryal, S., Ting, K.M., Wells, J.R., et al.: Improving iForest with relative mass (2014)
21. Liu, D., Zhao, Y., Xu, H., et al.: Opprentice: towards practical and automatic anomaly detection through machine learning. In: Proceedings of the 2015 Internet Measurement Conference, pp. 211–224. ACM Press, New York (2015)
22. Zhao, N., Zhu, J., Liu, R., et al.: Label-less: a semi-automatic labelling tool for KPI anomalies. In: IEEE INFOCOM 2019 - IEEE Conference on Computer Communications. IEEE (2019)
23. Taylor, S.J., Letham, B.: Forecasting at scale. Am. Stat. (2017)
24. Chalapathy, R., Chawla, S.: Deep learning for anomaly detection: a survey (2019)
25. Williams, R.J.: Complexity of exact gradient computation algorithms for recurrent neural networks. Technical report, Technical report NU-CCS-89-27. Northeastern, Boston (1989)
26. Hochreiter, S., Schmidhuber, J.: Long short-term memory. Neural Comput. **9**(8), 1735–1780 (1997)
27. Cho, K., et al.: Learning phrase representations using RNN encoder-decoder for statistical machine translation. arXiv preprint arXiv:1406.1078 (2014)
28. Bai, S., Kolter, J.Z., Koltun, V.: An empirical evaluation of generic convolutional and recurrent networks for sequence modeling (2018)
29. Krizhevsky, A., Sutskever, I., Hinton, G.E.: ImageNet classification with deep convolutional neural networks. In: Advances in Neural Information Processing Systems, pp. 1097–1105 (2012)
30. Nguyen Thi, N., Cao, V.L., Le-Khac, N.A.: One-class collective anomaly detection based on LSTM-RNNs. In: Hameurlain, A., Küng, J., Wagner, R., Dang, T., Thoai, N. (eds.) Transactions on Large-Scale Data- and Knowledge-Centered Systems XXXVI. LNCS, vol. 10720, pp. 73–85. Springer, Berlin, Heidelberg (2017). https://doi.org/10.1007/978-3-662-56266-6_4
31. Bontemps, L., Cao, V.L., McDermott, J., Le-Khac, N.A.: Collective anomaly detection based on long short-term memory recurrent neural networks. In: Dang, T., Wagner, R., Küng, J., Thoai, N., Takizawa, M., Neuhold, E. (eds.) FDSE 2016. LNCS, vol. 10018, pp. 141–152. Springer, Cham (2016). https://doi.org/10.1007/978-3-319-48057-2_9
32. Banjanovic-Mehmedovic, L., Hajdarevic, A., Kantardzic, M., Mehmedovic, F., Dzananovic, I.: Neural network-based data-driven modelling of anomaly detection in thermal power plant. Automatika **58**(1), 69–79 (2017)
33. Pal, S.K., Mitra, S.: Multilayer perceptron, fuzzy sets, classification (1992)
34. Saurav, S., et al.: Online anomaly detection with concept drift adaptation using recurrent neural networks. In: Proceedings of the ACM India Joint International Conference on Data Science and Management of Data, pp. 78–87. ACM (2018)
35. Guo, T., Xu, Z., Yao, X., Chen, H., Aberer, K., Funaya, K.: Robust online time series prediction with recurrent neural networks. In: 2016 IEEE International Conference on Data Science and Advanced Analytics (DSAA), pp. 816–825. IEEE (2016)
36. Qin, Y., Song, D., Chen, H., et al.: A dual-stage attention-based recurrent neural network for time series prediction. arXiv preprint arXiv:1704.02971 (2017)
37. Zhang, W., et al.: LSTM-based analysis of industrial IoT equipment. IEEE Access **6**, 23551–23560 (2018)

38. Chauhan, S., Vig, L.: Anomaly detection in ECG time signals via deep long short-term memory networks. In: IEEE International Conference on Data Science and Advanced Analytics (DSAA), pp. 1–7. IEEE (2015). 36678
39. Park, D., Kim, S., An, Y., Jung, J.-Y.: LiReD: a light-weight real-time fault detection system for edge computing using LSTM recurrent neural networks. Sensors **18**(7), 2110 (2018)
40. Hundman, K., Constantinou, V., Laporte, C., et al.: Detecting spacecraft anomalies using LSTMs and nonparametric dynamic thresholding. In: Proceedings of the 24th ACM SIGKDD International Conference on Knowledge Discovery & Data Mining, pp. 387–395 (2018)
41. Taylor, A., Leblanc, S., Japkowicz, N.: Anomaly detection in automobile control network data with long short-term memory networks. In: 2016 IEEE International Conference on Data Science and Advanced Analytics (DSAA), pp. 130–139. IEEE (2016)
42. Cheng, M., et al.: MS-LSTM: A multi-scale LSTM model for BGP anomaly detection. In: 2016 IEEE 24th International Conference on Network Protocols (ICNP), pp. 1–6. IEEE (2016)
43. Fu, R., Zhang, Z., Li, L.: Using LSTM and GRU neural network methods for traffic flow prediction. In: Youth Academic Annual Conference of Chinese Association of Automation (YAC), pp. 324–328. IEEE (2016)
44. Munir, M., Siddiqui, S.A., Dengel, A., Ahmed, S.: DeepAnT: a deep learning approach for unsupervised anomaly detection in time series. IEEE Access **7**, 1991–2005 (2018)
45. Danielsson, P.E.: Euclidean distance mapping. Comput. Graph. Image Process. **14**(3), 227–248 (1980)
46. Cui, Y., Ahmad, S., Hawkins, J.: Continuous online sequence learning with an unsupervised neural network model. Neural Comput. **28**(11), 2474–2504 (2016). http://arxiv.org/abs/1512.05463
47. Ahmad, S., Purdy, S.: Real-time anomaly detection for streaming analytics. arXiv:1607.02480 [cs], July 2016
48. Ahmad, S., Lavin, A., Purdy, S., Agha, Z.: Unsupervised real-time anomaly detection for streaming data. Neurocomputing **262**, 134–147 (2017). http://www.sciencedirect.com/science/article/pii/S0925231217309864
49. Wu, J., Zeng, W., Yan, F.: Hierarchical temporal memory method for time-series-based anomaly detection. Neurocomputing **273**, 535–546 (2018). http://www.sciencedirect.com/science/article/pii/S0925231217313887
50. Baldi, P., Hornik, K.: Neural networks and principal component analysis: learning from examples without local minima. Neural Netw. **2**(1), 53–58 (1989)
51. Vincent, P., Larochelle, H., Bengio, Y., et al.: Extracting and composing robust features with denoising autoencoders. In: International Conference on Machine Learning. ACM (2008)
52. Kingma, D.P., Welling, M.: Auto-encoding variational bayes (2014)
53. Goodfellow, I., Pouget-Abadie, J., Mirza, M., et al.: Generative adversarial nets. In: Advances in Neural Information Processing Systems, pp. 2672–2680 (2014)
54. Bengio, Y., Courville, A., Vincent, P.: Representation learning: a review and new perspectives. IEEE Trans. Pattern Anal. Mach. Intell. **35**(8), 1798–1828 (2013)
55. Sakurada, M., Yairi, T.: Anomaly detection using autoencoders with nonlinear dimensionality reduction. In: Proceedings of the MLSDA 2014 2nd Workshop on Machine Learning for Sensory Data Analysis, p. 4. ACM (2014)
56. Kieu, T., Yang, B., Jensen, C.S.: Outlier detection for multidimensional time series using deep neural networks. In: 2018 19th IEEE International Conference on Mobile Data Management (MDM). IEEE (2018)
57. Meng, C., Jiang, X.S., Wei, X.M., et al.: A Time convolutional network based outlier detection for multidimensional time series in cyber-physical-social systems. IEEE Access **8**, 74933–74942 (2020)
58. Zhang, C., Song, D., Chen, Y., et al.: A deep neural network for unsupervised anomaly detection and diagnosis in multivariate time series data (2018)

59. Kieu, T., Yang, B., Guo, C., et al.: Outlier detection for time series with recurrent autoencoder ensembles. In: Twenty-Eighth International Joint Conference on Artificial Intelligence IJCAI-19 (2019)

60. Luo, T., Nagarajany, S.G.: Distributed anomaly detection using autoencoder neural networks in WSN for IoT. In: 2018 IEEE International Conference on Communications (ICC), pp. 1–6. IEEE (2018)

61. Yuan, Y., Jia, K.: A distributed anomaly detection method of operation energy consumption using smart meter data. In: 2015 International Conference on Intelligent Information Hiding and Multimedia Signal Processing (IIH-MSP), pp. 310–313. IEEE (2015)

62. Araya, D.B., Grolinger, K., ElYamany, H.F., Capretz, M.A.M., Bitsuamlak, G.: An ensemble learning framework for anomaly detection in building energy consumption. Energy Build. **144**, 191–206 (2017)

63. Fan, C., Xiao, F., Zhao, Y., Wang, J.: Analytical investigation of autoencoder-based methods for unsupervised anomaly detection in building energy data. Appl. Energy **211**, 1123–1135 (2018). http://www.sciencedirect.com/science/article/pii/S0306261917317166

64. Fu, X., Luo, H., Zhong, S., Lin, L.: Aircraft engine fault detection based on grouped convolutional denoising autoencoders. Chin. J. Aeronaut. **32**, 296–307 (2019)

65. Filonov, P., Lavrentyev, A., Vorontsov, A.: Multivariate industrial time series with cyber-attack simulation: fault detection using an LSTM-based predictive data model. arXiv preprint arXiv:1612.06676 (2016)

66. Kim, D., et al.: Squeezed convolutional variational AutoEncoder for unsupervised anomaly detection in edge device industrial internet of things. In: 2018 International Conference on Information and Computer Technologies (ICICT), pp. 67–71, December 2018

67. Guo, Y., Liao, W., Wang, Q., Yu, L., Ji, T., Li, P.: Multidimensional time series anomaly detection: a GRU-based Gaussian mixture variational autoencoder approach. In: Asian Conference on Machine Learning, pp. 97–112 (2018)

68. Park, D., Hoshi, Y., Kemp, C.C.: A multimodal anomaly detector for robot-assisted feeding using an LSTM-based variational autoencoder. IEEE Robot. Autom. Lett. **3**(3), 1544–1551 (2018)

69. Xu, H., Chen, W., Zhao, N., et al.: Unsupervised anomaly detection via variational auto-encoder for seasonal KPIs in web applications. In: Proceedings of the 2018 World Wide Web Conference, pp. 187–196 (2018)

70. Li, D., Chen, D., Goh, J., Ng, S.: Anomaly detection with generative adversarial networks for multivariate time series. arXiv preprint arXiv:1809.04758 (2018)

71. Li, D., Chen, D., Jin, B., Shi, L., Goh, J., Ng, S.-K.: MAD-GAN: multivariate anomaly detection for time series data with generative adversarial networks. In: Tetko, I.V., Kůrková, V., Karpov, P., Theis, F. (eds.) ICANN 2019. LNCS, vol. 11730, pp. 703–716. Springer, Cham (2019). https://doi.org/10.1007/978-3-030-30490-4_56

72. Lim, S.K., Loo, Y., Tran, N.T., et al.: Doping: Generative data augmentation for unsupervised anomaly detection with GAN. In: 2018 IEEE International Conference on Data Mining (ICDM), pp. 1122–1127. IEEE (2018)

ExitSniffer: Towards Comprehensive Security Analysis of Anomalous Binding Relationship of Exit Routers

Qingfeng Zhang[1,2], Xuebin Wang[1,2(✉)], Jinqiao Shi[3], Meiqi Wang[1,2],
Yue Gao[1,2], and Can Zhao[1,2]

[1] Institute of Information Engineering, Chinese Academy of Sciences, Beijing, China
wangxuebin@iie.ac.cn
[2] School of Cyber Security, University of Chinese Academy of Sciences,
Beijing, China
[3] School of Cyberspace Security, Beijing University of Posts
and Telecommunications, Beijing, China

Abstract. Tor exit relays are operated by volunteers and the trust-worthiness of Tor exit relays need to be revisited in a long-term manner. In this paper, we monitored the Tor network by developing a fast and distributed exit relay scanner (ExitSniffer) to probe all exit relays over a period of 16 months continuously, seeking to expose the anomalous binding relationship phenomena of exit routers simply by comparing the returnIP and consensusIP. We totally find 1983 malicious exit relays which average contribute 10.12% bandwidth of total Tor exit relays bandwidth monthly, resulting tremendous threaten for Tor user's anonymity according to the current path-relay selecting algorithm. There exits two types of anomalous binding relationship consists 35 exit relay families, with different size ranging from 2 to 230, which are neither announced in the consensus document or detected by the Tor network.

Keywords: Malicious exit nodes · Exit sniffer · Tor network

1 Introduction

Tor provides a safe and concealed channel for clients to access the clear network. As of August 2021, there are approximately 1,300 exit relay nodes in the Tor network to provide services for clients [1]. Since the exit relay node is the last hop from the Tor network to the target website [2], it means that Tor's onion encryption algorithm will not be able to protect the traffic between the exit relay node and the target website. This may directly expose some client traffic without encryption means (such as HTTP requests) [3,4] to the attacker's vision. Therefore, the identity of the exit relay node is very sensitive, which is directly related to the security and privacy of client traffic.

Since the relay nodes of Tor are contributed by volunteers, attackers can implant malicious nodes with different roles into tor network at a very small

© The Author(s) 2022
W. Lu et al. (Eds.): CNCERT 2021, CCIS 1506, pp. 93–109, 2022.
https://doi.org/10.1007/978-981-16-9229-1_6

cost to realize their attacks, such as sybil attack [7]. A lot of work has proved that attackers have caused great harm to the anonymity and stability of tor network by manipulating controlled nodes [6–8]. Because the exit node acts as the middleman between the client and the target website, it is common for attackers to attack by controlling the exit node. [12], The reason why attackers are happy to implant malicious exit nodes may be that some government or school researchers try to destroy the anonymity of tor network; Another kind of attacker is for benefit. The attacker can hijack the transaction traffic and fake the content in the traffic by implementing man in the middle attack [8], so as to gain profits.

Tor officials and some researchers have launched defense against some common exit node attacks, such as traffic sniffing, DNS pollution and SSL based attacks [9,19] through practical work. For example, Tor officials launched Tor Metric project [10] to measure the ecology in Tor network. Philipp Winter et al. designed the ExitMap tool to detect malicious exit nodes [9]. In 2016, Philipp Winter's team again designed Sybilhunter tool to detect the sybil nodes of the Tor network [11]. These works have achieved remarkable results, but in the face of some new malicious exit node attacks, the results of the above methods are not satisfactory. When we observed the behavior of exit nodes in tor network for a long time, we find a phenomenon: the host IP address directly connected to the target website is inconsistent with the consensus IP address of exit nodes. We define it as a new attack mode of exit nodes. Unfortunately, the existing exit node probing tools can not detect this malicious behavior, because this silent attack method cannot trigger the detection module of the detection tool.

We have developed ExitSnifer system based on Python language, which depends on Ubuntu 16.04 system environment. ExitSniffer is designed with the idea of distributed clustering. It consists of three cloud hosts (with 1 core CPU and 4 GB of RAM) distributed in different countries, and can control multiple Tor clients to complete operations at the same time. The frequency of scanning nodes can be controlled by setting the timing module of ExitSniffer.

The principle of ExitSniffer is: use the exit node to be tested to access the website with the function of detecting IP through the Stem control protocol. It will compare the IP address returned by the website with the IP address of the exit node in the consensus file to judge whether the exit node is malicious.

By analyzing the results returned by exitsnifer, we find that the consensus IP of the malicious exit node has a malicious binding relationship with the IP returned by the website. Another phenomenon is that the IP returned by the website is in the same/24 network segment as the consensus IP of the exit node. However, we cannot distinguish whether the actual IP and consensus IP are different network cards of the same host, or different hosts. However, this malicious binding relationship indicates that there is a co-owner relationship between exit nodes.

To sum up, we make the following key contributions:

- We find that the exit node is not directly connected to the target website, and defined this type of exit node as: a malicious exit node with a proxy.
- We designed and implemented ExitSniffer, which is capable of detecting malicious exit node with proxies in consensus files in real time. It adopts distributed design, and is lightweight and easy to deploy.

– We analyze the influence of these malicious exit nodes with proxies on Tor networks and explore the co-owner relationship of these nodes.

2   Related Work

Due to the low threshold of implanting nodes into tor network, it promotes the continuous growth of tor network, but it will also make tor network absorb some malicious nodes. Up to now, tor network has been subject to Traffic Association attacks and node attacks by attackers, such as traffic confirmation attack, DoS attack, sybil attack, etc. However, some researchers have always supported the development of tor, and the communities involved in tor have been active. They have developed many tools to defend against tor attacks through their practical work.

Murdoch et al. [22] verified the IX level attack. By sampling the real traffic and extracting the statistical characteristics such as message sending rate and message length, the entity communication relationship was confirmed. Nasr et al. [23] Designed a traffic association system deepcorr, which uses the deep learning architecture to learn the traffic association function suitable for tor complex networks, and can connect Tor. Ling et al. [24] control the sending law of Tor cell on the controllable OR node. Wang et al. [25] proposed an attack scheme. Once the attacker finds that the target page of his exit node responds to traffic, he can inject malicious network links with empty images to make the browser on the client side download these links to generate specific traffic model.

However, there are some researchers who have been working on the defense of Tor. Akhoondi et al. [26] designed an efficient algorithm to judge whether the tor link can be associated by as traffic, and designed a new Tor client LASTor based on this algorithm. LASTor can avoid establishing tor links that can be associated by as traffic, so as to improve the security of tor dark network. Philipp Winter et al. designed the ExitMap tool to detect malicious exit nodes [9]. In 2016, Philipp Winter's team again designed Sybilhunter tool to detect the sybil nodes of the Tor network [11]. Sybilhunter integrates the functions of exitmap tool and adds HTML and HTTP injection detection.

By observing the exit nodes in the Tor consensus document for a long time, we find a malicious exit node with a proxy (MENP). However, the existing node scanning tools ignore this malicious node. Therefore, we designed a special software ExitSniffer to detect MENP nodes, which can scan all exit nodes in the consensus file in a short time. We hope that the ExitSniffer tool can become an extension of ExitMap and other tools to make up for the defense mechanism of malicious exit nodes. Next we will introduce the composition of ExitSniffer and analyze the behavior of MENP nodes.

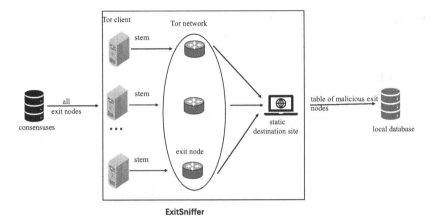

Fig. 1. It shows the schematic diagram of ExitSniffer. With a distributed design, Exit-Sniffer can start multiple Tor clients at the same time, create Tor links through Stem libraries, visit websites with IP detection function, and finally output the results to the specified database.

3   The Design of ExitSniffer and Phenomenon

3.1   The Design of ExitSniffer

Before using exitsnifer, it is necessary to introduce its working principle. As shown in Fig. 1, ExitSniffer will download the exit node information in the latest consensus file every hour, use Stem control protocol [14] to create the circuits, judge whether the exit node is evil by using the target exit node to access the website with IP query function, and finally output the result to the specified database. Stem is a Python controller library for Tor. With it we can use Tor's control protocol to script against the Tor process, or build things such as Nyx. We use the Stem library to control Tor's circuit creation process. For example, we can decide when to establish a circuit and which exit node to choose as the last hop of the circuit. The target website we use also has special functions. It can return the IP of the host directly connected to it. We can deploy a website with this function ourselves, because it is more secure. But using public web-sites(such as https://jsonip.com/) is more labor-saving, as long as we would like to take some security risks. Generally speaking, the exit node is directly connected to the target website. Therefore, the IP of the exit node obtained by the target website should be consistent with the IP of the exit node in the consensus document. If this condition is not established, we believe that there is a problem with the exit node.

ExitSniffer is a distributed sniffer tool developed in Python can that detect malicious exit nodes with proxies. We use a distributed setup, utilizing 3 Virtual Machines (VMs) on cloud environment provided by Vultr[1]. These virtual

---

[1] http://vultr.com.

machines are located in different countries including Singapore, France and the United States, so as to ensure the diversity of traces. Each VM is configured with 1 core CPU and 4 GB of RAM. On each VM, 10 docker instances are deployed, and each docker with a separate Tor process (version 0.4.4.6). Next, we will introduce the data set captured using exitsnifer.

3.2   Dataset

We set the detection frequency of ExitSniffer to be executed every two hours. A total of 7125,133 data records were collected from 2020-02-18 to 2021-08-18 by ExitSniffer system. Unfortunately, due to machine failure and other reasons, our data collection process was interrupted during the two months from 2021-02-18 to 2021-04-18, but this did not affect the following work. This dataset has 10 fields:

consensus-IP:IP address of the exit node in the consensus file.
actual-IP:ExitSniffer actually obtains the IP address of the exit node.
bandwidth:Bandwidth of the exit node in the consensus file.
flags:The labels of the exit node in the consensus file.
or-port:The OR port of the exit node in the consensus file.
fingerprint:The fingerprint of exit node in consensus file.
nickname:The nickname of the exit node in the consensus file.
spent-time:The time it takes the ExitSniffer to scan an exit node.
status:ExitSniffer detects the result of an exit node.
recording-time:The local time when the ExitSniffer scans an exit node.

It is worth noting that the data set mainly contains the information of exit nodes in the consensus file, so it depends on the accuracy of the consensus file.

4   Experimental Analysis

By testing exit node behavior for a long period of time, we find a hidden phenomenon: the IP address in the consensus document of the exit node is inconsistent with the IP address connected to the target website. This is similar to adding an proxy between the exit node and the target website. We believe that this behavior is malicious and mark the exit node with this behavior as MENP(a malicious exit node with a proxy). The inconsistency between the consensus IP address and the actual IP address may be caused by malicious operations of the trunk owner, such as man-in-the-middle attacks. Figure 2 shows that MENP nodes can reroute traffic to Tor network or route it to hosts outside the Tor network. By analyzing the IP actually returned by ExitSniffer, we find that some of MENP nodes route the client traffic to nodes outside the Tor network. Furthermore, the attacker may control multiple malicious exit nodes, and first aggregate the traffic relayed through these controlled exits to a controlled node outside the Tor network, and then route it to the client's target website. The behavior has a

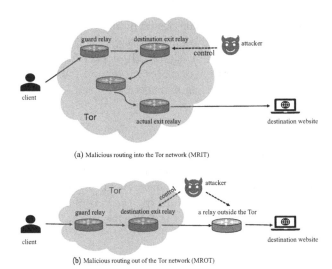

(a) Malicious routing into the Tor network (MRIT)

(b) Malicious routing out of the Tor network (MROT)

Fig. 2. MENP nodes can decide whether to route the traffic that flows through them into or out of the Tor network. In Fig. 2(a), MENP nodes route traffic into the Tor network, and traffic eventually arrives at the target website from a random exit node. Figure 2(b) shows the MENP node routing traffic to a conspiracy host outside the Tor network

negative impact on the privacy protection of the client, because we don't know what happed between malicious exit node and the target website.

For malicious exit nodes with proxy (MENP) that route traffic outside the Tor network, there are two cases for Actual exit node IP (actual-IP) scanned by ExitSniffer:

1) Actual-IP is another IP address in the same/24 network segment of the Consensus IP address (Consensus IP) of the exit node. For example, by searching the Consensus file, the IP address of the exit node is 109.70.100.9, while the IP address detected by ExitSniffer is 109.70.100.27. It is impossible to tell whether such a node is a malicious one, even if its consensus IP is different from the one detected by the ExitSniffer, because there may be multiple network cards on the machine.
2) Actual-IP and the consensus IP address of the exit node are not in the same/24 network segment. As shown in Fig. 2(b), the client traffic is routed by the malicious exit node to other relays that are not part of the Tor network, during which the attacker is likely to carry out a man-in-the-middle attack.

Perhaps MENP nodes do nothing but route the traffic between the client and the target website to the proxy, which may also be a kind of goodwill behavior.

According to the work of Zhao Zhang et al., some websites have implemented IP blocking on Tor exit nodes [13]. Adding a proxy outside the Tor network behind the exit node can circumvent a site's blocking of Tor, but this is potentially risky because it could expose more traffic from clients and target sites to attackers.

4.1   The Size of the Malicious Exit Nodes

We analyze the data of MENP nodes (malicious exit node with a proxy) since 2020-02-18 to 2021-08-18 (where 2021-02-18 to 2021-04-18 data is missing). We totally find 1983 malicious exit relays. Figure 3 shows the proportion curve of the number of malicious exit relays to the total number of exit nodes in the consensus file. It can be seen that the proportion curve (green line) has relatively large fluctuations, which means that the MENP node has a large churn rate, that is, the attacker deploys the MXNO malicious node and implements malicious behavior in a short period of time. However, from 2020-07-18 to 2020-08-18, the number of MENP nodes accounted for 16% of all exit nodes, which has reached a very large scale.

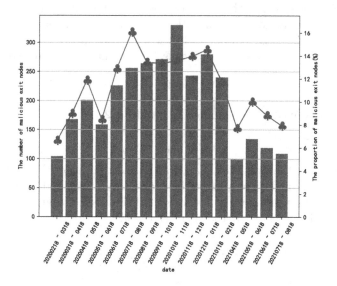

Fig. 3. This figure shows the loss of MENP nodes over time. It can be clearly seen that many MENP nodes run for a short time, so the proportion curve (green line) fluctuates greatly. (Color figure online)

4.2   Bandwidth Ratio of MENP Nodes

Tor's selection of exit nodes follows the routing selection algorithm [15]. The client randomly selects a node as the exit node from the relay node set that meets the exit node label rules by using the bandwidth weighting algorithm [16]. The calculation method of weight$_{final}$ of each alternative node is shown in the formula:

$$weight_{final} = weight * bw_n = \begin{cases} I_n * (W_{db})) * W_d * bw_n, & n \in S_{guard,exit} \\ I_n * (W_{gb})) * W_g * bw_n, & n \in S_{guard} \\ I_n * (W_{eb})) * W_e * bw_n, & n \in S_{exit} \\ I_n * (W_{mb})) * W_m * bw_n, & else \end{cases} \tag{1}$$

$$I_n(x) = \begin{cases} x, n \in S_{dir} \\ 1, esle \end{cases} \tag{2}$$

Where S is the set of all nodes in the consensus file, n is a node in the set S, and bw_n is the consensus bandwidth of node n. $S_{guard,exit}$ is a set of nodes with Guard and Exit labels in set S. S_{guard} is set of nodes with only Guard labels in set S. S_{exit} is set of nodes with only Exit labels in set S. W_{db}, W_{gb}, W_{eb}, and W_{mb} can be obtained from the consensus file. W_{db} is the bandwidth weight with Guard and Exit tags, W_{gb} is the bandwidth weight with Guard tags, W_{eb} is the bandwidth weight with Exit tags, W_{mb} is the bandwidth weight without Guard or Exit tags, W_d is the W_{ed} parameter in the consensus file, W_g is the W_{eg} parameter in the consensus file, W_e is the W_{ee} parameter in the consensus file, and W_m is the W_{me} parameter in the consensus file.

Query parameters related to consensus files and make standardized discovery:

$$W_g = W_{gb} = W_m = W_{mb} = W_e = W_{eb} = W_d = W_{db} = 1 \tag{3}$$

It can be obtained by combining Eq. 1 and Eq. 2:

$$weight_{final} = bw_n \tag{4}$$

According to the weighted bandwidth selection algorithm, the greater weight$_{final}$ of the node, the greater the probability of the node being selected. This means that the greater the bandwidth of the node, the greater the probability P_n of being selected by the client as the last hop of the circuit.

$$P_n = \frac{weight_{final,n}}{\sum_{i=0}^{m} weight_{fina,il}} = \frac{bw_n}{\sum_{i=0}^{m} bw_i}, i \in (0, m) \tag{5}$$

In the above formula, P_n is the probability that the client selects exit node n, bw_i is the consensus bandwidth of exit node i, and m is the number of exit nodes in the consensus file.

Algorithm 1 is the weighted bandwidth algorithm of the exit node, and Algorithm 2 shows the algorithm for selecting the index of each node according to the weighted bandwidth value of each node. Therefore, we can deduce Eq. 1 and Eq. 5.

In Algorithm 2, even if the index of the selected node is found, the loop will not jump out immediately. This is to resist the attack of time consumption, and the attacker cannot calculate the value of *rand_value* through the running time of the algorithm.

Algorithm 1. Exit node compute weighted bandwidth

Input: all of relays in consensus file S

Output: the list of weighted bandwidths for exit nodes Bw_out

1: $Bw\_out \leftarrow$ an empty list
2: $We \leftarrow$ get_bw_weight("Wee") / 10000
3: $Wm \leftarrow$ get_bw_weight("Wem") / 10000
4: $Wd \leftarrow$ get_bw_weight("Wed") / 10000
5: $Wg \leftarrow$ get_bw_weight("Weg") / 10000
6: $Wgb \leftarrow$ get_bw_weight("Wgb") / 10000
7: $Wmb \leftarrow$ get_bw_weight("Wmb") / 10000
8: $Web \leftarrow$ get_bw_weight("Web") / 10000
9: $Wdb \leftarrow$ get_bw_weight("Wdb") / 10000
10: **for** each $n \in S$ **do**
11:     **if** n is guard and n is exit **then**
12:         $weight \leftarrow$ (is dir ? $Wdb * Wd : Wd$)
13:     **else if** n is guard **then**
14:         $weight \leftarrow$ (is dir ? $Wgb * Wg : Wg$)
15:     **else if** n is exit **then**
16:         $weight \leftarrow$ (is dir ? $Web * We : We$)
17:     **else**
18:         $weight \leftarrow$ (is dir ? $Wmb * Wm : Wm$)
19:     **end if**
20:     $weight_{final} \leftarrow weight * bw\_n$
21:     $Bw\_out.\text{add}(weight_{final})$
22: **end for**

Algorithm 2. Choose an exit node by weight

Input: the list of weighted bandwidths for exit nodes Bw_out

Output: the index of the selected exit node idx

1: $total \leftarrow \text{sum}(Bw\_out)$
2: $rand\_value \leftarrow \text{randint}(0, total)$
3: $idx \leftarrow -1$
4: $total\_so\_far \leftarrow 0$
5: **for** each $bw \in Bw\_out$ **do**
6:     **if** $total\_so\_far > rand\_value$ **then**
7:         $idx \leftarrow Bw\_out.\text{index}(bw)$
8:     **else**
9:         $total\_so\_far \leftarrow total\_so\_far + bw$
10:     **end if**
11: **end for**

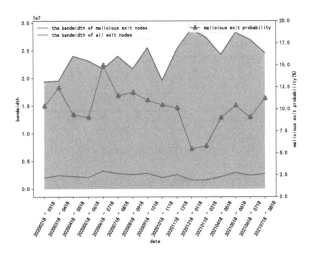

Fig. 4. It shows the bandwidth capabilities of MENP nodes.

Figure 4 shows that the bandwidth curve of the MENP node is basically stable. But it fluctuates greatly in the proportion of the total exit bandwidth. This is because the large churn rate at the Tor exit point causes the total export bandwidth to fluctuate greatly [11]. Through statistical analysis, the bandwidth of MENP nodes accounts for 10.12% of the total exit bandwidth. According to Eq. 5, it can be concluded that the probability of clients selecting these malicious exit nodes as the last hop is 10.12%. This is a very scary thing, malicious exit nodes listen to or hijack about 10.12% of the exit traffic without being detected by Tor officials.

4.3   Behavior Exploration of MENP Nodes

After 16 months of observation and data collection, We find that MENP nodes have two forms when routing client traffic: 1) rerouting traffic to Tor network; 2) routing traffic to hosts outside the Tor network.

Traffic Is Routed to the Tor Network (MRIT, Malicious Routing into the Tor Network). When using the ExitSniffer system to scan the exit nodes, we find that many exit nodes reroute client traffic to the Tor network. We suspect that the reasons for this are as follows: 1) The circuit is replaced. When Tor detects a circuit failure, it will select another circuit. Therefore, the exit node IP detected by exitsnifer is inconsistent with the target exit node's consensus IP 2) Malicious operations by node owners. Some researchers reroute traffic to tor network in order to collect more traffic information.

Traffic Is Routed Outside the Tor Network (MROT, Malicious Routing Out of the Tor Network). The attacker manipulated the exit node to route the traffic of the client to the outside of Tor network. Although it is not ruled out that the exit node is innocent, it may be that the connection between the exit node and the target website is hijacked by the attacker. We cannot distinguish it, so we uniformly believe that the malicious exit node leads to such behavior.

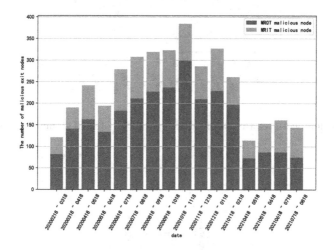

Fig. 5. It shows the ratio of MRIT malicious nodes to MROT malicious nodes.

Figure 5 shows that the number of MROT malicious exit nodes accounts for 67.59% of the total number of MROT malicious exit nodes. Figure 6 shows the bandwidth capacity of MROT malicious exit nodes, which accounts for 68.30% of the total number of MROT malicious exit nodes. Therefore, we turn more attention to MROT malicious exit nodes. We were surprised to find that when ExitSniffer scanned the malicious exit node with MROT behavior, the actual IP address obtained was in the same/24 network segment as the consensus IP address of the exit node. We were inclined to think that the ExitSniffer system had errors in obtaining the real IP address. We obtained the IP addresses of other network cards under the host, because we assume that if two IP addresses are in the same/24 network segment. We will aggregate them into one IP address. Such data records are common in our data set. For example: Consensus IP is on the same/24 network segment as actual IP, and ACutal IP1 is on the same/24 network segment as actual IP2.

Figure 7 shows the comparison of the number of malicious nodes with MROT behavior on whether the actual returned IP and the consensus IP are in the same/24 network segment. Most of the malicious exit node consensus IP and the actual measured IP are not in the same subnet. Moreover, the consensus IP and the actual returned IP present a one-to-one, one-to-many, many-to-one,

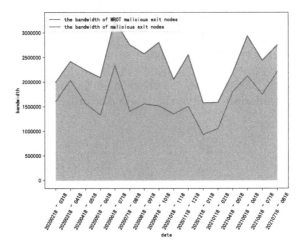

Fig. 6. It demonstrates the bandwidth capabilities of MROT malicious nodes.

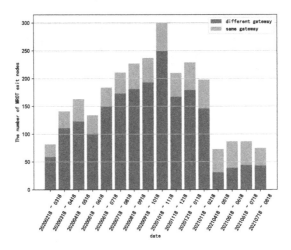

Fig. 7. This figure shows the number of malicious nodes with MROT behavior that actually return IP addresses versus consensus IP addresses in the same/24 network segment.

and many-to-many malicious binding relationship. Table 1 shows the one-to-one relationship between consensus IP and actual IP, and Fig. 8 shows an exit node may be bound to multiple hosts outside the Tor network. Figure 9 shows that multiple exit nodes are bound to one or more hosts outside the Tor network. Our intuition is that multiple exit nodes are bound to one or more nodes outside the Tor network, which means that these exit nodes have a "co-owner" relationship [17, 18], which we will discuss in the next section.

Table 1. Consensus IP and actual IP have a one-to-one mapping relationship.

Consensus IP	Actual IP
93.133.12.195	2.243.1.65
83.236.208.78	95.223.285.221
117.222.107.93	61.1.215.1
191.34.116.131	177.18.199.95
31.13.195.173	87.120.37.148
73.174.133.218	67.163.135.106
82.202.170.31	82.146.55.139
86.128.30.92	81.151.109.84
158.69.35.227	54.39.101.136

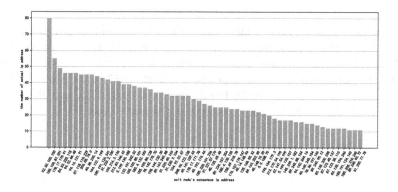

Fig. 8. It shows that a consensus-IP corresponds to multiple actual-IP.

4.4 The co-owner Relationship of the Malicious Exit Node

Multiple exit nodes route traffic to one or more IP addresses outside the Tor network, and we suspect that these exit nodes are held by the same person or organization, i.e., there is a "co-owner" relationship. We used graph algorithm and Gephi tool to display the results of family aggregation. A total of 35 co-host families were found, and the largest family included 230 exit nodes.

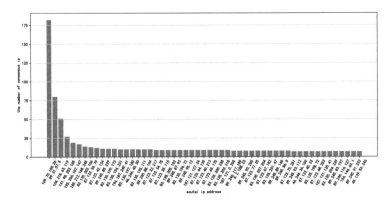

Fig. 9. It shows multiple consensus-IP corresponding to one or more actual-IP.

We can see that there is a large family in Fig. 10, which may seem inconceivable, but through deep analysis of the data, we find that the multiple acutal IP bound exit nodes have a large overlap, as shown in Table 2. Acutal IP 109.70.100.32 overlapped 66 exit nodes bound to 89.31.57.5. We believe that the same attacker controls host 109.70.100.32 and host 89.31.57.5, and their bound exit nodes jointly carry out malicious acts at the same time.

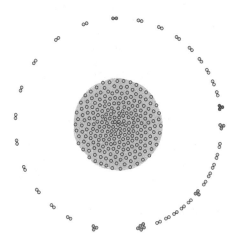

Fig. 10. We grouped the exit nodes of the same family together and identified them in the same color. (Color figure online)

As mentioned by Zhao Z. [13, 21], many websites [20] block the IP address of exit node. The malicious exit nodes detected in this paper may be a well-intentioned bridge between the client and the target website built by the owner of the exit node, but such behavior may bring more security risks. It will expose

Table 2. Different actual-IPS are bound to the same group of consensus-IPS. It means that these actual-IPS can be aggregated after exceeding the overlap threshold. Finally, cousensusIPs will form a large family.

Actual IP1	Actual IP2	The number of overlapping consensus IP addresses
109.70.100.32	109.70.100.33	79
109.70.100.32	89.31.57.5	66
109.70.100.32	104.218.63.119	43
109.70.100.33	195.206.107.147	17

more users' traffic to attackers, so it is reasonable for us to define this kind of node as malicious exit node.

5 Conclusion

In this paper, we revisited the trustworthiness of Tor exit relays. We designed and developed the ExitSniffer tool to continuously pay attention to scale and bandwidth of malicious exit relay nodes, the consensus IP is inconsistent with the actual returned IP, over a period of 16 months. By analyzing the anomalous binding relationship phenomena of malicious exit nodes, we totally find 1983 malicious exit relays which average contribute 10.12% bandwidth of total Tor exit relays bandwidth monthly, resulting tremendous threaten for Tor user's anonymity according to the current path-relay selecting algorithm. Besides, according to our results, there exits two types of anomalous binding relationship consists 35 exit relay families which are neither announced in the consensus document or detected by the Tor network.

Acknowledgements. This work is supported by the Key Research and Development Program for Guangdong Province under grant (No. 2019B010137003), Fundamental Research program of National Defence (JCKY2019211B001) and the Strategic Priority Research Program of Chinese Academy of Sciences (XDC02040400).

References

1. The number of exit nodes. https://metrics.torproject.org/relayflags.html. Accessed 18 Aug 2021
2. Dingledine, R., Mathewson, N., Syverson, P.: Tor: the second-generation onion router. In: USENIX Security. USENIX Association (2004)
3. Bernstein, D.J.: Curve25519: new Diffie-Hellman speed records. In: Yung, M., Dodis, Y., Kiayias, A., Malkin, T. (eds.) PKC 2006. LNCS, vol. 3958, pp. 207–228. Springer, Heidelberg (2006). https://doi.org/10.1007/11745853_14
4. Huber, M., Mulazzani, M., Weippl, E.: Tor HTTP usage and information leakage. In: De Decker, B., Schaumüller-Bichl, I. (eds.) CMS 2010. LNCS, vol. 6109, pp. 245–255. Springer, Heidelberg (2010). https://doi.org/10.1007/978-3-642-13241-4_22

5. Douceur, J.R.: The Sybil attack. In: Druschel, P., Kaashoek, F., Rowstron, A. (eds.) IPTPS 2002. LNCS, vol. 2429, pp. 251–260. Springer, Heidelberg (2002). https://doi.org/10.1007/3-540-45748-8_24

6. Marlinspike, M.: Sslstrip. http://www.thoughtcrime.org/software/sslstrip/

7. Ryan, P.: Security expert used tor to collect government e-mail passwords (2007)

8. TOR exit-node doing MITM attacks. http://www.teamfurry.com/wordpress/2007/11/20/tor-exit-node-doing-mitm-attacks/

9. Winter, P., et al.: Spoiled onions: exposing malicious tor exit relays. In: De Cristofaro, E., Murdoch, S.J. (eds.) PETS 2014. LNCS, vol. 8555, pp. 304–331. Springer, Cham (2014). https://doi.org/10.1007/978-3-319-08506-7_16

10. The Tor Project. Tor Metrics. https://metrics.torproject.org/

11. Winter, P., et al.: Identifying and characterizing Sybils in the Tor network. ArXiv abs/1602.07787 (2016)

12. How Malicious Tor Relays are Exploiting Users in 2020 (2020). https://nusenu.medium.com/how-malicious-tor-relays-are-exploiting-users-in-2020-part-i-1097575c0cac

13. Zhang, Z., Zhou, W., Sherr, M.: Bypassing tor exit blocking with exit bridge onion services. In: ACM Conference on Computer and Communications Security (CCS) (2020)

14. The Tor Project. Stem Docs (2013). https://stem.torproject.org

15. Hanley, H., Sun, Y., Wagh, S., Mittal, P.: DPSelect: a differential privacy based guard relay selection algorithm for tor. Proc. Priv. Enhancing Technol. **2**, 166–186 (2019). https://doi.org/10.2478/popets/20190025

16. The Tor Project. Relays with Exit, Fast, Guard, Stable, and HSDir flags (2013). https://metrics.torproject.org/network.html

17. Sanatinia, A., Noubir, G.: Honey onions: a framework for characterizing and identifying misbehaving Tor HSDirs. IEEE Conf. Commun. Netw. Secur. (CNS) **2016**, 127–135 (2016)

18. Chen, M., Wang, X., Shi, J., Yue, G., Gan, Z.: Towards comprehensive secuity analysis of family phenomenon of Tor hidden service. In: ICICS 2019 (2019)

19. Hodges, J., Jackson, C., Barth, A.: RFC 6797: HTTP Strict Transport Security (HSTS) (2012). https://tools.ietf.org/html

20. Alexa: The top 500 sites on the web (2013). http://www.alexa.com/topsites

21. Singh, R., et al.: Characterizing the nature and dynamics of tor exit blocking. In: USENIX Security Symposium (USENIX) (2017)

22. Murdoch, S.J., Zieliński, P.: Sampled traffic analysis by internet-exchange-level adversaries. In: Borisov, N., Golle, P. (eds.) PET 2007. LNCS, vol. 4776, pp. 167–183. Springer, Heidelberg (2007). https://doi.org/10.1007/978-3-540-75551-7_11

23. Nasr, M., Bahramali, A., Houmansadr, A.: Deepcorr: strong flow correlation attacks on Tor using deep learning. In: Proceedings of the ACM SIGSAC Conference on Computer and Communications Security, pp. 1962–1976 (2018)

24. Ling, Z., Luo, J., Yu, W., et al.: A new cell counter based attack against Tor. In: Proceedings of the 16th ACM conference on Computer and Communications Security, pp. 578–589 (2009)

25. Wang, X., Luo, J., Yang, M., et al.: A potential HTTP-based application-level attack against Tor. Futur. Gener. Comput. Syst. **27**(1), 67–77 (2011)

26. Akhoondi, M., Yu, C., Madhyastha, H.V.: LASTor: a low-latency AS-aware Tor client. In: 2012 IEEE Symposium on Security and Privacy, pp. 476–490. IEEE (2012)

Traffic Analysis

Efficient Classification of Darknet Access Activity with Partial Traffic

Xuebin Wang[1,2], Meiqi Wang[1,2], Jinqiao Shi[3(✉)], Zeyu Li[3], Kexin Zou[3], and Binxing Fang[1,4]

[1] Institute of Information Engineering, Chinese Academy of Sciences, Beijing, China
[2] School of Cyber Security, University of Chinese Academy of Sciences, Beijing, China
[3] School of Cyberspace Security, Beijing University of Posts and Telecommunications, Beijing, China
shijinqiao@bupt.edu.cn
[4] Institute of Electronic and Information Engineering of UESTC in Guangdong, Dongguan, China

Abstract. In this paper we propose a novel approach to classify darknet-access traffic with only partial traffic data, which significantly reduces resource consumption and is as accuracy as prior work. Besides, in order to keep up with the users' real access activity, we simulate new and old user by simply whether delete the cached consensus document before each access and apply our approach. The experiment results confirm that there does exist a window of cell sequence contributes greatly to distinguish darknet-access traffic. With the window size 75 and the start point 67, we can achieve 95.97% accuracy for new user access scenario. Similarly, with the window size 85 and the start point 44, we achieve 94.43% accuracy for old user access scenario.

Keywords: Tor · Hidden service · Traffic analysis

1 Introduction

Tor [14], a low-latency anonymity network, has emerged as an important privacy-enhancing tool protecting users' online privacy, i.e. hiding the users' IP address while communicating on the Internet. Nowadays, with more than two million users daily [1], Tor is considered to be one of the most popular anonymous communication systems consisting of nearly 7000 volunteer-operated relays, which are run from all around the world.

Besides protecting client's privacy, Tor also allows servers to operate anonymously by offering hidden services (HSs). HSs allow users, in particular those living in oppressive regimes, e.g., human right activists and whistle-blowers, to bypass censorship and to exercise freedom of speech by publishing and offering access to sensitive content without the fear of being targeted, arrested or forced to shut down. As a result, many sensitive contents are hosted and only accessed

© The Author(s) 2022
W. Lu et al. (Eds.): CNCERT 2021, CCIS 1506, pp. 113–128, 2022.
https://doi.org/10.1007/978-981-16-9229-1_7

through HSs, forming a deep-dark cyberspace for criminals [4]. Hence, it is necessary to comprehensively evaluate the level of protection provided by this novel anonymity mechanism.

Unfortunately, attackers can classify whether a user is accessing hidden service and even infer which specific hidden service a user has visited. With malicious nodes controlled, attacker performs circuit fingerprinting attack can easily distinguish hidden service related circuits both at the guard [8] and middle [6] position of a circuit, the attack significantly depends on the number of nodes controlled. What's more, a local observer which eavesdrops traffic between the sender and the first anonymization relay node, can distinguish whether a user is accessing hidden service [11] and guess the user's destination without decryption, called Website Fingerprinting attack (WF attack) [5,10,12,13,15–17]. With the help of machine-learning or deep learning models, prior works treat each whole traffic trace as input to extract features, which is not suitable for online classification scenario.

In this paper we propose a novel approach to classify darknet-access traffic with only partial traffic data, which significantly reduces resource consumption and is as accuracy as prior work. Besides, in order to keep up with the users' real access activity, we simulate new and old user by simply whether delete the cached consensus data before each access. Moreover, we collect direct cell logs by modifying Tor source code to record the basic information of each cell, and use the direct cell logs as ground truth to analysis the nuance between darknet-access and general access activity. By digging into the access process thoroughly, we find that there exists a window of cell sequence contributes greatly to distinguish darknet-access related traffic. With the window size 75 and the start point 67, we can achieve 95.97% accuracy for new user access scenario. With the window size 85 and the start point 44, we can achieve 94.43% accuracy for old user access scenario.

The contributions of this paper are listed as follows:

- As far as we know, as a network level attack, we are the first to use partial traffic data to classify darknet-access activity, which is also much more practical and applicable in online manner.
- In order to verify our method, we capture a large and practical dataset by simulating new and old user access activity. Besides, we make the generated dataset publicly available[1], allowing researchers to replicate our results and systematically evaluate new approaches in the future.
- Based on the dataset we collected, we use the direct cell logs to determine the proper window size and the start point of the darknet-access activity. Then, we transform traffic traces into cell sequences and conduct activity classification experiments, the experimental results verify that it does work that with a proper window size and start point can effectively distinguish darknet-access activity from general access activity.

---

[1] The dataset can be found on the following URL: https://github.com/Meiqiw/mingan/.

Organization. The rest of the paper is organized as follows. In Sect. 2, we illustrate the background on Tor and hidden service design as well as the attacker threat model. In Sect. 3, we describe the data collection and processing methodology, generating the dataset for analysis. We next present, in Sect. 4, our observations and experiment results regarding differences between darknet-access activity and general access activity. We introduce the related work in Sect. 5 and the conclusion in Sect. 6.

2   Background

In this section, we will provide the necessary background on Tor as well as the functionality of the Tor hidden services. Then, we describe the threat model of our attack.

2.1   Tor

A user starts the anonymous journey by simply unzipping the Tor browser bundle, which contains the Onion Proxy (OP) and a customized Firefox browser. The OP performs as an bridge between users' applications and the Tor network. Before user sends his application data over the Tor network, the OP must learn about Tor's relays, Onion Routers, by downloading the network consensus document from directory servers. And then select three relays: an entry guard, middle and exit node, creating circuits incrementally and interactively. The OP encapsulate application data into 514-byte fixed-size cells as its communication data unit, forwarded though the created circuit hop by hop. Tor builds circuits hop by hop like an onion, and the details of the circuit construction process as follow. Firstly, the OP sends a *create2* cell to establish the circuit with the guard relay, which responds with a *created2* cell. Secondly, the OP sends an *extend2* command cell to the guard relay, which parses the cell and correspondingly sends a create cell to the middle relay node to establish the circuit on behalf of the user, thus a tunnel between the user and the middle relay has been created. Finally, the OP sends another *extend2* command cell to the middle relay through the tunnel just created, causing the middle relay sends a create cell to the exit node correspondingly. And then the circuit between the OP and the exit relay has been created, then a *begin* cell is relayed the exit node building a TCP connection to the final destination. Figure 1 demonstrates the 3 hop circuit construction process as well as the cells exchanged between OP and the guard relay for general Tor connections.

The TCP connection between each hop of a Tor circuit is secured with TLS. Moreover, Tor multiplexes circuits within a single TCP connection. Precisely, An OP-OR TCP connection multiplexes all circuits from the same user while an OR-OR TCP connection multiplexes circuits for various users simultaneously. An ISP level attacker who monitors the OP-OR TCP connection can not distinguish which TCP packet belongs to which circuit as all circuits exists in the same one TCP connection.

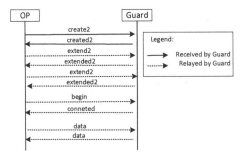

Fig. 1. Circuit construction details

2.2 Hidden Service Components

Hidden service was introduced in 2004 as a feature of Tor, providing anonymity of responders by hidden the location information while offering service. According to the protocol specification [2], the hidden service architecture consists of the following five components, as shown in Fig. 2:

- **HS:** Hidden Server is the information provider which hosts various services, such as WEB, MAIL.
- **OP:** User accesses the Tor network by running Tor client instance name as Onion Proxy (OP).
- **RP:** Rendezvous Point is the Tor relay which is chosen by the OP randomly, forwarding traffic on behave of OP while concealing the location at the same time.
- **IP:** Introduction Point maintains a long-term circuit and forwards the requests from clients to the hidden service.
- **HSDir:** Hidden Service Directory is a Tor relay which has the flag **HSDir**, acting as a database for storing and retrieving hidden service information.

Next, we describe the steps to set up a hidden service in Tor and establish a connection to it.

- Firstly, the HS chooses three onion routers as its IPs, and then builds circuits to each IPs by sending a *relay-establish-intro* cell respectively. Upon receiving such a cell, the IPs send back *relay-intro-established* cell with an empty payload to inform that the circuits have been successfully established.
- After establishing circuits to IPs, the HS builds a circuit to the HSDirs chosen to advertise the service descriptor, the cell sequences exchanged is shown in Fig. 3. After that, the HS owner can advertise the onion address in the surface Web with the form z.onion.
- After receiving an onion address, the Tor client creates circuits to HSDirs responsible for the specific HS and retrieves HS descriptor from which the client learns the information about IPs.

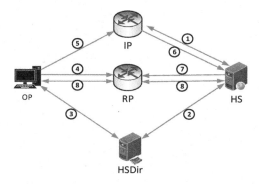

Fig. 2. Hidden service architecture

– The Client randomly chooses a pre-created circuit and picks the last hop as the RP and builds a circuit to that onion router by sending a *relay-establish-rendezvous* cell which carries the rendezvous cookie, and the RP replies with an empty *relay-rendezvous-established* cell, indicating that the rendezvous circuit has been successfully built.
– The Client then builds separate circuits to one of the IPs extracted from the HS descriptor. The Client sends a *relay-introduce1* cell contains the rendezvous cookie, the fingerprint of RP and the hash of the public key of the HS along the introduction circuit.
– Once the IP receiving *relay-introduce1* cell, it sends the *relay-introduce2* cell to corresponding HS, according to the hash of the public key. The *relay-introduce2* cell also contains the rendezvous cookie generated by Client and the fingerprint of RP.
– Upon receiving the *relay-introduce2*, HS decrypts it with the private key and extract rendezvous cookie and RP's fingerprint. Then, the HS extends a circuit to RP according to the fingerprint and sends a *relay-rendezvous1* cell containing rendezvous cookie.
– At last, RP binds two circuits which have the same rendezvous cookie, so as to deliver relay cells from each of the two circuits to the other, and sends a *relay-rendezvous2* cell to Client which denotes the beginning of communication between Client and HS.

In this way, the OP and HS communicates successfully without any leakage of their anonymity. Figure 4 demonstrates the cell exchange process in detail. From the description introduced above, there does exist significant differences between hidden service related activity and general access activity, indicating that it is possible to distinguish hidden service related activity from others.

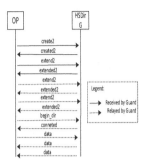

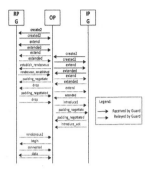

Fig. 3. Client-HSDir circuit cell exchanges

Fig. 4. Client-HS circuit cell exchanges

2.3   Threat Model

In this work, we assume a network level attacker which is: local, meaning that he has access only to the connection between the OP and the guard relay node, and passive, i.e., he can only collect the network packets and can not delay, drop, modify or decrypt even them. Precisely, we assume the attacker is the Internet Service Providers (ISP). Figure 5 illustrates the attack scenario: the user access both general web service and hidden service over the Tor network and intercepts the traffic between the user and the Tor network. We assume that the attacker knows the user's identity and only aims at distinguishing the darknet-access activity from numerous connections.

Within this attack scenario, we make several assumptions about the attacker goals and capabilities.

Traffic Parsing: The ISP attacker has access to all OP-OR TCP connections built by huge amount users concurrently, and able to record the traffic packet meta-data of the both direction, including timestamp, srcIP, srcPort, dstIP, dst-Port, packetSize, direction. As what has been mentioned above, the ISP attacker can only distinguish each OP-OR TCP connection but can not identify each circuit multiplexed in one TCP connection while a node level attacker does.

Goals: In this work, we assume the ISP level attacker only focus on identifying that a user is connected to hidden service (darknet-access activity) within huge amount TCP connections as effective as possible, or even the real time scenario. Identifying which website the user surfs is out of the coverage of this work.

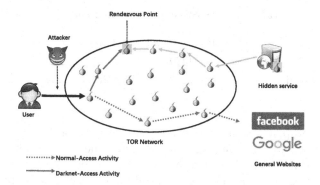

Fig. 5. The threat model

3 Data Collection and Processing

In this section, we propose our new data collection method and describe our experimental setup. Then we describe the data extraction procedure as well as giving a brief introduction of our dataset.

3.1 Data Collection

In order to simulate users' access activity over the Tor network more realistically, we define two scenarios: delete Tor cached documents and not delete. The former scenario aims at simulating a user who use Tor network for the first time, while the latter scenario for simulating a user who use Tor network access the Web just now. The reason is that new user needs download Tor consensus document before building circuits while the old user not needs, making totally difference in the number connection built as well as packet pattern transferred.

We use a distributed setup, utilizing 3 Virtual Machines (VMs) on cloud environment provided by Vultr[2]. These virtual machines are located in different countries including Singapore, France and the United States, so as to ensure the diversity of traces. Each VM is configured with 2 CPUs and 8 GB of RAM. On each VM, 10 docker instances are deployed, and each docker with a separate Tor process (version 0.4.4.6). To access the Tor network, we use **Selenium**[3] (version 3.12.0) to control headless browser **Firefox** (version 60.0.2), utilizing a SOCKS5 proxy listened by Tor. We recorded the traces of web pages leveraging **tcpdump**[4]. Web pages are given 120 s to load, and upon loading the page, it was left open for an additional 10 s, after which the browser is closed and the Tor process is killed. As for new user scenario, the cached data in the DataDirectory such as cached consensus, server descriptors, is deleted automatically each time. Next, **tcpdump** and Tor process are restarted. A script to monitor the bootstrap status of the Tor process is deployed ensuring Tor is ready before each visit.

---

[2] http://vultr.com.

[3] http://www.seleniumhq.org/.

[4] http://www.tcpdump.org/.

Table 1. Data collection for both scenarios

	Website	WebsiteTrace	Onion	OnionTrace
Delete cache	8155	13504	8755	14594
Not delete	7754	20622	8267	22255

With this setup, new connections and circuits are established each time as the client visits a website, ensuring that we never used the same circuit to download more than one instance of a single page. What to be mentioned is that one trace may contains multi connections, we split all connections and build dataset for our attack as the network level attacker does. While recording the traffic trace, we also record the connection creation, circuit construction, stream info, cell sequences into the notice log file by modifying Tor source code, aiming at showing light on the real activity Tor instance occurs during darknet-access as well general-access activity. By performing statistics on the connection, circuit, stream as well as cell, we reveal the difference between darknet-access activity and general-access activity in two scenarios described above. Those statistic results have theoretical significance for the attack approach we proposed.

Following our data collection method, we use Alexa Top websites and Tor hidden services[5] as our target website for both scenarios, each with 10,000 websites. Similar to the previous work, after data collection, we filtered out invalid traces and outliers, which caused by timeout or crash of the browser or Selenium driver. Eventually, we obtained huge amount of traces as shown in Table 1, each trace accomplished with one corresponding notice log file.

3.2   Data Extraction and Processing

In general, as in many previous work [12,13,17], we represent the data as a sequence of $[+1, -1]$, where each $+1$ or -1 represents a cell, which is the most basic communication unit of Tor, and the sign indicates whether the direction of the cell is from the client to the Tor entry node or vice versa. As a result, an input instance of our model is a series of 1 and -1. In the experiment, we truncated the input sequences to a fixed length, and filled the sequences less than this length with 0. As asserted in [12], neural networks generally work with real numbers from the compact interval $[-1, 1]$ due to the nature of the mathematical operations they perform. Moreover, by providing the input data in such a format, we avoid having to rescale and/or normalize the values and thus mitigate a possible information loss coupled with the preprocessing step.

---

[5] As the prior work, we chose hidden services based on the list provided by the .onion search engine http://www.ahmia.fi/.

Our dataset contains two type of data: **traffic traces** and **cell records**. With the cell records, we split the cell sequences according to different connectionID, generating cell sequences of one specific connection, which commonly multiplexed with multiple circuits. For the traffic traces, we split each traffic trace into different flows. And then transfer each flow into TCP packet sequences, TLS record sequences as well as cell sequences. The detail processing procedure described as follows respectively.

Cell Record Processing. By parsing the notice log file, many basic information about the connection, circuit, cell are extracted, including connection creation time, connectionID, circuitID, cell command and direction etc. Firstly, we order cells of each circuit with timestamp and tag the circuit with different flags according to the circuit purpose. We divide circuit into five categories: **create-fast**, meaning that this circuit is built for downloading consensus documents at bootstrapping process, **client-data**, meaning that this circuit is built for access non-hidden service related data, **client-ip, client-rp, client-hsdir**, those three are hidden service related, and others. Secondly, we select circuits belongs to the same connection and put corresponding cells together, generating the cell sequence of one specific connection. At last, we tag each connection according to the circuits categories multiplexed in the same connection.

Traffic Trace Processing. As shown in Fig. 6, at the application layer, Tor embeds the encrypted data into a fixed-size (514-byte) packet, which is called a cell. And the cell is further embedded into the TLS record. Multiple cells can be grouped into a single TLS record. Finally, in the transport layer, TLS records are typically fragmented into multiple TCP packets, the size of which is limited by the Maximum Transmission Unit (MTU). Note that several TLS records can be within a single TCP packet. As for collected traffic traces, our process performs as follows: Firstly, we cut each visit traffic trace file into multi flows according to four-meta tuple (srcIP, srcPort, destIP, destPort), ensuring each flow contains and only contains one connection. Secondly, we tag each connection the same category as the connection recorded in the notice log file which processed in the prior subsection. What's more, we parse the single flow pcap files into TCP packet sequences and TLS record sequences, with the help of Tshark[6] (version 1.12.1), an industrial grade widely used tool for network traffic analysis. At last, we extract cell sequences from the TLS record sequences following the method proposed by [17], thus translating each connection traffic packet traces into cell sequences tagged with corresponding categories. A slight difference from [17] is that we divide the length of the TLS record by 514 instead of 512, because with the upgrade of the Tor protocol, the length of the cell has changed from a fixed 512 bytes to 514 bytes. Therefore, we believe that this treatment is much more closer to the real situation.

DATASET MingAn21. After completing the above operation, we eventually obtained *MingAn21*, consisting of two subsets: (i) 15,000 instances of hidden service related, general website related and others each, corresponding

---

[6] https://www.wireshark.org/docs/man-pages/tshark.html.

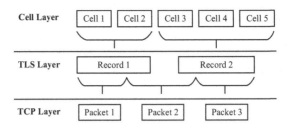

Fig. 6. Layers of data transport in Tor

to the delete cache scenario (ii) 10,000 instances of hidden service related and general website related each, corresponding to the not delete cache scenario. Our dataset contains both direction and time information of each cell.

4   Evaluation and Discussion

In this section, we firstly perform location statistic of hidden service related cell commands with the real cell record parsed from the notice log file, revealing the possible position of **establish_rendezvous** and **rendezvous2** cell in one single connection. Next, we provide an evaluation of the different classification methods of prior work with proper length of cell sequences, finding the state-of-the-art as the one we use in this paper. At last, we perform iterative experiments to learn the best choice of the start point and window size to perform our attack.

4.1   Position Distribution Observation

According to our data collection method, we record two type of data for every connection: raw traffic packets and real cell sequences. We record some basic cell data including cell command name, cell direction and timestamp. With the cell command name, we can clearly notice the activity the Tor instance is doing. As for hidden service related activity, **establish_rendezvous** and **rendezvous2** cell are import functional cells during the OP-HS connection construction procedure, indicating the start and success signals correspondingly. In order to have a clear understanding the position of those two functional cells within one single connection, we perform statistics on all the record cell sequences parsed from the notice log file for both two scenarios. In detail, we statistic the absolute position of establish_rendezvous and rendezvous2 as well as the interval distance in the unit of one connection.

As shown in Fig. 7, in most cases establish_rendezvous cells are send after 69 and receive rendezvous2 cell before 147 with a window size of 72 in the delete cache document scenario. However, in not delete cache document scenario, most establish_rendezvous cells are send after 45 and receive rendezvous2 cell before 130 with a window size of 73. It is oblivious that, in most cases, hidden service related functional cell signals of not delete document scenario occur much earlier

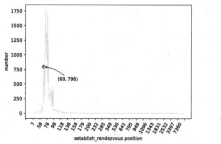

(a) Establish_Rendezvous Cell Position Distribution of Delete Scenario

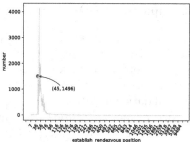

(b) Establish_Rendezvous Cell Position Distribution of Not Delete Scenario

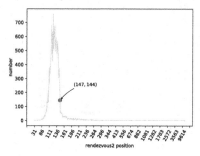

(c) Rendezvous2 Cell Position Distribution of Delete Scenario

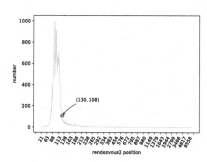

(d) Rendezvous2 Cell Position Distribution of Not Delete Scenario

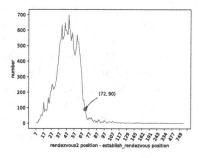

(e) Interval Distance Distribution of Delete Scenario

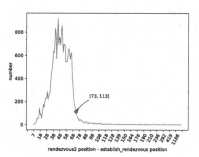

(f) Interval Distance Distribution of Not Delete Scenario

Fig. 7. Position statistic results on both scenarios

than that of delete cache document scenario. From the statistic results, we draw the conclusion that there does exist a fragment of cell sequences contribute significantly on distinguishing hidden service related activity and that it is possible to filter hidden service related activity only with partial cell sequences.

4.2   Comparison of Different Classification Methods

In this subsection, we reproduce the classification methods of prior work on our dataset **MingAn21**, finding the state-of-the-art as the method we use in this paper. In order to check the robustness and accuracy, we increase the cell sequences from 40 to 140 with a step by 10 iteratively by setting the radio of training, validation and testing as 1:1:2. With the above setting, we perform our experiments on both scenarios with different classification methods, including CNN [12], LSTM [12], SDAE [12], DF [13], k-NN [16], CUMUL [10] and k-FP [5].

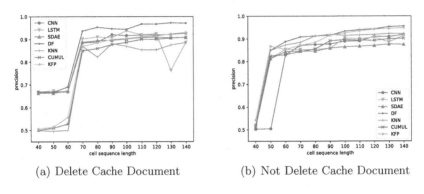

(a) Delete Cache Document   (b) Not Delete Cache Document

Fig. 8. Different classification on both scenarios

As shown in Fig. 8, the DF classification method performs the best with excellent robustness as well as accuracy for both scenarios. As for the delete cache document scenario, with the cell sequences length at 40, deep learning related classification methods achieve much better accuracy than that of machine learning methods do. As the increase of the cell sequence length more than 70, the performance of DF method increases rapidly and keeps stable. As for the not delete cache document scenario, KFP and DF both achieve better accuracy and stability as the cell sequence increases. As DF achieves better performance in both scenarios, we take DF as our classification method used in this paper.

4.3   Classification with Partial Cell Fragment

In this section, we try to search the best value of the start point and window size for the DF classification method for both scenarios. We refer the search space as $S * W$, which S indicates the space of start point and W indicates the window size. According to the observation described above, we set S belongs to [start_point-2, start_point, start_point+2] and W belongs to [window_size-2, end_point-start_point]. In delete cache document scenario, S belongs to [67, 68, 69, 70, 71] and W belongs to [70, 71, 72, 73, 74, 75, 76, 77, 78]. And in not delete cache document scenario, S belongs to [43, 44, 45, 46, 47] and W belongs to [71, 72, 73, 74, 75, 76, 77, 78, 79, 80, 81, 82, 83, 84, 85]. Then, by setting the radio of training, validation and testing as 1:1:2, we perform experiments with DF classification method iteratively by increase the S and W parameter with a step by 1. The final results are illustrated in Fig. 9, with the window size 75 and the start point 67, we can achieve 95.97% accuracy for delete cache document scenario. With the window size 85 and the start point 44, we can achieve 94.43% accuracy for not delete cache document scenario. The result verifies that it is possible to classify hidden service access and general service access activity as efficient as prior work while significantly reduce the resource cost. With 75 and 85 cell sequences respectively, in both scenarios, a network level attacker can distinguish whether a user is accessing hidden service or general service with a high accuracy without decrypting the packets.

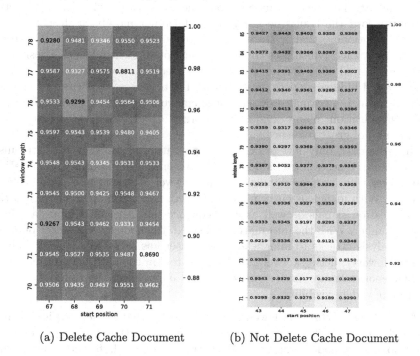

(a) Delete Cache Document   (b) Not Delete Cache Document

Fig. 9. Different classification on both scenarios

The most relative work to us is Panchenko et al. [11], in contrast to this work, our approach only use 75 or 85 cell sequences of each trace while achieving as good performance as the prior work. Moreover, in terms of training time, with much less data for training, our approach is also much effective than the prior work.

5 Related Work

Many attacks have been proposed to challenge the security of Tor hidden services. Most of these threat models assume that the attacker is active, that is, the adversary has the ability to modify the monitored traffic, or influence the routing of relays. For example, Biliukov et al. [3] proposed that when a malicious RP receives *relay-introduce1* sent by the hidden service, it sends a message to the hidden service consisting of 50 padding ucells. This signal allows another malicious OR along the circuit from the hidden service to the RP to identify the hidden service or its entry guard on the circuit. Another example, Jansen et al. [7] proposed a memory-based DoS attack. The attacker identifies and disables the entry node of the target HS, thereby forcing the server to choose a new guard. Chen et al. [9] proposed a novel approach discovering the hidden service or its entry guard in a parallel manner by embedding numerous hidden services identification into rendezvous cookie.

In contrast, the adversary in our threat model is passive, that is, the attacker can only record the traffic he monitors, but cannot modify or drop them. It is worth mentioning that a study similar to our research method is Website Fingerprint Attack, which uses traffic classification to identify which website Tor users have visited. The difference is that we need to answer whether Tor users have accessed hidden services, or just used Tor to access a website that can be accessed through a normal browser. Although we have different granularities of traffic classification, many outstanding works [5,10,12,13,15–17] in the WFP field are also of great reference value.

Unfortunately, only few prior studies pay attention to how to distinguish whether a user is accessing a hidden service. According to the ability and location of attackers, they can be divided into node level attackers and network level attackers. With malicious entry node controlled, node level attackers record the circuit creation signals as well as cell sequences silently and traffic data in a passive manner. With the information collected, the node level attacker perform traffic analysis attacks to infer whether the user has accessed a specific hidden service. However, network level attackers located on the path between user and the first anonymization node, can collect and only collect the traffic data with much more widely visibility.

Node Level Attacker. Kwon et al. [8] showed that hidden services' traffic can be distinguished from regular websites with more than 90% accuracy from a malicious entry node perspective. Recently, Jansen et al. [6] performed circuit fingerprinting attach from the middle relay position, demonstrating that traffic fingerprinting techniques are as effective as prior works shown from a guard relay perspective. However, the result of this kind of attack significantly depends on the number of nodes attacker controlled.

Network Level Attacker. Hayes and Danezis [5] find that the onion sites can be discriminated from other regular web pages with 85% true positive rate and only 0.02% false positive from a dataset of 100,000 sites. Panchenko et al. [11] use machine learning methods to distinguish hidden service related traffics accurately and scales well, with a precision more that 0.9 and a recall at least 0.8. With the help of machine-learning or deep learning models, prior works treat each whole traffic trace as input to extract features, which is not suitable for online classification scenario.

In our paper, we innovatively examine the existence of the fragment of cell sequences and explore the effectiveness of only use partial traffic data for distinguishing darknet-access activity from general access activity.

6   Conclusion

In this paper we have analyzed the susceptibility of darknet-access activity to the traffic analysis attack. To this end, we proposed a novel approach to classify darknet-access traffic with only partial traffic data, which significantly reduces resource consumption and is as accuracy as prior work. In order to verify the effectiveness and applicable for practical scenario, we conduct experiments both on new and old user scenario. The results depict that there does exist a window of cell sequences contribute greatly to distinguish darknet-access traffic. Moreover, our approach performs as well as state-of-the-art methods with respect to classification accuracy. Thus, with only partial traffic data we can distinguish darknet-access activity effectively with much less resources, which can be applied in online classification scenario.

Acknowledgements. This work is supported by the Key Research and Development Program for Guangdong Province under grant (No. 2019B010137003), Fundamental Research program of National Defence (JCKY2019211B001) and the Strategic Priority Research Program of Chinese Academy of Sciences, Grant No. XDC02040400.

References

1. Tor project, users - tor metrics. https://metrics.torproject.org/userstats-relay-country.html?start=2021-02-25&end=2021-05-26&country=all&events=off. Accessed May 2021
2. Tor specification. https://gitweb.torproject.org/torspec.git/tree/rend-spec-v2.txt
3. Biryukov, A., Pustogarov, I., Weinmann, R.P.: Trawling for tor hidden services: detection, measurement, deanonymization. In: 2013 IEEE Symposium on Security and Privacy, pp. 80–94 (2013). https://doi.org/10.1109/SP.2013.15
4. Christin, N.: Traveling the silk road: a measurement analysis of a large anonymous online marketplace. Arch. Neurol. **2**(3), 293 (2012)
5. Hayes, J., Danezis, G.: k-fingerprinting: a robust scalable website fingerprinting technique. In: USENIX Security Symposium, pp. 1187–1203 (2016)
6. Jansen, R., Juárez, M., Galvez, R., Elahi, T., Díaz, C.: Inside job: applying traffic analysis to measure tor from within. In: 25th Annual Network and Distributed System Security Symposium, NDSS 2018, San Diego, California, USA, 18–21 February 2018. The Internet Society (2018)
7. Jansen, R., Tschorsch, F., Johnson, A., Scheuermann, B.: The sniper attack: anonymously deanonymizing and disabling the tor network. In: 21st Annual Network and Distributed System Security Symposium, NDSS 2014, San Diego, California, USA, 23–26 February 2014 (2014)
8. Kwon, A., Alsabah, M., Lazar, D., Dacier, M., Devadas, S.: Circuit fingerprinting attacks: passive deanonymization of tor hidden services. In: USENIX Security Symposium, pp. 287–302 (2015)

9. Muqian, C., Wang, X., Liu, T., Shi, J., Yin, Z., Fang, B.: SignalCookie: discovering guard relays of hidden services in parallel, pp. 1–7, June 2019. https://doi.org/10.1109/ISCC47284.2019.8969639

10. Panchenko, A., et al.: Website fingerprinting at internet scale. In: NDSS (2016)

11. Panchenko, A., Mitseva, A., Henze, M., Lanze, F., Wehrle, K., Engel, T.: Analysis of fingerprinting techniques for tor hidden services. In: Proceedings of the 2017 on Workshop on Privacy in the Electronic Society, Dallas, TX, USA, 30 October–3 November 2017, pp. 165–175. ACM (2017)

12. Rimmer, V., Preuveneers, D., Juarez, M., Van Goethem, T., Joosen, W.: Automated website fingerprinting through deep learning. In: Network and Distributed System Security Symposium (NDSS) (2018)

13. Sirinam, P., Imani, M., Juarez, M., Wright, M.: Deep fingerprinting: undermining website fingerprinting defenses with deep learning. In: Proceedings of the 2018 ACM SIGSAC Conference on Computer and Communications Security, pp. 1928–1943 (2018)

14. Syverson, P., Dingledine, R., Mathewson, N.: Tor: the second-generation onion router. In: USENIX Security (2004)

15. Wang, M., Li, Y., Wang, X., Liu, T., Shi, J., Chen, M.: 2ch-TCN: a website fingerprinting attack over tor using 2-channel temporal convolutional networks. In: 2020 IEEE Symposium on Computers and Communications (ISCC), pp. 1–7 (2020). https://doi.org/10.1109/ISCC50000.2020.9219717

16. Wang, T., Cai, X., Nithyanand, R., Johnson, R., Goldberg, I.: Effective attacks and provable defenses for website fingerprinting. In: USENIX Security Symposium, pp. 143–157 (2014)

17. Wang, T., Goldberg, I.: Improved website fingerprinting on tor. In: Proceedings of the 12th ACM Workshop on Privacy in the Electronic Society, pp. 201–212. ACM (2013)

Research and Application of Security Situation Awareness Platform for Large Enterprises

Zhanyu Wang[✉]

China Mobile Tietong Co. Ltd., Room 1105, Jinze Building, No. 2, Guangningbo Street,
Xicheng District, Beijing 100033, China
wangzhanyu@cmtt.chinamobile.com

Abstract. This paper analyzes the international and domestic security situation and major security threats, including those faced by large enterprises. In order to improve the security management level of large enterprises, the construction of safety management system which takes the safety situation awareness platform as the command core is puts forward. The technical framework, evolution route, main functions, core technologies and three-stage models of detection, perception and prediction, closed-loop rectification, and threat information sharing are discussed. At the same time, the author analyzes the organization mechanism, the research and development guarantee, the sustainable application, the introduction of ecology and so on, and puts forward the solution.

Keywords: Security · Situational awareness · Detection · Prediction · Sharing

1 Introduction

Under the impetus of the fourth industrial revolution, informatization and intellectualization are becoming the core driving force for large enterprises to continuously improve their informatization level and efficiency. It is becoming common that who master information will win the competition. Network security and informatization complement each other; Network security and informatization are two wings of one body and two wheels of one drive. Without network security, there will be no national security, and without informatization, there will be no modernization. The overall development of informatization and information security is indispensable. As the lifeline of national security and national economy, large enterprises have invested a lot of money, manpower and material resources in security, and generally built their own information network, system and information security equipment. However, there are still problems in information security, such as fragmentation, information island and poor perception, It is difficult to deal with complex security problems with one or several security technologies alone. The focus of network security personnel has developed from solving single security problem to studying the security state and its changing trend of the whole network. Building a complete security situation awareness platform is the core of the unified smart security command system of large enterprises. It will lead the overall situation, quickly and quantitatively perceive enterprise security and various threats, and greatly improve the response and disposal level.

W. Lu et al. (Eds.): CNCERT 2021, CCIS 1506, pp. 129–139, 2022.
https://doi.org/10.1007/978-981-16-9229-1_8

2   General Status and Problems of Information Security in Large Enterprises

2.1   General Situation of Information Security in Large Enterprises

With the development and popularization of information technology, most large enterprises are gradually applying the latest information technology to better promote the improvement of work efficiency, making the development of enterprises in line with the development characteristics of the times. At present, China's large enterprises have basically completed the information construction, which is reflected in the corresponding information technology at all stages of the daily operation of enterprises, such as personnel management system, industrial control system, computer room construction, network construction and enterprise portal, involving all aspects of enterprise development. At the same time, large enterprises have added security construction investment for information construction, and issued corresponding management system for the security of technology application.

Different enterprises have different aims of information security protection. The technical system of information security management center needs to contain a variety of elements to play the corresponding role of information protection, including host, terminal, network, information system, technology application and data. The corresponding security products of each link are different. The information security technology architecture can be summarized into seven subsystems: host security, terminal security, application security, 4A security, information system security, data security and network security. The information management security of the whole enterprise can be guaranteed with the joint assistance of multiple subsystems.

In practice, most large enterprises use following equipments to build information security protection system: 4A, VPN, firewall, WAF, IPS/IDS, EDR, sandbox, honeypot, asset management system, anti-virus software, leak scanning system, etc., forming four basic conditions of secure communication network, regional boundary, management center and computing environment, providing enterprises with terminal access, interface security guarantee, application access and management, system security interconnection, safe operation guarantee Safety management ability.

2.2   Analysis of Information Security Situation of Large Enterprises

According to the analysis of China's Internet security situation by the national Internet Emergency Response Center and the statistics of the national information security vulnerability sharing platform, threats and risks such as denial of service attacks, high-risk vulnerabilities, phishing emails, personal information and important data leakage are still prominent in the first half of 2019–2020, and the risks remain high [1, 2].

The key infrastructure of large enterprise has become the key target of network attacks, and the network security risks such as vulnerability attacks and blackmail software are becoming more and more serious. The government, education, medical care, telecommunications, scientific research institutions and other important industries have become the hardest hit areas of network attacks.

From 2019 to the first half of 2020, the risk of personal information leakage continues to increase. In addition to the Internet industry, hotels and other service industries and industrial enterprises have become major risk areas of personal information leakage, and data security is facing serious challenges [1, 2].

Although the network security protection ability of large enterprises has been improved, there is still a certain gap between the security technology innovation and the international advanced level. In particular, with the wide application of emerging technologies such as artificial intelligence and blockchain, new types of network crimes are also escalating. In the face of the increasingly severe situation of attack and defense, the network security protection concept, ideas and technology implementation path of large enterprises need to be integrated and innovated.

For enterprises, the challenges of information security are mainly reflected in the following four aspects:

Decentralized security management; too many network devices; isolated information. The security incidents are analyzed and handled by different departments independently, which is impossible to analyze the security incidents end-to-end and make corresponding decisions.

Internal leakage: driven by interests, internal employees can easily disclose confidential information to competitors. Leakage means such as terminal copy, printing, e-mail delivery, etc.

Internal and external malicious attacks: the enterprise network is becoming more and more complex, and the enterprise terminal, network, server and so on have become the targets of internal and external attacks.

Vires abuse. Operation and maintenance personnel or business management personnel can easily use it system, ultra vires (fake, unauthorized access) access to enterprise confidential information.

2.3 Analysis of Information Security Problems in Large Enterprises

Among many information security problems that need to be solved, the most important one is the intelligent interconnection of various security devices. On the whole, all kinds of security equipment and capabilities are still in the state of decentralized construction and decentralized operation. There is a lack of interconnection between systems. Logs and other data are separated from each other and are actually "isolated islands" of data. It has some effect on the static and low-intensity information security attacks in the past, but it is not enough for the new situation attacks such as APT.

In addition, the sharing of security information with the outside of the enterprise is also an important factor affecting the ability of security protection, mainly because the security threat intelligence, virus database, rule base and other information of authoritative institutions and manufacturers can not enter the enterprise and play a role in a short time.

The lack of deep data correlation and analysis leads to the lack of means for high-level information security events and threats such as persistent and advanced network attacks and leaks. It emphasizes the single, flat and passive security protection, lacks the organic integration of personnel, process and means, and has three-dimensional, multi-dimensional and active cyberspace confrontation thinking. It has no perception of the attacker's "when to come, when to go, what to do, what to take, why to do and how to do" in the whole process.

The means of operation are out of date. Security protection relies heavily on 4A and the traditional equipments. Enterprise relies on the deployment of firewall, intrusion detection system, vulnerability scanner, and then combines with 4A system for asset management, authentication and access control. The construction of security means is mainly piled up and isolated, and the security system is lack of systematization and coordination, so it is difficult to form an effective response to network threats.

All of these need to build a security situation awareness platform as soon as possible, effectively connect various security devices, and eliminate data islands.

3   Status and Role of Security Situation Awareness Platform

3.1   Relationship Between Security Situation Awareness Platform and Security Management System

The concept of situation awareness (SA) was put forward by Endsley in 1988. SA is the acquisition and understanding of environmental factors in a certain time and space, and the short-term prediction of the future (Fig. 1).

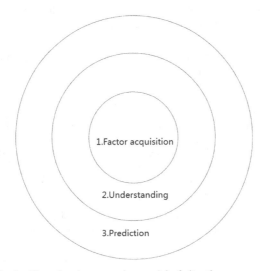

Fig. 1. Three level progressive model of situation awareness.

Security situation awareness is to use all kinds of data from the network and terminals, use the advanced big data architecture, through artificial intelligence algorithm, take the analysis of personnel and terminal behavior as the main line, detect and find the security incidents that threaten the enterprise, and provide a complete evidence chain of traceability and forensics, so as to comprehensively guarantee the enterprise information security.

Security situation awareness platform is a comprehensive solution platform for unified management of network information security situation awareness, security monitoring, notification and early warning, threat intelligence, tracing, traffic detection and emergency response. Through the orderly operation of the platform, enterprises can comprehensively grasp the key information infrastructure, important portal websites, information system network security situation, the dark network traffic within the jurisdiction, trace the source of IP, and carry out early warning, emergency disposal and comprehensive network security management. Network security situation awareness is a means of quantitative analysis of network security and a fine measurement of network security.

Security situation awareness platform, security management platform, security communication network and security equipment together constitute the enterprise security management system, which acts on the enterprise information system and information network, realizes the control command and data interaction, completes the operation of monitoring, warning, testing, configuration and switching, and realizes the corresponding disposal of security threats, security incidents and security. With the security situation awareness platform, it will provide accurate control instructions for the security management platform to achieve effective control. Security situation awareness platform becomes the core of enterprise security management system (Fig. 2).

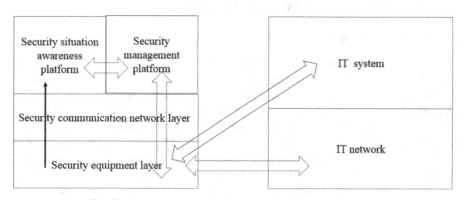

Fig. 2. Schematic diagram of enterprise security architecture.

3.2 Main Functions of Security Situation Awareness Platform

Comprehensive collection of detailed data based on logs, traffic, etc., to build a basic security information base;

The whole enterprise shares the threat intelligence of social organizations and provides the enterprise security threat intelligence for social organizations;

Basic awareness of external and internal threats to achieve rapid security incident analysis, monitoring and situational awareness;

Comprehensive management and control of exposed assets, dynamic management and control of cyberspace to achieve spatial mapping;

Build enterprise wide intrusion analysis and monitoring capabilities with intrusion monitoring, website attack, self owned app protection and other functions;

Build the ability to analyze and monitor intranet intrusion, such as preventing penetration from all directions, password cracking, illegal information access and unauthorized access;

Provide the whole network linkage interface for emergency disposal to realize the whole process of rapid disposal; Establish a unified network security situation awareness platform and enterprise wide integrated command and dispatch system;

Build the ability of abnormal event traceability based on log and traffic data;

Connect and share with the relevant monitoring and sensing system of the superior unit; Support the security operation and simulation operation for different scenarios such as daily threat, major guarantee and emergency disposal.

Expand the scope of threat monitoring, detect, prevent or limit the network attacks from inside or outside at the key network nodes; And take technical measures to analyze, record information, optimize the ability of technical means, optimize the emergency response mechanism, and improve the monitoring, early warning and disposal level of the whole enterprise.

4 Technology Implementation Scheme and Evolution Route of Security Situation Awareness Platform

4.1 Platform Structure

It is mainly through extracting the network security situation analysis index system, establishing the network security situation analysis and prediction system based on complex network behavior model and simulation, and then obtaining quantitative or qualitative network security situation assessment results, and forecasting the evolution of network security situation in the future by analyzing and modeling the historical situation, In order to make reasonable adjustment and upgrading of the security elements, security equipment and information system in the network by the network security management personnel, and to cope with the changes of the network security situation. The network security situation awareness platform mainly includes six levels, namely data acquisition layer, preprocessing layer, label and storage layer, modeling and analysis prediction layer, visual display layer, application command layer, and two basic levels, knowledge base and rule base. The technical structure is shown in Fig. 3.

Data Acquisition Layer. Data acquisition is connected to different equipment, systems and products through various communication means, and the security data of a wide range and deep level is collected, and the protocol conversion and processing of heterogeneous data are collected, and the data base of enterprise network security situation awareness platform is constructed. The platform has many probe acquisition methods, such as active detection, log collection and flow analysis, to obtain real-time security data. The data collected from the daily management of the equal protection data, threat intelligence data and the third-party standard interface constitute the total data on the data acquisition level. The acquisition system must identify many device protocols such as syslog, SNMP, NetFlow, EDR, VSS, and analyze the protocol in depth, support data collection of various

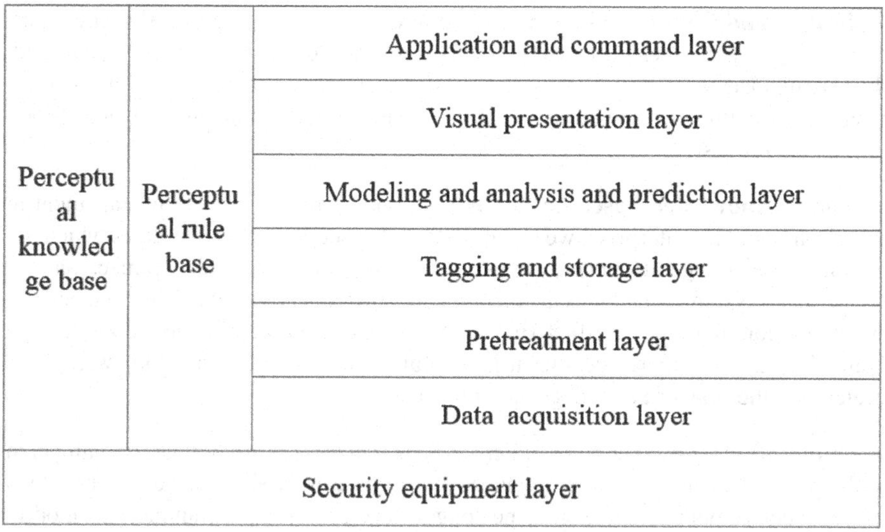

Perceptu al knowled ge base	Perceptu al rule base	Application and command layer
		Visual presentation layer
		Modeling and analysis and prediction layer
		Tagging and storage layer
		Pretreatment layer
		Data acquisition layer
Security equipment layer		

Fig. 3. Security situational awareness platform architecture.

information including terminal behavior, threat alarm data, log data, and support output to the flat platform in a variety of standard formats.

Pretreatment Layer. The data collected in various formats are pre processed in a standardized and unified way, and abnormal data and duplicate data are eliminated to improve the data quality and improve the efficiency, quality and accuracy of data analysis.

Tagging and Storage Layer. Classify and analyze data, label data according to rule base and knowledge base. Data storage and index can realize data aggregation, storage and index function of detection data, monitoring data and knowledge base resources, and provide open interface for data acquisition at data modeling layer.

Modeling and Analysis and Prediction Layer. The preprocessing data is associated with knowledge base and rule base, and relevant security information data is extracted for modeling. Combined with machine learning and deep learning algorithm, it analyzes the identification information, asset information, attack event, attack trace information, attack path information and attack source header information, and displays threat situation and data association mining.

According to the historical and current status information, the analysis model is established in line with the network and business scenarios, and the situation prediction is carried out based on the combination of network threat and asset situation.

Visual Presentation Layer. The paper presents the quantitative status and prediction results of network situation through data visualization. With the help of powerful processing ability, logical thinking and judgment ability in graphics and images, the paper realizes the artificial global visualization analysis and drilling analysis of enterprise security situation, threat situation, attack source, attack event and asset security status, as well as qualitative judgment and prediction.

Application and Command Layer. The comprehensive analysis of the detection, perception and prediction results of safety events is completed, and the solution is proposed, which is divided into control tasks and control instructions. It is sent to the security management platform through the interface to interact and command the closed-loop rectification process.

Perceptual Knowledge Base. According to the needs of the security management in the industry and the enterprise, we should establish a set of knowledge slices which are structured, easy to operate and easy to use, and are organized to store, organize, manage and use in the system. It includes the theoretical knowledge, fact data, detection, perception, prediction and other verified knowledge related to the field, heuristic knowledge obtained by expert experience, etc. It is helpful to share and exchange knowledge by accelerating the flow of knowledge and information.

Perceptual Rule Base. The rules of detection, perception, prediction and visualization involved in the sensing system are managed by rule base as database management. When business requirements change, it is no longer necessary for programmers to modify individual code, but to manage them in the rule base. It is provided to each system and technical use as the basis of rules.

4.2 Main Capabilities of Network Security Situation Awareness Technology

Threat Intelligence Disposal and Sharing. Collect and dispose threat information data from various sources, and transform the format internally and transfer all to the knowledge base and rule base; the core system of driving detection, perception and prediction dynamically adjusts the processing logic and makes closed-loop correction. To the outside world, the threat information sharing based on internal success cases is provided to external organizations. Threat information includes: IP asset portrait, domain name portrait, lost host data, regional security report, illegal organization and activity threat information.

Network Intrusion Detection. The platform analyzes the intrusion detection of the collected data and gives timely alarm. The intrusion response evaluates the security situation of the system according to the system attack alarm and abnormal alarm perceived by real-time intrusion detection, and makes and implements the optimal security strategy in time to alleviate the impact of intrusion attack. Intrusion response includes two parts: security policy decision and policy execution.

The Analysis of Safety Events and Situation Evaluation. According to the degree of harm and the ability of regional security protection, the paper uses decision tree, Bayesian network and other technologies to analyze the security events comprehensively. Neural network and fuzzy reasoning are introduced into situation assessment. The knowledge base and rule base of network security attributes are used to comprehensively evaluate the status and development trend of security events, and reasonable judgment, decision-making suggestions and protective preparation measures are put forward. Including perception of rigid creeping network, vulnerability situation, etc.

Network Security Situation Forecast. The platform uses the current and historical detailed and massive collection data, knowledge base and rule base to learn and analyze the big data in depth. It finds the rules of hacker invasion. According to the intrusion behavior, the platform predicts the intrusion behavior, the purpose of hacker invasion and the equipment that may be threatened in the future, and takes effective targeted measures to prevent it.

Invasion Tracing. The platform uses the intrusion trace data, the collection data, the knowledge base and the rule base, combined with threat information, to quantitatively and trace the security events, determine the intrusion entrance, path, scope, measures, etc., recover the intrusion process, propose targeted rectification measures and modify the knowledge base, rule base and perception and prediction system.

Disposal and Closed Loop Correction. The platform issues control orders to the safety management platform based on the results of detection, perception and prediction. The safety management platform issues manual and automatic work orders to safety organizations and safety equipment for security defense disposal; The platform conducts closed-loop evaluation based on the completed status of work order and collected data, and the closed-loop correction detection, perception, prediction knowledge base and rule base are closed-loop.

Core Analysis Model of Situation Awareness. Network security situation awareness includes three elements: perception, understanding and prediction. The following four models are mainly used in the analysis process:

Endsley model, which senses the information of the state, attribute and dynamic of the important components in the network environment, and the continuous updating, prediction and evolution process of the integration and sorting of the elements.

OODA model refers to observation, Orient, decision and act, which is a concept in the field of information warfare. OODA is a process of continuously gathering information, assessing decisions and taking action.

The JDL model is to analyze the data and information from different data sources, to identify the target, to estimate the identity, to evaluate the situation and to evaluate the threat. The accuracy of the evaluation is improved by refining the evaluation results.

RPD model (Recognition primed decision) defines situation perception into two stages: perception and evaluation. Perception compares the existing situation with the past to select the past situation with high similarity. Evaluation is the process of analyzing the past to speculate the current situation evolution.

4.3 Platform Evolution Route

Based on the Specific Organization, Complete the Internal Situation Awareness Infrastructure. It includes: data and alarm collection, threat intelligence platform, event analysis platform, internal disposal management platform, and visualization application to present and assist these work. In this way, a complete security operation can be supported within an enterprise. The required security analysts can be obtained by purchasing external services, or they can be trained by themselves.

Establish Vertical Support System and Intelligence Data Sharing System. It includes vertical malicious code analysis center, enhanced event analysis center, intelligence sharing mechanism and vertical Threat Intelligence Center. Malicious code analysis and major event analysis need high-level security analysts to participate in order to achieve the effect. The intelligence sharing mechanism ensures the synchronization of information and social organizations, and enables key intelligence to be used more quickly and effectively in enterprises. Security analyst resources are mainly self-cultivation.

Building Integrated Automatic Defense Capability. With the enhancement of the vertical support system and the overall intelligence analysis ability, when encountering key events, we can carry out integrated protection, more quickly and efficiently suppress attacks, and strive for time to clear attacks. At the same time, security analyst resources have formed a scale and can be provided for external use.

5   Problems Needing Attention

After the completion of the security situation awareness platform, we must strengthen the continuous use and continuous optimization, and pay attention to solve the following problems:

5.1   Organization Mechanism Guarantee, Forming a Virtuous Circle

We should establish a special safety management team to manage in parallel with the information management team, improve the three synchronous principles of synchronous planning, synchronous construction and synchronous operation of the information system and safety system, and realize a good and benign mechanism that can be managed and used well.

Strengthen the training of internal high-level security analyst resources to form a strong personnel base.

5.2   Devops Guarantee

Around the situation awareness platform, the core engine of security management, a technical team integrating development, maintenance and technical support is established to control the R & D quality and agile iteration ability of security business.

5.3   Institutional Constraints to Reduce Employee Risk

Hierarchical protection of business security. We will improve and formulate the business security classification protection system and work standards, and strengthen the business security evaluation management mechanism and technical level.

5.4   Persevere and Introduce Ecology (Good Partner)

Business security process embedding. Realize the whole life-cycle embedding and centralized continuous management of enterprise key business security management and control; Introduce professional consulting agencies and professional security service providers as partners, establish a sound enterprise security situation awareness system, take me as the main, share partner experience, and improve together.

6   Conclusion

Through the construction and deployment of security situation awareness platform, large enterprises will intelligently connect the existing security equipment, form the ability of defense in advance, active management, three-dimensional protection and efficient response, quickly and comprehensively sense the security threats faced by enterprises, comprehensively improve the level of enterprise information security governance, and eliminate all kinds of hidden dangers in the bud. Through long-term operation, the security situation awareness platform has accumulated experience and data, which will continuously improve the comprehensiveness, accuracy, timeliness and judgment of perception, and provide a strong information security guarantee for the development of enterprise informatization and more efficient investment in the tide of digital economy. It will also bring information security revenue for enterprises through data sharing and ecological co construction!

References

1. China Internet Network Security Monitoring Data Analysis Report for 2019. National Computer Network Emergency Response Technical Coordination Center, Beijing (2020)
2. China Internet Network Security Monitoring Data Analysis Report for first half of 2020. National Computer Network Emergency Response Technical Coordination Center, Beijing (2020)

Social Network Security

Research on the Relationship Between Chinese Nicknames and Accounts in Social Networks

Yi Han, Xiangyu Liu, Yanhui Du[(✉)], and Tianliang Lu

People's Public Security University of China, Beijing 100038, China
duyanhui@ppsuc.edu.cn

Abstract. With the increasing integration of mobile Internet into people's daily life, generally a user will register several different network applications at the same time. Therefore, there are many virtual identities belonging to one person on the Internet, and the similarity analysis of cross-platform network identities is of great significance in the field of network security. This paper studied the Chinese user nicknames and virtual identity recognition in domestic social networking. Considering that account nicknames, to some extent, can reflect the characteristics of the account owners' naming habits and preferences, and that the information of nickname is easier to obtain than other registration information, we collected the nickname information of users who registered on three application platforms: WeChat, Weibo and Alipay. At the same time, according to the characteristics of account nicknames and their probability distribution, we determined the characteristic indicators that can be used to calculate the similarity of nicknames. Finally, this paper optimized the Jaro distance and Jaro-Winkler distance algorithms, and proposed an identity algorithm suitable for domestic social networks, especially calculating the similarity of Chinese nicknames, and verified the effectiveness of the algorithm on the basis of large-scale real data.

Keywords: User nickname · Similarity · Jaro distance · Virtual identity

1 Introduction

With the rapid development of mobile Internet, various social software has greatly enriched people's lives, and the scale of Internet users in China is also growing. By December 2020, the total number of Internet users in China has reached 940 million [1]. Research shows that about 84% of Internet users have more than one social networking account [2]. At the same time, with the characteristics of multiple identities, virtualization and anonymity of social networks becoming more and more obvious, some lawless elements spread extreme remarks through the network, which seriously endangered social order.

In recent years, a lot of attention has been paid to the study of social network user identity, and the analysis of network account association can provide necessary information for the safety supervision of public opinion in social networks. Considering that user nicknames are easier to obtain than other registration information, and to some extent, it

W. Lu et al. (Eds.): CNCERT 2021, CCIS 1506, pp. 143–156, 2022.
https://doi.org/10.1007/978-981-16-9229-1_9

can reflect the naming habits and feature preferences of account holders. Therefore, this paper collects user nicknames from domestic mainstream social networking sites, and proposes a method for calculating account similarity based on Chinese user nicknames.

- This paper investigates the similarity of social network accounts, and finds that most of the current research results are oriented to foreign social platforms such as Twitter, Facebook, Myspace [3–5], which is not applicable to account analysis of the top Apps in the domestic application market, and designs a prototype system that can push users' nicknames in batches by using the address book matching and friend recommendation functions of App, and constructs a database for studying the similarity of domestic SNS accounts.
- This paper summarizes some features of Chinese nicknames, analyzes the consistency of the features of the same natural person on different platforms, and selects character features as the only index of the algorithm. Specifically, the paper converts Chinese characters into English characters by the way of phonetic conversion, which solves the problems of homophones and homophones in account similarity judgment.
- This paper proposes a similarity algorithm suitable for Chinese nicknames, aiming at the common characters in different strings, such as "head-head", "tail-tail" and "head-tail". Improve the calculation weights when the calculation weight when the characters of "tail-tail" and "head-tail" are consistent, and the effectiveness of the algorithm is verified on the experimental data set.

In the first section, the paper introduces the relevant research work. The second section introduces the method of obtaining account nickname data and its implementation process; The third section sorts out some characteristics of Chinese accounts, and analyzes the consistency of characteristics of accounts on different platforms; In the fourth and fifth sections, an account similarity algorithm suitable for Chinese nicknames is proposed, and the effectiveness of the proposed algorithm is verified by real data Finally, the sixth section summarizes the full paper.

2 Related Work

2.1 Research Status

At present, researchers usually design network account association analysis based on three different dimensions: user attribute, user behavior and user relationship. Among them, user attribute features mainly include user nickname, avatar, birthday, place of residence, personality signature, etc. User behavior characteristics mainly include online speech, behavior track, participation topic, etc. The characteristics of user relationship mainly include attention, interaction between fans and friends, joining groups and so on. In the research field of user nickname association analysis, most of them are related to English-speaking users such as Twitter and Facebook, and have achieved good results. In view of the unequal information that can be collected by the above-mentioned user characteristics in different social networks, this paper mainly studies the research status of user nicknames in China and abroad.

Reza Zafarani et al. [6] listed 414 potential features related to user names, and proposed a calculation method of multi-platform virtual identity association by calculating the most important 10 features. Siyuan Liu et al. [7] give weight to user names, and then carry out association analysis on user virtual identities based on statistical analysis method. Perito et al. [8] used n-gram model to measure the uniqueness of user names, and finally analyzed the similarity of user names by editing distance. Dong Liu et al. [9] made statistics according to the user's explicit length, the frequency of using special characters, the use of numeric characters, the combination mode of keyboard input mode and user name, and obtained probability distribution and feature analysis, and then proposed a method of identity verification. Y Li et al. [10] have done more detailed feature engineering on the username of Chinese users, considering the existence of the user name in simplified and traditional Chinese or English letters and homophones, a language mapping method based on Pinyin is proposed. Siyuan Liu et al. [11] mentioned the situation of Chinese characters in the study of association analysis of virtual accounts, but in fact, they did not carry out in-depth discussion and did not propose corresponding solutions.

2.2 Existing Problem

Although the research on user-oriented nickname association analysis has important research significance, the research based on Chinese user nicknames is still in its infancy, and literature and research results at home and abroad are extremely scarce. At present, Chinese-oriented research fields mostly focus on natural language analysis, semantic understanding and other corpus studies with a certain length, but there are few short Chinese analyses on user nicknames, and the feature extraction and correlation analysis techniques of Chinese user nicknames are quite different from those of English users. Therefore, the research on nickname association of Chinese users is facing great challenges, and there are also many problems to be solved, among which the most prominent ones are as follows:

1. Traditional Chinese characters. When registering account nicknames, mainland users prefer simplified Chinese, while users in Taiwan Province, Hong Kong and Macau generally use traditional Chinese.
2. Disassembly of Chinese characters. For example, the same natural person has registered usernames "弓长佩" and "张博佩"" on different social platforms, so how to establish account association with user names with such characteristics is a problem worthy of in-depth study. For another example, accounts such as "萌正灬太King" and "默念你的爱卄" also take the dismantling of Chinese radical as a part of nicknames. How to effectively identify and classify them is also of great significance in the analysis of users' nickname features.
3. Homophonic. The problem of homophonic words has always been a hot spot in the field of Chinese research, and there is also the problem of homophonic words in the research of nickname of Chinese users. For example, "橙丸村" and "陈婉春" are different network accounts belonging to the same natural person. How to solve Chinese homophones and homophones is also one of the problems that need to be solved in this paper.

4. Emoji expression. With the gradual liberalization of character restrictions on user nicknames in different social platforms, some post-90s, post-95s and even post-00s network users have added personalized characters to their nicknames, and many personalized nicknames such as "西瓜红烧才好吃🐌 ", " Eva😊的母后" and "董婷🐱 ₀🐱ᵔᵔᵉ " have brought great difficulties to Chinese account analysis.

2.3 Research Opportunities

In the early days, the data sources of virtual identity account research were scarce, and most experimental data sets were mainly collected by web crawlers to obtain attribute information related to users, such as name, gender, birthday, occupation and so on. Most of this kind of characteristic information is incomplete, and its authenticity is difficult to verify, so it is difficult for researchers to obtain it for research on high-quality dataset. As for user nicknames, literature [12] has high credibility in associating different usernames of the same user through social investigation, but this method consumes manpower and time, and the respondents are generally unwilling to provide their account information to others. There are also some social platforms that allow registration-free login through other website accounts, but the jump view function is limited on the personal homepage of this account, and researchers cannot obtain the account information associated with the target account on other platforms. In addition, some public data sets, such as Google+, Facebook, Twitter, etc., are mainly English-speaking and native-speaking users in the West and Europe, and are not the research objects of this paper.

In recent years, with the promotion of real-name registration system, a user of social networks in China, more and more social platforms need to bind their mobile phone numbers when registering. Although the mobile phone numbers are not public, it virtually provides the possibility for the research of virtual identity association analysis. Literature [13] introduces that most network applications provide the function of "address book matching", and through this function, the mapping relationship between mobile phone number and virtual account number is established. In addition, literature [14] introduces many cases of personal privacy leakage, and literature [15] puts forward a method of obtaining account related information by using network App communication traffic, and makes use of it. Therefore, the above-mentioned real data related to the user's mobile phone number and nickname provide a new idea for the experimental data research of virtual identity account association analysis.

3 Data Collection and Implementation

In order to construct nickname samples in China, this paper selects three applications with the highest download volume in Android mobile phone application market: Weibo, WeChat and Alipay as data sources (Table 1), and filter users who register and customize nicknames in the three applications at the same time as seed samples.

In addition, the paper randomly selects 7296 accounts from the leaked user data of Sina Weibo in March 2020, and forms the mapping relationship between nicknames and mobile phone numbers of Weibo users according to the corresponding user nicknames associated with Weibo account id.

Table 1. Statistics of monthly active users of different network applications

Network applications	Number of monthly active users	Date	Reference
Weibo	530 million	2021.5.10	Second-quarter earnings in 2020
Wechat	1.242 billion	2021.5.20	Second-quarter earnings in 2020
Alipay	711 million	2020.6	Prospectus of Ant Group

3.1 Information Acquisition and Integration Analysis

Literature [8] introduces the method of network account matching. The paper matches the address book of the above 7296 mobile phone numbers, and obtains the account nicknames of WeChat and Alipay. The specific methods are as follows (Fig. 1):

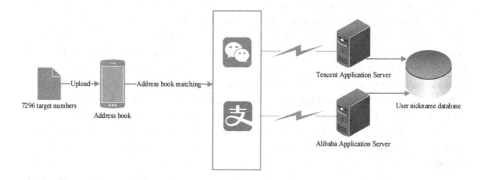

Fig. 1. The flow chart of matching mobile phone number with network account

- Step 1 Import the mobile phone number to be processed into the mobile phone address book, and view/add friends in the address book through the target application.
- Step 2 App uploads the address book information to the application server in the form of original text or abstract information.
- Step 3 Server returns the user account information matching with the mobile phone number in the address book (registration binding).

The statistics of account number matching results are shown in Table 2.

Table 2. Network platform account matching results

Total	Weibo	Wechat	Alipay	All the three platforms
7296	7296	5683	6055	5050

3.2 Acquisition Module Design and Implementation

This paper designs and implements the matching function based on mobile phone address book. The prototype system for obtaining user nicknames is divided into three modules, namely, address book import module, information acquisition module and content extraction module. The address book import module is responsible for automatically loading the target mobile phone number and inputting it in the standard format readable by the address book; The information acquisition module is responsible for uploading the address book information to the target application server and acquiring the address book user account information from the server; Based on the analysis of the target application, the content extraction module realizes the automatic collection of nickname information of user accounts in the address book.

The prototype system acquisition terminal realized in this paper is based on Google Pixel equipped with Android native system version. This choice is mainly due to the following considerations: First, the Android system has a high market share of mobile devices, and it has a wider application value to use Android system as the target system. Second, most networks apps developers provide Android version of application software, so there will be no shortage of application collection coverage; More importantly, Android system is an open source software project, and the system carried by Google Pixel is a native operating system, so there is no version customization and secondary development, which greatly facilitates the design and implementation of the prototype system.

The specific method is as follows: firstly, the mobile phone number to be analyzed is processed into VCF format file, empty the original address book in the mobile phone; And then Import VCF format file into the phone address book; The information acquisition module pre-analyzes the trigger mode of the address book reading function in the target application, automatically triggers the function, and realizes the acquisition of address book user account information from the server; The content extraction module obtains user nicknames by analyzing the target application interface, and the module can extract user nicknames in batches; Finally, the user nickname and the corresponding mobile phone number are stored in the database (Fig. 2).

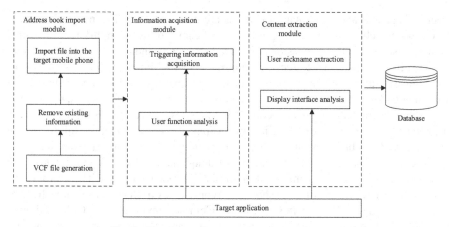

Fig. 2. The frame diagram of acquisition module

4   Data Collection and Implementation

4.1   Universal Feature

As a hot research direction of social network, account association technology usually adopts account characteristics including: 1) length characteristics. The length of most usernames is within a specific range, which is generally not too short or too long, which can visually show the length characteristics of user names. 2) Character type. Chinese characters are the main nicknames of domestic social network users. Compared with the western language system with only 26 English letters, any character or a group of characters in the nicknames of domestic network users have unique symbols for judging a natural person. 3) Special characters. Some nicknames containing numbers and symbols can reflect the naming habits and preferences of users. 4) Combination mode. Combination mode can also be used as one of the characteristic indexes in judging nickname similarity, that is, the same natural person should have the same or similar combination mode on different platforms. In order to further apply the above features to the Chinese language environment, the paper also needs to make statistics on the above features, as shown in Table 3.

Table 3. Consistency analysis of user nickname features in different platforms

Length characteristic	Character type	Special characters	Combination mode
0.047	0.652	<0.001	0.076

4.2   Feature Selection

Through the statistics of the above characteristics of WeChat, Weibo and Alipay, it is found that users register nicknames on different platforms. The length characteristics, special characters and combination patterns are not consistent. The main reasons are as follows: the character types supported by nicknames of users on different platforms are inconsistent, and the expressions of special characters and emoji are quite different among different operating systems, coding methods and input methods; Weibo nicknames have the unique characteristics of the whole network. In order to avoid duplication with other nicknames, users often add numbers, letters and other characters, resulting in long overall characters and diverse combination modes. However, this kind of situation rarely occurs in nicknames of WeChat and Alipay. Therefore, length features, special characters and combination patterns are not considered as similarity calculation factors.

In terms of character features, due to the uniqueness of Chinese characters, users are usually accustomed to using fixed or similar Chinese characters. Therefore, in the above statistical results, most users show good consistency in character features. In addition, every Chinese character in Chinese has Chinese Pinyin, and the Chinese Pinyin Scheme published in 1958 clearly stipulates that Chinese Pinyin adopts the internationally accepted Latin alphabet. Therefore, this paper takes character features as the core index to calculate similarity, converts Chinese into English writing form by the method of phonetic conversion, and then calculates account similarity by calculating text similarity. This method can effectively solve the conversion between simplified Chinese and traditional Chinese characters, and at the same time, it can play a better conversion effect in homophonic words with the same pronunciation and similar pronunciation.

5 Algorithm Design

5.1 Jaro Distance

Jaro distance is one of the most commonly used methods to judge the similarity of short texts based on the number and sequence of commonly used characters. It was originally used to judge whether two names of health records are the same in census, so it is the best selection for matching user names. This section is further optimized based on Jaro distance algorithm to improve nickname recognition ability suitable for domestic network users.

For any two strings, the matching window under Jaro algorithm is defined first as follows: the comparison between characters should be limited to a certain range or condition, besides if two characters are equal in this range, indicates a successful match; If it exceeds this range, the match fails. In Jaro algorithm, it is defined as formula (1), that is, mw does not exceed the value of the following expression:

$$w \leq \frac{max(|S_i|, |S_j|)}{2} - 1 \tag{1}$$

Where, $|S\_i|$ and $|S\_j|$ represent the lengths of the string S_i and S_j. At the same time, if the matching sequence characters are reversed, the number of characters in the reversed sequence is recorded as the transposition number (tn for short) in Jaro algorithm. Therefore, based on the logic of matching window mw and transposition number tn, the Jaro distance calculation formula of string S_i and S_j is as follows:

$$JD_{ij} = \begin{cases} 0 & \text{if } m = 0 \\ \frac{1}{3}\left(\frac{m}{|S_i|} + \frac{m}{|S_j|} + \frac{m-t}{m}\right) & \text{otherwise} \end{cases} \tag{2}$$

Where m represents the number of matching characters of two strings based on the matching window logic; t represents $\frac{1}{2}tn$ under transposition number logic.

5.2 Jaro-Winkler Distance

Given the importance of English prefixes, Jaro-Winkler distance is further modified basis on Jaro distance, meaning that, if two strings of the first few characters are the same, they will be more similar. The formula of the algorithm is shown as formula (3):

$$JWD_{ij} = JD_{ij} + lp\left(1 - JD_{ij}\right) \tag{3}$$

In which JD_{ij} represents Jara distance based on Jaro algorithm; l indicates the number of common prefix characters of two strings (maximum no more than 4); p is a scale factor constant, that describes the contribution of common prefix to similarity. The larger the p is, the greater the weight of common prefix is (the maximum value not more than 0.25, and the default value is 0.1).

It can be seen that jaro-winkler distance algorithm is more friendly to prefix matching, but there is still a certain degree of misjudgment when calculating the similarity of user nicknames. For example, "芸" and "白芸" are nicknames of the same natural person on different platforms, but their Jaro-Winkler similarity is 0, so they are judged to be a group of unrelated accounts, which is a misjudgment. From here, we can make a conclusion that Jaro-Winkler distance algorithm has an obvious error in nickname similarity analysis, in particular when a group of nicknames keywords are at the end of a string, and the likelihood of this occurrence is relatively high. Therefore, the Jaro-Winkler distance is further optimized.

5.3 Text Algorithm

Taking into account the habit of bidirectional combination of last name and first name in nicknames, the matching weights of key characters of "first-first", "tail-last" and "first-last" should be considered at the same time. Therefore, the two algorithms are further revised in this paper, and the modified distance formula is as shown in formula (4). The paper is called Jaro-Winkler-Plus distance algorithm:

$$JWPD_{ij} = JD_{ij} + max\left(l_h p_h, l_t p_t, max\left(l_{ih}, l_{jh}\right)\frac{(p_h + p_t)}{2}\right)\left(1 - JD_{ij}\right) \tag{4}$$

In which: JD_{ij} is Jaro distance based on Jaro algorithm.

l_h represents the number of character with common prefix of two strings, where l_{ih} and l_{jh} represent the number of common S_i prefix and S_j suffix, and the number of common S_i suffix and S_j prefix, l_t represent the number of common suffix of two strings, and satisfy the minimum value of arbitrary $l_i(i = h, t, ih, jh)$ is no less than the minimum number of characters 1 (such as 'a') and the maximum number is no more than the maximum number of characters 6 (such as "Zhuang").

p_h is a common prefix scaling factor constant, and p_t is a common suffix scaling factor constant, any $p_i(i = h, t)$ satisfy $0.1 \leq p_i \leq 0.165$, in order to ensure $max\left(l_h p_h, l_t p_t, max\left(l_{ih}, l_{jh}\right) \frac{(p_h + p_t)}{2}\right) \leq 1$ Therefore, under the premise of $l_i \leq 6$, the maximum value is also reduced from the initial 0.25 to 0.165.

It can be seen that Jaro-Winkler-Plus distance has obvious advantages in measuring text similarity compared with Jaro and Jaro-Winkler distance, which is shown as follows: First, it is better suitable for different habits of different users writing surnames + firstnames (such as "张三疯、" and "疯子张"), especially Chinese people pay special attention to the last names, and are willing to use it repeatedly in social media or daily communication; Second, adding "tail-to-tail" and "head-to-tail" influencing factors on the basis of "head-to-head" instead of summary and induction, but adopts the principle of giving priority to the maximum value can avoid the excessive influence of head-to-head strategy on total Jaro distance.

6 Experiment and Analysis

6.1 Data Description

The data sources used in this paper are 5050 groups of user data processed in Sect. 3.1, all of which are registered on Alipay, Weibo and WeChat, and their nicknames are customized. In order to facilitate the calculation, this paper converts the nicknames of each user on three platforms, that is, the phonetic sequences without tones are recorded as strings. By random selection, this paper constructs three experimental data sets, each of which contains 5000 positive examples (user name pairs belonging to the same natural person) and 5000 counterexamples (randomly combining user name pairs of different natural persons).

6.2 Index Evaluation

Precision, Recall and F-Score are used as evaluation criteria to measure the performance of the algorithm. Specific definitions are shown in formulas:

$$Precision = tp/(tp + fp) \tag{5}$$

$$Recall = tp/(tp + fn) \tag{6}$$

$$F - Score = 2 \times pc \times rc/(pc + rc) \tag{7}$$

F-Score is the harmonic mean of Precision and Recall, and it is the total evaluation index of the algorithm performance. The three evaluation indicators in the above formulas are based on the following three indicators: tp (true positive) refers to the number of account pairs that are correctly judged as the same user by this algorithm. fp (false positive) is the number of account pairs incorrectly judged as the same user. fn (false negative) represents the number of account pairs that are judged to be different users but are the same user. In our experiment, a threshold is required to be set to determine whether two nicknames belong to the same user account. If the distance is greater than the threshold, it is determined that the two nickname strings participating in the comparison belong to the same natural person. If the distance is less than or equal to the threshold, it is determined that the two nickname strings participating in the comparison do not belong to the same natural person. Here, the paper needs to flexibly adjust the threshold to balance the Precision and Recall. As shown in Fig. 3, Fig. 4 and Fig. 5, with the increase of the judgment threshold, Precision of the three groups of data also increases correspondingly, while Recall decreases obviously. The main reason for this result is that when the threshold is increased, the more severe the judgment condition is set, the number of username pairs that the algorithm judges to be a match also decreases. In addition, the number of misjudged username pairs also increased, resulting in a decrease in Recall.

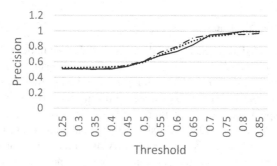

Fig. 3. Precision value

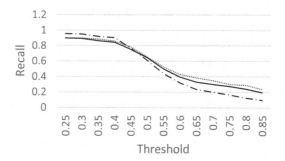

Fig. 4. Recall value

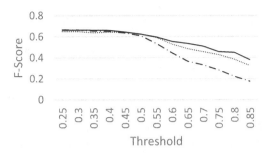

Fig. 5. F-Score value

Through the trend analysis of the value, it seems that 0.5–0.55 is a reasonable threshold range. Here, the paper defines 0.5 as the threshold for judging account similarity.

6.3 Comparison of Methods

After the threshold is determined, Jaro distance and Jaro-Winkler distance are used to calculate nickname similarity, About 7.07% of the data distance increases slightly, but the influence degree does not change for judging whether they belong to the same user, Therefore, the results of the two distance algorithms are consistent. The algorithm proposed in this paper not only greatly improves the distance value, but also improves the judgment accuracy by about 9.12%. This shows that the nickname similarity calculation method proposed in this paper can better quantify user nicknames, and better identify and discover different network accounts belonging to the same natural person in Chinese environment (Table 4).

Table 4. F-Score of different algorithm

Algorithm	F-Score		
	Data Set 1	Data Set 2	Data Set 3
Jaro	0.6085	0.6238	0.6262
Jaro-winkler	0.6085	0.6238	0.6262
Jaro-winkler-plus	0.6921	0.7082	0.7319

In this paper, the proposed nickname similarity calculation method is applied to the user data of the three platforms of WeChat, Weibo and Alipay. Since the nickname custom rules of each platform are quite different, this paper can distinguish account similarity only by analyzing the character characteristics, indicating that this research direction has good value potential. In the future, better judgment results will be obtained by combining more platforms and larger-scale user data and extracting more feature attributes that can be used to calculate similarity, such as gender, age, birthday, hobbies and other features.

7 Conclusion

In view of the difficulty in identifying multiple virtual identities of domestic social network users, and the lack of data resources in domestic research on virtual identity accounts, considering that account nicknames can reflect the naming habits and feature preferences of holders to a certain extent, and the nickname information is more open and transparent than other information, this paper studies the similarity analysis of online accounts First of all, the paper uses the "address book matching" and "friend recommendation" functions of social software to collect nickname data from three mainstream apps in China; Secondly, the paper puts forward some common characteristics of account nicknames, and makes statistics and consistency analysis on the nicknames registered by the same user on three platforms, and determines the characteristic indexes for calculating account similarity; Finally, Jaro distance algorithm is improved, and an account similarity calculation method suitable for Chinese nicknames is proposed.

Through experimental data verification, it is concluded that the proposed similarity calculation method based on account nickname character features is 9.12% more effective than the traditional Jaro distance algorithm, which is better applicable to the Chinese language environment dominated by Chinese characters and provides effective support for the identification of domestic netizens. In the next step, we can make a more in-depth study on the similarity determination of network virtual identity by combining the characteristics of users in other aspects, such as gender, age, friend relationship and other account attributes.

References

1. The 46th China Statistical Repot on Internet Development[R/OL], 29 September 2020. http://www.cnnic.net.cn/hlwfzyj/hlwxzbg/hlwtjbg/202009/P020200929546215182514.pdf
2. Bartunov, S., et al.: Joint Link-attribute user identity resolution in online social networks. In: Poceedings of the 6th International Conference on Knowledge Discovery and Data Mining, Workshop on Social Network Mining and Analysis, pp. 104–109. Beijing, China (2012)
3. User identification across multiple social networks based on information entropy. J. Comput. Appl. **37**(8), 2374–2480 (2017)
4. Motoyama, M., Varghese, G.: I seek you-searching and matching individuals in social networks. In: Proceedings of the 11th International Workshop on Web Information and Data Management, pp. 67–74. Hong Kong, China (2009)
5. You, G.W., Hwang, S.W., Nie, Z., Wen, J.R.: SocialSearch: enhancing entity search with social network matching. In: Proceedings of the 14th International Conference on Extending Database Technology, pp. 515–519. Uppsala, Sweden (2011)
6. Zafarani, R., Liu, H.: Connecting users across social media sites: a behavioral-modeling approach. In: Proceedings of the 19th ACM SIGKDD International Conference on Knowledge Discovery and Data Mining. ACM (2013)
7. Kumar, S., Zafarani, R., Liu, H.: Understanding user migration patterns in social media. In: AAAI'11
8. Perito, D., Castelluccia, C., Kaafar, M.A., Manils, P.: How unique and traceable are usernames? In: Fischer-Hübner, S., Hopper, N. (eds.) Privacy Enhancing Technologies. PETS 2011. LNCS, vol. 6794, pp. 1–17. Springer, Berlin, Heidelberg (2011). https://doi.org/10.1007/978-3-642-22263-4_1

9. Liu, D., Wu, Q.Y., Han, W.H., Zhou, B.: User identification across multiple websites based on username features. Chin. J. Comput. **38**(10) (2015)
10. Li, Y., et al.: Connecting Chinese users across social media sites. In: ICMIA, pp. 1273–1279 (2015)
11. Liu, S., Wang, S., Zhu, F., Zhang, J., Krishnan, R.: HYDRA: large-scale social identity linkage via heterogeneous behavior modeling. In: Proceedings of the ACM SIGMOD (2014)
12. Liu, J., et al.: What's in a name an unsupervised approach to link users across communities. In: Proceedings of the International Conference on Web Search and Web Data Mining, pp. 495–504. Rome, Italy (2013)
13. Cheng, Y., et al.: Research on user privacy leakage in mobile social messaging applications. Chin. J. Comput. **37**(1), 87–100 (2014)
14. Jin, P.-Y.: The leakage and protection of personal privacy data in the era of big data. J. Tongji Univ. (Soc. Sci. Sect.) **31**(3), 18–29 (2020)
15. Yue, H.-Z., Zhang, Y.-Q.: Vulnerability analysis and exploitation of location privacy leakage in webcasting platforms. Chin. J. Comput. **37**(1), 87–100 (2014)
16. Zhang, J.: Design of patient identity matching method and implementation of EMPI system (Social Science Section) **31**(3), 18–29 (2020)

TFC: Defending Against SMS Fraud via a Two-Stage Algorithm

Gaoxiang Li[1(✉)], Yuzhong Ye[1], Yangfei Shi[1], Jinlin Chen[2,3], Dexing Chen[2,3], and Anyang Li[4]

[1] National Computer Network Emergency Response Technical Team/Coordination Center of China Guangdong Branch, Guangzhou, China
jerishi@icloud.com
[2] Guangzhou Institute of Forensic Science, Guangzhou, China
[3] Guangzhou Anti-Fraud Center, Guangzhou, China
[4] Department of Mathematics, New York University, New York, USA
al5861@nyu.edu

Abstract. With the increasing of the telecom network fraud in China, SMS (Short Message Service) has became an important channel exploited by the criminals to contact victims. Due to the tiny amount compared with normal SMS, the high proportion of malicious adversarial characters, and the lack of knowledge to specific fraud types, it is still challenging to identify the fraud SMS efficiently. In this paper, we firstly conduct a measurement study to explore the characteristics of the fraud SMS. Based on the exploration, we propose a two-stage algorithm called TFC. TFC can quickly filter out normal SMS in the first stage with two indicator functions, and then easily identifies the category of fraud SMS in the second stage by combining the semantic deep features and the domain-knowledge based artificial features. We conduct two real-world SMS datasets for extensive experiments, and the results show that TFC successfully reduces calculation cost and achieves better performance in distinguishing various categories of fraud SMS.

Keywords: Telecom network fraud · SMS classification · Domain knowledge

1 Introduction

The evolution of the information society has brought great changes to the structure of crime, as traditional contact crimes keep declining, the new paradigm crime represented by telecom network fraud increases sharply in China. The average growing rate of telecom network fraud has reached 34% over the years [1], which has become the most prominent crime reported by the citizens. SMS is an important first-contact channel in many telecom network fraud cases, especially in the Loan Fraud, Part-time Fraud and Investing Fraud, etc. As shown in Fig. 1, if victims perform corresponding operations with fraud SMS, such as replying SMS or adding QQ, WeChat (the top 2 popular social media software in China) mentioned in the texts, the criminals would make further contact with victims in other communication channels where the real identities are

W. Lu et al. (Eds.): CNCERT 2021, CCIS 1506, pp. 157–175, 2022.
https://doi.org/10.1007/978-981-16-9229-1_10

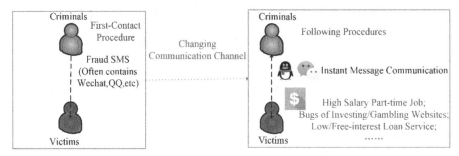

Fig. 1. Communication channel under different fraud procedures.

difficult to be traced. Therefore, the identification and prevention of fraud SMS has become a crucial issue.

Despite of some studies that have investigated detecting spam text already, these methods can not be applied in Chinese fraud SMS classification problem ideally due to the following reasons:

- Unlike the giant scale of normal SMS, the number of fraud SMS is relatively small. According to [2] and [3], the number of Smishing (SMS Phishing) for telecom network fraud only accounts for 0.05% of the whole SMS in China during 2020. It's important to design an effective method to filter out numerous normal SMS before the fraud SMS detection. Such scenarios are quite common and important for telecom operators, which are required to curb the fraud SMS by regulatory departments.
- Compared with English which has a relatively small alphabet, Chinese is logographic with a large set of characters. Besides, the battle between criminals and polices is extremely fierce, and the attack methods in fraud SMS, which has huge difference with English could be updated quickly in several hours. Typical attack methods contain Word Split (split a character into several characters), Homophony (different words or characters have the same PINYIN [4]) and Glyph Similar (obfuscated characters have similar structures with the original characters), etc.
- Differing from the traditional spam text (such as Gambling, Porn, Abuse, etc.) and Smishing (which mainly aims at collecting sensitive data from people), the domain-knowledge plays an important role in the identification of the specific type of fraud SMS. For example, there are lots of zeros in the Loan fraud SMS, but the SMS with many zeros could be the normal SMS of banking notice as well. The fraud domain-knowledge related studies are very limited in the previous work.

To tackle these challenging problems, we firstly conduct a measurement study to obtain a better understanding about the fraud SMS, then we design a novel two-stage algorithm called *TFC* to classify the Chinese fraud SMS. In the first stage, we utilize the key insights found in our measurement to quickly filter out the normal SMS. In the second stage, we exploit BERT-wwm [5] to obtain the semantic features, and thoughtfully designed 61-dim features base on the fraud domain-knowledge to capture the various attack methods and different kinds of abnormal SMS characteristics. By conducting extensive experiments with real-world SMS dataset, we prove that *TFC* is able to achieve the best performance compared with five alternative algorithms, and the generated features are robust to many kinds of classification algorithms in the meanwhile.

The main contributions of this paper can be summarized in three aspects:

- We conduct a comprehensive analysis on the labeled telecom network fraud SMS and discover some interesting insights. To mitigate the problem of lack of Chinese fraud SMS datasets, we release part of our labeled dataset online [6] for research convenience.
- We propose a novel two-stage algorithm to address the fraud SMS classification problem. The algorithm can rapidly filter out normal SMS in Stage 1. After composing deep features and domain-knowledge related features in stage 2, five types of SMS (namely, normal SMS, Loan fraud SMS, Part-time fraud SMS, Investing fraud SMS and Gambling SMS) can be effectively classified with simple machine learning algorithm.
- We demonstrate our algorithm's performance through real-world data driven experiments. Compared with various algorithms, our algorithm is able to obtain the highest F1-score and accuracy. Impacts of the Stage 1 and domain-knowledge keywords, and the performance of different ML classifiers with *TFC* are also included.

The rest of the paper is organized as follows. In Sect. 2, we review the previous work of SMS fraud and spam text related problems. In Sect. 3, we conduct a comprehensive measurement analysis with fraud SMS and obtain several interesting insights. We introduce our two-stage algorithm and detailed feature construction procedures in Sect. 4. Section 5 presents the results of experiments using real-world data. Section 6 concludes the paper.

2 Related Work

SMS fraud related problems have gained lots of attention for many years. *Joo et al.* [7] proposed an enhanced security model for detecting Smishing attack in smart devices. *Goel et al.* [8] designed a algorithm framework consist of three phases for Smishing attack detection. *Mishra et al.* [9] investigated Smishing detection problem through SMS Content, URL and Source Code, then a prototype of the proposed system with 96.29% overall accuracy is developed. *Pervaiz et al.* [10] investigate the scope and scale of the problem of SMS fraud in Pakistan, *Delany et al.* [11] and *Abdulhamid et al.* [12] reviewed and summarized the SMS spam filtering method. As for the fraud detection in the telecom area, previous works mainly use Call Detail Record (CDR) to identity the fraudulent user. For example, *Olszewski* [13] proposed an approach based on user profiling with Latent Dirichled Allocation (LDA), and detecting fraudulent behavior on the basis of threshold type classification with use of the KL-divergence. *Farvaresh et al.* [14] employed a hybrid approach consisting of preprocessing, clustering and classification phases to identifying customers' subscription fraud. The studies of SMS fraud from telecom operator's perspective are very limited.

There are several attack methods in spam text, such as adversarial text, wrong-spell words etc. Another thread of research studied the related problem from different aspects.

Wang et al. [15] proposed an adversary-generation algorithm for increasing the variance of adversarial training data; *Ebrahimi et al.* [16] investigated the robustness of models with adversarial examples trained by the proposed two translation-specific types of attacks. *Li et al.* [17] presented an adversarial defense framework designed for Chinese based deep learning model, all the results of experiments show that these methods could improve model performance to defend against adversarial text attacks. *Yeh et al.* [18] presented a novel spelling error detection and correction method based on N-gram ranked inverted index; *Xiong et al.* [19] designed a unified framework HANSpeller for Chinese text spelling error detection and correction. *Karan et al.* [20] and *Nobata et al.* [21] investigated the abusive language detection problem with Cross-Domain method and NLP features based classification methodology separately. All these works focused on the characteristics of the spam text, and the differences between spam text and fraud SMS are not considered.

Differing from the previous work, our work focuses on two aspects. Firstly, we aim at addressing the fraud SMS classification problem from telecom operator's perspective, rather than identifying the fraud with CDR [13, 14] or detecting Smishing from the view of mobile devices [7–9]. Secondly, while previous works focus on English [15, 16] and Chinese [17–19] spam text related studies, our work studied the Chinese fraud SMS classification problem which can not be applied by many proposed methods in other languages due to the huge Chinese grammatical difference and the unique characteristics between fraud SMS and spam text.

3   Measurement Analysis

In this section, we mainly conduct the measurement analysis with fraud SMS dataset, which are reported by massive citizens and collected by the Guangzhou Anti-Fraud Center from 11/02/2020 to 11/11/2020, named **RD1**. Figure 2(a) plots the fraud SMS daily count over a week, and we can observe that the average fraud SMS count is larger in weekdays compared to the weekends. As shown in Fig. 2(b) (We use '#' as the abbreviation of word 'number' in this paper), in terms of the fraud SMS types, Part-time fraud, Loan fraud and Investing fraud accounted for 85% of the whole **RD1**, and the Part-time fraud SMS has the highest proportion, nearly 50% .

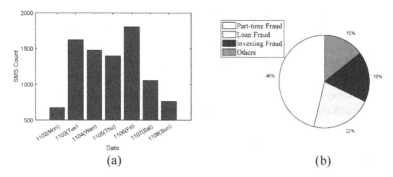

Fig. 2.   (a) Daily fraud SMS count of **RD1**. (b) # of fraud samples percentage.

Table 1. Examples of attack methods and corresponding # of *Uncommon Chinese Characters* and *Other Characters*

Attack Method	Example	# of the *Uncommon Chinese Characters*	# of the *Other Characters*
Word Split	加我微信→力口我微信	0	0
Homophony	微信→V信	0	1(V)
Glyph Similar	做事→做偉	1(偉)	0
Homophony+Glyph Similar	做事→作事→筰偉	2(筰,偉)	0
Homophony+Word Split	微信→V信→\/信	0	2(\,/)
Word Split+Homophony+Glyph Similar	加微做事→加V做事→+\/筰偉	2(筰,偉)	3(+,\,/)

Before stepping into further analysis, we define five types of characters in the SMS as follows:

- *Common Chinese Characters.* Define the common words and sub-common words in the List of *Commonly Used Characters in Modern Chinese* [22] as *Common Chinese Characters*, and the dict size is 3500.
- *Uncommon Chinese Characters.* Define Chinese characters that not belong to the *Common Chinese Characters* as *Uncommon Chinese Characters*.
- *Numeric Characters.* Define the number characters from 0 to 9 as *Numeric Characters*.
- *English Characters.* Define the alphabet characters from a to z and their upper case A to Z as *English Characters*.
- *Other Characters.* Define the characters in SMS that do not falling into 4 types mentioned above are *Other Characters*, such as symbolic characters like $! #, etc..

After we dive into the **RD1**, we obtained two interesting insights. One is that *Uncommon Chinese Characters* and *Other Characters* often appear in the fraud SMS. As shown in Fig. 3, to pass the keywords based spam detection methods and systems, the criminals tend to modify the SMS with several adversarial attacks, such as Word Split, Word Homophony, Glyph Similar, or combination of them. Therefore *Uncommon Chinese Characters* and *Other Characters* would have a considerable amount. Some examples of attack methods are presented in Table 1. Figure 4(a) plots the CDF (Cumulative Distribution Function) of the sum of *Uncommon Chinese Characters* and *Other Characters* in the fraud SMS. We can observe that only 22% of them have less than 10 *Uncommon Chinese Characters* and *Other Characters*. It even exceeds 30 in some fraud SMS samples, which proves that *Uncommon Chinese Characters* and *Other Characters* are frequently adopted in fraud SMS.

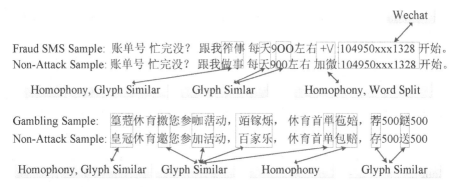

Fig. 3. Fraud SMS and Gambling SMS sample.

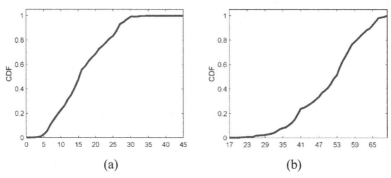

Fig. 4. (a) The CDF of sum of *Uncommon Chinese Characters* and *Other Characters*. (b) The CDF of SMS length in **RD1**.

Another insight is that there are often contained some contact information in the fraud SMS, which increases the count of *Numeric Characters* and *English Characters*. Table 2 shows that 99.41% of the fraud SMS have *Numeric Characters* and 69.54% of them have *English Characters*, it's reasonable that the proportion with *Numeric Characters* is much higher than the *English Characters*, because the fraud SMS often contains QQ or Wechat which represented by 5–11 digit numbers directly. From Fig. 4(b), we can observe that the minimal length of the fraud SMS in **RD1** is 17, and around 60% of the samples are longer than 50 characters. We argue that the length of the fraud SMS are commonly longer than normal one because of the expressions of contact information and the adversarial attacks (e.g., Word Split) in the fraud SMS.

Table 2. Statistics of *Numeric Characters* and *English Characters* in **RD1**.

Conditions	Percentage
# of *Numeric Characters* > 0	99.41%
# of *Numeric Characters* > 0 & # of *English Characters* > 0	69.02%
# of *English Characters* > 0	69.54%
# of *Numeric Characters* = 0 & # of *English Characters* = 0	0.03%

Given the above measurement results, the most intuitive idea is that we can design features based on the appearance of *Uncommon Chinese Characters* or *Other Characters*, *Numeric Characters* or *English Characters* to classify the fraud SMS. However, the authors found out that some other abnormal SMS have the same characteristics. Taking the Gambling SMS sample in Fig. 3 for example, the # of *Uncommon Chinese Characters* is 12, and the # of *Numeric Characters* and *English Characters* are also greater than 0. If only these two types of features are considered, too much Non-fraud SMS will be recalled in practice. What's more, we plan to classify fraud SMS in a fine-grained manner, i.e., classifying the Part-time fraud, Loan fraud and Investment fraud SMS separately. For this purpose, a much more accurate and robust algorithm needs to be developed.

4 Algorithm Design

4.1 Model Overview

The goal of fraud SMS classification problem is to design a classification algorithm $cls(\cdot)$ for any input text $x \in X$, $x = \{x_1, x_2, \ldots, x_n\}$ and output its fraud category. In this paper, we propose an algorithm composed by two stages, which can be defined as:

$$cls(x) = cls_{ml}(V(cls_{s1}(x)); \theta) = \hat{y} \tag{1}$$

where Stage 1 $cls_{s1}(\cdot)$ is used to quickly filter out normal SMS, i.e. SMS not belongs to any fraud category. $cls_{ml}(V(\cdot); \theta)$ would be noted as stage 2, where $V(\cdot)$ is a feature extraction function that convert SMS into continuous or discrete features, $cls_{ml}(\cdot; \theta)$ is a machine learning classifier aims at obtaining the specific category of the SMS, and θ are the parameters of the classifier.

The procedures of our method are shown in Fig. 5. Concretely, Stage 1 is introduced Subsect. 4.2, and we presents the b) of Fig. 5 in the **Deep Model** of Subsect. 4.3. Figure 5's part c) and d) are explained in the **PINYIN and BISHUN** and **Hard Matching** of Subsect. 4.3 separately.

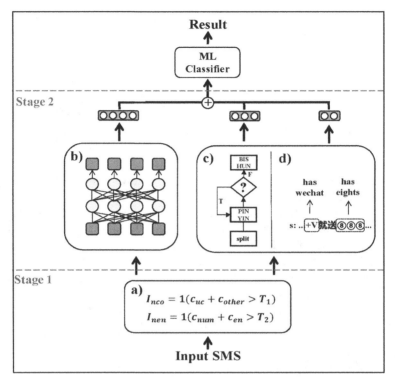

Fig. 5. Algorithm procedures.

4.2 Stage 1 - Normal SMS Filter

In Stage 1, we plan to use simple method to filter out massive normal SMS quickly while keeping the algorithm's recall at a high level. Based on the measurement analysis in Sect. 3, two indicators are considered as follows:

$$I_{nco}(x) = \mathbf{1}(c_{uc}(x) + c_{other}(x) > T_1) \qquad (2)$$

$$I_{nen}(x) = \mathbf{1}(c_{num}(x) + c_{en}(x) > T_2) \qquad (3)$$

where $c_{uc}(x)$ is the count of *Uncommon Chinese Characters* in SMS x, $c_{other}(x)$ denoted the count of *Other Characters* in x, $c_{num}(x)$ and $c_{en}(x)$ stand for the count of *Numeric Characters* and *English Characters* in x respectively, T1 and T2 are the threshold parameters. As mentioned in Sect. 3, differing from the normal SMS, the fraud SMS often uses obfuscated characters to avoid detection. Many of these obfuscated characters are homophony or glyph similar compared with original characters, and majority of them are *Uncommon Chinese Characters* and *Other Characters*. Given this context, we argue that when the sum of *Uncommon Chinese Characters* and *Other Characters* is bigger than 0, i.e. T1 is 0, x could be a fraud SMS in a certain extent. On the other hand, criminals often need more contact channels to deliver information to victims other than SMS, and the information of network communicating channels is frequently appeared in the SMS. So $I_{nen}(x)$ is introduced to catch these information indirectly, which has already been explained in Sect. 3. The final output of Stage 1 is given by Eq. 4

$$cls_{s1}(x) = x \odot (I_{nco}(x) \wedge I_{nen}(x)) \tag{4}$$

i.e. only the SMS with *Uncommon Chinese Characters* or *Other Characters* appearance, and *Numeric Characters* or *English Characters* appearance simultaneously will be sent to the stage 2. For simplicity, we set T1 and T2 equal to 0, and the detailed analysis of threshold setting will be discussed in the ablation study.

4.3 Stage 2 - Fraud SMS Classification

In stage 2, we aim to classify the SMS provided by previous stage in a find-grained manner. Due to the impressive advantage of a huge corpus in text classification, we exploited a deep neural model trained from Chinese corpus to extract semantic information. Besides, for the reason that there are lots of attacked texts in the fraud SMS, which are able to fool the deep model trained by the normal SMS, we design an artificial extractor, which can match specific keywords defined by anti-fraud professionals. Finally, features from deep model and artificial extractor were combined and fed into a machine learning model, e.g. SVM (support vector machine) to obtain the final classification results. The entire progress of stage 2 can be expressed as:

$$V(x) = f_{deep}(x) \oplus f_{pb}(x, k_1) \oplus f_{hm}(x, k_2) \tag{5}$$

$$cls_{s2}(x) = cls_{ml}(V(x); \theta) \tag{6}$$

where cls_{ml} is a machine learning classifier, f_{deep} is deep model, f_{pb} is PINYIN and BISHUN similarity extractor, and f_{hm} is hard matching extractor. $\oplus$ represents feature combination. We define $f_{pb}(x, k_1) \oplus f_{hm}(x, k_2)$ as artificial feature because it depends on pre-defined keywords group k_1 and k_2.

Deep Model. In the field of natural language processing, pre-trained deep language models have became a very important basic technology. We use the BERT-wwm, which released by Harbin Institute of Technology and IFlytek, for deep feature extraction [5]. BERT-wwm is one of the best open source deep models trained on Chinese wikipedia (including simplified Chinese and traditional Chinese) data and have better performance in formal text modeling. Specifically, we directly use the pre-trained model for deep feature extraction, i.e. taking the SMS as input, and use the corresponding output vector of the first symbol ('[CLS]') as the semantic representation.

PINYIN and BISHUN. Fraud SMS commonly use attacks against detection, and these transformed words could disturb the semantic meaning of sentences, affecting the accuracy of semantic features. Inspired by [23], we propose a strategy based on PINYIN [4] and BISHUN (stroke order) to recognize attack methods of some specific fraud keywords. Detailed procedures of our similarity judgement strategy are shown in Fig. 6.

Firstly, the algorithm will search the Word Split attack in the SMS, and make correspond-ing corrections if such obfuscated characters exists. Then the keywords generated by anti-fraud specialists will be searched in the SMS, and output a boolean vectors whether each keyword exists. We argue that two words can be regarded as same only when they are same or highly similar in some aspects. Concretely, two perspectives for judgement are considered in our strategy:

- *SAME PINYIN*. For homophony attack, one character would be transformed to others that has the same pronunciation. Since that Chinese characters can be pronounced base on their PINYIN, two words with the same PINYIN (without tones) could be regarded as the same word.
- *BISHUN similarity*. A Chinese character has five basic writing strokes, i.e. 横 (hor-izontal), 竖 (vertical), 撇 (left-falling), 捺 (right-falling) and 折 (turning). By cit-ing each basic stroke as number 1–5 and arranging them in writing order, BISHUN (stroke order) can uniquely identify a number sequence of a Chinese character. For glyph similar attack, transformed character usually shares some similar structure with the original one. For this reason, two words with high BISHUN similarity would be regarded as the same word in our method. The BISHUN similarity is calculated by adding the length of left common substring and the length of right common substring, then dividing by the length of keyword character composition string.

To explain our strategy clearly, we construct an example to further illustrate the process. Given an attacked SMS '徼亻言' and a keyword '微信' (wechat). Our method will try to combine each two adjacent characters first. In this case '亻言' would be corrected to '信'. Though the PINYIN of '徼' (hui) is different to '微' (wei), their BISHUN '徼' (33225215542343134) and '微' (3322521353134) maintain long left common substring (3322521) and right common substring (3134). We calculate the BISHUN similarity as Eq. 7:

$$(len(left) + len(right))/len(keyword) \approx 0.846 \qquad (7)$$

Due to the reason of the high BISHUN similarity, the strategy would determine '徼亻言' as an attack form of '微信'. Designed by anti-fraud specialists, we obtain 54 keywords in total from different fraud categories, therefore a 54-dim boolean features will be generated finally.

Hard Matching. Although PINYIN and BISHUN are able to catch the majority attack methods of words, there are still some attack methods that could bypass the detection, such as non-Chinese special characters. Due to the limited non-Chinese special char-acters which could be used for attack, we adopt a hard matching method to determine whether these keywords exist in the SMS. As shown in Table 3, we design 6 hard matching expressions to search pre-defined keywords. We also use the SMS length as an additional feature since the number of special characters is also related to the SMS length (which has been partially investigated in Fig. 4(b)), and thus obtain a 7-dim hard matching feature. Finally, these hard matching features are combined with PINYIN and BISHUN features, resulting in a 61-dim artificial feature.

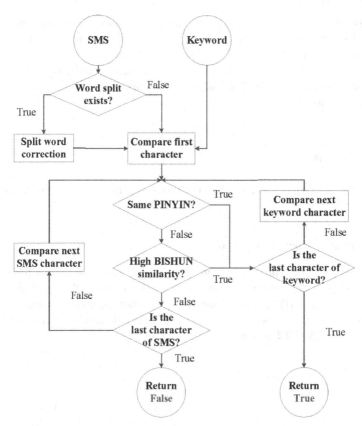

Fig. 6. PINYIN and BISHUN similarity judgement procedures.

Table 3. Hard matching expressions.

Hard Matching expression	Keyword	Non-Chinese Attack Form	Design principle
Has Phone or QQ	5-11 digits	+Q, tel:	Criminals needs phone, QQ, wechat, website to further contact with victims
Has website	Website	.com, .net, .cc, ...	
Has Wechat	微信	+V, +\ /, VX, ...	
# of 0	零	0,0, o, ○, °, ₀	Fraud SMS usually contains lots zeros to indicate the amount
# of 8	八	8,⑧, ⁸ , ₈	Gambling SMS usually contains lots eights, which means '发'(lucky)
# of numeric numbers	1-9	①,②,③,④,⑤,⑥,⑦,⑧,⑨,x, X, ...	'x' or 'X' is used to replace numbers in some desensitization data

ML Classifier. After the deep features and artificial features extraction, each SMS is represented as continuous or discrete features. Any multi-class classifier can be deployed to learn feature distribution and give its prediction. In the experiments, we commonly use SVM in one-versus-all manner to train on SMS features with all hyper-parameter of the SVM set to default. The detailed analysis of ML classifier selection is also discussed in the ablation study.

5 Experiments

In this section, we conduct real-world data experiments to estimate the performance of our algorithm.

5.1 Dataset and Experiments Setting

Since we only have the fraud samples provided from citizens, the normal SMS and the gambling SMS samples need to be collected in another channel. We randomly sampled some normal SMS from [26] and [27] datasets and further gathered some gambling SMS from volunteers. Table 4 summarizes statistics of the two datasets explored in this paper, and we made **DATASET2** available [6] for research usage.

Table 4. Sample statistics of two datasets.

Dataset Name	Normal	Gambling	Fraud
DATASET1	31640	6793	10300
DATASET2	1317	646	517

As for the experiments with **DATASET1**, the fraud and gambling samples in training and testing set are separated based on the collected date, the normal samples are randomly distributed in the training and testing set. Due to the limited sample size of **DATASET2**, we choose the entire **DATASET1** as training set, and the whole **DATASET2** as testing set for **DATASET2** related experiments.

5.2 Comparison of Different Algorithms

For comparison with our proposed algorithm *TFC*, five strategies are considered as follows:

- *JWE* [24], in which exploiting stroke-level information for improving the learning of Chinese word embeddings. We get the sentence embedding vectors by averaging the word embedding vector obtained from the algorithm and Chinese word-split tools \cite{Jieba}.

- *cw2vec* [25], in which jointly embed Chinese words as well as their characters and fine-grained subcharacter components. The sentence embedding vectors are obtained with the same procedures in *JWE*.
- *BERT-wwm*, we feed the SMS into BERT-wwm model directly to get the deep features.
- *Stage 1 + BERT-wwm*, we utilize Stage 1 to filter some normal SMS, and feed the rest SMS into BERT-wwm model to get the deep features.
- *PyCor + BERT-wwm*, we use an open source Chinese text error correction tool Pycorrector [29] to correct the obfuscated characters in the SMS, and exploit BERT-wwm model to get deep features of the corrected SMS.

All the features calculated from *TFC* and the above five strategies will be sent to SVM with the same parameters to obtain the final classification result.

Table 5 presents the performance of different algorithms with **DATASET1** and **DATASET2**, among them our proposed algorithms (*TFC without Stage 1* and *TFC*) achieve best performance on both datasets. Particularly, we can observe that strategy with *BERT-wwm* has better performance compared with *JWE* and *cw2vec*. From the comparison of *TFC without Stage 1* and *PyCor + BERT-wwm*, we conclude that our artificial features outperform than *PyCor*, which is able to deal with the obfuscated characters more effectively. From the comparison of *TFC without Stage 1* and *TFC*, we can find that Stage 1 has negative effects on the overall performance. We argue that the result is reasonable, because the main purpose of Stage 1 is quickly filtering out the normal SMS, and it's inevitable that some fraud SMS samples may have 0 *Uncommon Chinese Characters* and *Other Characters*, so these samples will be misclassified as normal in Stage 1. Meanwhile, it's quite easy to identify the filtered normal SMS in stage 2, which further enhances the performance of *TFC without Stage 1*.

Table 5. Performance of different algorithm.

Algorithm	DATASET1		DATASET2	
	F1-score	Accuracy	F1-score	Accuracy
JWE	0.84	0.922	0.591	0.757
cw2vec	0.764	0.894	0.437	0.65
BERT-wwm	0.9942	0.982	0.833	0.906
Stage 1 + BERT-wwm	0.941	0.949	0.832	0.902
Pycor + BERT-wwm	0.94	0.982	0.835	0.906
TFC without Stage 1	**0.952**	**0.986**	**0.851**	**0.923**
TFC	**0.948**	0.956	**0.843**	**0.915**

Table 6 demonstrates the effectiveness of domain-knowledge related features. TFC uses three types of features, i.e. deep features from *BERT-wwm*, PB features from **PINYIN and BISHUN** extractor and HM features from **Hard Matching** principle. Deep features extracts semantic information of SMS and provides the basic classification performance. HM features and PB features further improve accuracy on **DATASET1** and

Table 6. Performance comparison of different domain-knowledge features.

Features	DATASET1		DATASET2	
	F1-score	Accuracy	F1-score	Accuracy
Deep	0.942	0.982	0.833	0.906
Deep + PB	0.942	0.982	0.840	0.910
Deep + HM	0.947	0.984	0.833	0.906
Deep + PB + HM	**0.952**	**0.986**	**0.851**	**0.923**

Table 7. Classification examples under different algorithms.

No	SMS Samples	Ground Truth	TFC	JWE	cw2vec	PyCor+ Bert
(a)	Fraud SMS Sample：由于您的购物记录良，您来给我做事，·口260-580请 +Q：9213xxx27 Non-Attack Sample：·比下您的购物记录良，您来给我做事，一卜260-580请 加Q：9213xxx27	Part-time Fraud	Part-time Fraud	Loan Fraud	Normal	Part-time Fraud
(b)	SMS Sample：宋宋医疗费用预计xx万元	Normal	Normal	Loan Fraud	Loan Fraud	Normal
(c)	Fraud SMS Sample：戒俗宝，做款 十扣498xxx817秒卞 Fraud SMS Sample：借货宝，故款 加Q 498xxx817秒卞	Loan Fraud	Loan Fraud	Gambling	Gambling	Gambling
(d)	Fraud SMS Sample：嘿荮麽逊挂软件，泊动带注盈例，技攵网佬带梅天赚50%，涮 则呪涌溢虹。多柏赚多仟懒多万涌寸探检10-8888 +叩叩；1060xxx102 Non-Attack Sample：黑科技外挂软件，自动下注盈利。技术员私带每天赚50%，前 期无需分红。二百赚三千三千赚三万首充彩金10-8888 加QQ：1060xxx102	Investing Fraud	Investing Fraud	Gambling	Gambling	Gambling

DATASET2, respectively. After combining all three types of features (i.e. *TFC without Stage 1*), our algorithm achieves better performance on both datasets.

Here we give a few examples to illustrate the effectiveness of *TFC*. As shown in Table 7, for example (a) and (b), only a few of characters in the sentence are changed, and the algorithm based on large corpus (like *TFC* and *pycorrector + BERT*) can effectively extract the semantic information of the sentence and obtain good performance. In example (c) and (d), almost each character in the sentence has been changed to its attacked form. It's challenging to correct them by the algorithm based on transition probability, which further effects the performance of deep features. The artificial features added by *TFC* can effectively identify the keywords in various attack methods, which could guide the classifier to make the correct choices.

5.3 Ablation Experiment

Recall that the main purpose of Stage 1 is filtering out normal SMS precisely and quickly, so we relabeled the Gambling and Fraud SMS as abnormal SMS. Therefore the output of Stage 1 can be viewed as a binary classification problem, i.e., classify normal and abnormal SMS. We studied the effects of T1 (the right hand side of Eq. 2) and T2 (the right hand side of Eq. 3) with **DATASET1** train and test set in Fig. 7 and Fig. 8. From Fig. 7 we can find out when T2 is 0, changing T1 from 0 to 6 has trivial effects on the F1-score and Accuracy, but the results dropped significantly if T1 is greater than 7. Figure 8 shows the similar results when T1 is 0, and we can conclude that the reasonable value range for T2 is [0, 8]. Figure 9 plots the Stage 1's effect on total running time of *TFC* and # of samples. We can conclude that the total running time could be decreased 56.5% by simply setting T1 and T2 to be 0, which is quite important when the algorithm runs in the huge datasets. And the # of samples decreased 61.5% as well. The above results prove that the Stage 1 is able to effectively reduce the size of dataset while classifying the normal and abnormal SMS with satisfactory performance.

Given lots of domain-knowledge keywords are adopted in Stage 2, we also investigate their corresponding effects with **DATASET1**. We can change the problem into a binary classification problem for each fraud type, for example, Non Loan fraud SMS v.s Loan fraud SMS. Table 7 presents the results of binary classification with the impacts of the domain-knowledge keywords, we can observe that three types of fraud SMS have better performance when they exploit the related keywords. To explore the reason that both F1-score and accuracy are lower after utilizing the keywords for Part- time Fraud, the authors plot the percentage of samples that each fraud type's keywords appeared in the test set in Fig. 10. We can observe that the Part-time fraud keywords are appeared in 98.6% Part-time fraud SMS, but it also shown in 92.4% Investing fraud SMS and 75.5% Gambling SMS respectively, which means the uniqueness of the keywords is limited. As for the Investing fraud keywords, since the keywords appearance percentage in the Investing fraud samples is relatively higher, which helps the algorithm achieve bigger improving in both F1-score and accuracy (shown in Table 8).

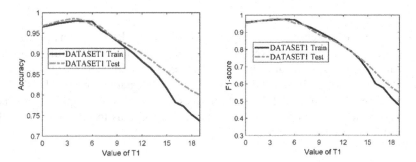

Fig. 7. Accuracy and F1-score under different T1 (T2 = 0).

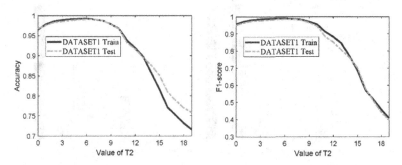

Fig. 8. Accuracy and F1-score under different T2 (T1 = 0).

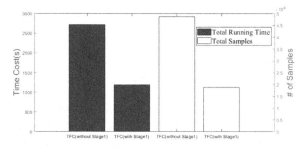

Fig. 9. Accuracy and F1-score under different T2 (T1 = 0).

Table 8. Impacts of the domain-knowledge keywords.

Fraud types	With keywords		Without keywords	
	F1-score	Accuracy	F1-score	Accuracy
Loan fraud	0.970	0.988	0.949	0.980
Part-time fraud	0.955	0.963	0.969	0.974
Investing fraud	0.910	0.967	0.885	0.958
Gambling	0.974	0.975	0.971	0.972

We modify the final classification algorithm from SVM to RF (Random Forest), MLP (Multi-Layer Perceptron) and KNN (K-Nearest Neighbor) to study the different types algorithm's performance, parameters of all the algorithms are used in default setting with scikit-learn [30], and Table 9 demonstrates that the features generated by *TFC* are robust to many algorithms, and the performances are quite close compared with each other. Researchers can apply advanced or parallel algorithms to further improve the performance or speed up the running time.

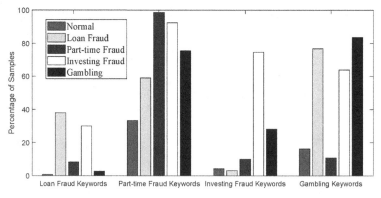

Fig. 10. The percentage of samples for each fraud type keywords.

Table 9. Performance of TFC with different ML algorithm.

ML algorithm	DATASET1		DATASET2	
	F1-score	Accuracy	F1-score	Accuracy
SVM	0.948	0.956	0.915	0.843
RF	0.931	0.937	0.877	0.779
MLP	0.933	0.944	0.879	0.807
KNN	0.939	0.948	0.773	0.693

6 Conclusion

This paper mainly investigates the fraud SMS classification problem. We conduct a comprehensive measurement study of the fraud SMS, and observe some interesting phenomena. In addition, we propose a two-stage algorithm called *TFC*, which is able to quickly filter out normal SMS in the first stage, and classifying fraud SMS precisely in the second stage with the semantic deep features and the domain-knowledge based artificial features. By comparing with other algorithms using real-world dataset, we demonstrate that our algorithm *TFC* achieves better performance on both F1-score and accuracy. In the future, we plan to study how to extract the domain-knowledge keywords precisely and automatically.

Funding. This work was supported by the Science and Technology Program of Guangzhou under Grant 2019030005.

References

1. Supreme People's Procuratorate sets up a steering group to crackdown the rapidly spread cybercrime. http://www.xinhuanet.com/legal/2020-04/08/c_1125829699.htm. Accessed 07 Apr 2021
2. The survey report shows that three telecom operators have achieved nearly 100% scam SMS processing in September 2020. https://www.sohu.com/a/430647655_287480. Accessed 07 Apr 2021
3. China public security department cracked 256,000 cases of telecommunications network fraud in 2020. http://www.gov.cn/xinwen/2021-01/02/content_5576223.htm. Accessed 07 Apr 2021
4. Wikipedia, PINYIN. https://en.wikipedia.org/wiki/Pinyin. Accessed 07 Apr 2021
5. Cui, Y., et al.: Revisiting pre-trained models for Chinese natural language processing. In: Proceedings of Conference on Empirical Methods in Natural Language Processing: Findings (2020)
6. DATASET Repo. https://github.com/leegdcert/TFCDATASET. Accessed 07 Apr 2021
7. Joo, J.W., Moon, S.Y., Singh, S., Park, J.H.: S-Detector: an enhanced security model for detecting smishing attack for mobile computing. Telecommun. Syst. **66**(1), 29–38 (2017). https://doi.org/10.1007/s11235-016-0269-9

8. Goel, D., Jain, A.: Smishing-classifier: a novel framework for detection of smishing attack in mobile environment. In: Bhattacharyya, P., Sastry, H.G., Marriboyina, V., Sharma, R. (eds.) Smart and Innovative Trends in Next Generation Computing Technologies, pp. 502–512. Springer, Singapore (2018). https://doi.org/10.1007/978-981-10-8660-1_38

9. Mishra, S., Soni, D.: Smishing detector: a security model to detect smishing through SMS content analysis and URL behavior analysis. Futur. Gener. Comput. Syst. **108**, 803–815 (2020)

10. Pervaiz, F., et al.: An assessment of SMS fraud in Pakistan. In: Proceedings of 2nd ACM SIGCAS Conference on Computing and Sustainable Societies (2019)

11. Delany, S., Buckley, M., Greene, D.: SMS spam filtering: methods and data. Expert Syst. Appl. **39**(10), 9899–9908 (2012)

12. Abdulhamid, S., et al.: A review on mobile SMS spam filtering techniques. IEEE Access **5**, 15650–15666 (2017)

13. Olszewski, D.: A probabolistic approch to fraud detection in telecommunications. Knowl.-Based Syst. **26**, 246–258 (2012)

14. Farvaresh, H., Sepehri, M.: A data mining framework for detecting subscription fraud in telecommunication. Eng. Appl. Artif. Intell. **24**(1), 182–194 (2011)

15. Wang, Y., Bansal, M.: Robust machine comprehension models via adversarial training. In: Proceedings of NAACL-HLT (2018)

16. Ebrahimi, J., Lowd, D., Dou, D.: On adversarial examples for character-level neural machine translation. In: Proceedings of 27th International Conference on Computational Linguistics (2018)

17. Li, J., Ji, S., Du, T., Li, B., Wang, T.: TEXTBUGGER: generating adversarial text against real-world applications. In: Proceedings of Network and Distributed Systems Security (NDSS) Symposium (2019)

18. Yeh, J., Li, S., Wu, M., Chen, W., Su, M.: Chinese word spelling correction based on N-gram ranked inverted index list. In: Proceedings of Seventh SIGHAN Workshop on Chinese Language Processing (2013)

19. Xiong, J., Zhang, Q., Zhang, S., Hou, J., Cheng, X.: HANSpeller: a unified framework for Chinese spelling correction. Comput. Linguist. Chin. Lang. Process. **20**(1), 1–22 (2015)

20. Karan, M., Snajder, J.: Cross-domain detection of abusive language online. In: Proceedings of 2nd Workshop on Abusive Language Online (2018)

21. Nobata, C., Tetreault, J., Thomas, A., Mehdad, Y., Chang, Y.: Abusive language detection in online user content. In: 25th International Conference on World Wide Web (2016)

22. Wikipedia, Commonly used words in Modern Chinese. https://zh.wikipedia.org/wiki/现代汉语常用字表. Accessed 07 Apr 2021

23. Li, J., et al.: TEXTSHIELD: robust text classification based on multimodal embedding and neural machine translation. In: Proceedings of 29th USENIX Security Symposium (2020)

24. Yu, J., Jian, X., Xin, H., Song, Y.: Joint embeddings of Chinese words, characters, and fine-grained subcharacter components. In: Proceedings of Conference on Empirical Methods in Natural Language Processing (2017)

25. Cao, S., Lu, W., Zhou, J., Li, X.: cw2vec: learning Chinese word embeddings with stroke n-gram information. In: Proceedings of AAAI (2018)

26. Chen, T., Kan, M.: Creating a live, public short message service corpus: the NUS SMS corpus. Lang. Resour. Eval. **47**(2), 299–335 (2013). https://doi.org/10.1007/s10579-012-9197-9

27. SpamMessage. https://github.com/hrwhisper/SpamMessage. Accessed 07 Apr 2021

28. Jieba. https://github.com/fxsjy/jieba. Accessed 07 Apr 2021

29. Pycorrector. https://github.com/shibing624/pycorrector. Accessed 07 Apr 2021

30. Scikit-learn. https://sklearn.org. Accessed 07 Apr 2021

Vulnerability Detection

Research Towards Key Issues of API Security

Ronghua Sun, Qianxun Wang, and Liang Guo$^{(\boxtimes)}$

Data Star Observatory Technology Co., Ltd., Beijing, China
guoliang@shuziguanxing.com

Abstract. With the mass application of virtualization, micro-services, and cloud-native technologies, the interaction between service entities through APIs has become a norm. Many platforms are still maintaining a large number of old APIs due to business needs. At the same time, many new APIs are gradually going online. Both of these statuses put forward higher requirements for API security. Focusing on old APIs' security protection and other issues, this article starts from the process of asset discovery, vulnerability detection, and security auditing. Aiming at the problem of API asset discovery, this article summarizes the technical methods of automatically clustering unowned API assets using the characteristics of various commonly used APIs. Aiming at new API vulnerability detection, a security analysis method based on finite state machine is proposed. For the first time, the cross-network communication taint propagation based on dynamic taint analysis technology and system-level simulation technology is realized, enabling sensitive data flow tracing in API communication become feasible. We designed a flowbased API security audit system to improve automated API protection. Finally, We analyzed technical opportunities and challenges of API security in detail and prospected for API security research's next direction and development trend.

Keywords: API security · Asset discovery · Vulnerability detection

1 Introduction

An application programming interface (API) is a collection of commands, functions, protocols, and objects. It interacts with external systems by performing common operations. API is flexible, easy to use, and efficient. As a bridge between modules, software, and developers, API is an integral part of modern mobile App, SaaS, and web applications. It is widely used in customer-oriented, partner-oriented, and internal applications [15], such as banking, retail, driverless cars, and smart homes. With the continuous deepening of various industries' networked processes, the API service model is becoming more and more popular.

Currently, using tools can quickly build applications, which means that even inexperienced developers can deploy or integrate applications. This kind of agile development generally doesn't have robust security design or application integration guidance, and they even fail to consider security impacts fully and may expose application logic vulnerability. For example, when designing and implementing extensions, improper constraints on resources or permissions may lead to denial of service attacks. Therefore, the

W. Lu et al. (Eds.): CNCERT 2021, CCIS 1506, pp. 179–192, 2022.
https://doi.org/10.1007/978-981-16-9229-1_11

widespread use of APIs has increased the risk of user safety and privacy leakage, and APIs have gradually become the target of cyber attackers [10].

Although the application may implement robust input validation and access control in the native code, these data are usually not copied in the same class when sent to the server over API. Therefore, an attacker can bypass the client's control. API attacks mostly log in with a legal identity and then simulate normal operations such as multi-source and low-frequency requests. Therefore, the security mechanisms provided by traditional API security gateways such as identity authentication, authority management, rate limiting, and request content verification can not meet the security requirements. API security is a fundamental part of network security. Without secure API, it is impossible to achieve rapid innovation.

2   API Asset Discovery Based on Traffic

With the digital transformation, enterprise apps, mini apps, and light applications on various platforms have developed rapidly. Programmers would like to use the web due to its versatility, economy, and independence from specific platforms or SDKs. Compared with the binary version, the functions of Web products are more comprehensive and reliable [1]. Jeff Atwood, the founder of the StackOverflow website, once asserted, "All programming will be Web programming." According to the 2020 StackOverflow annual developer survey, JavaScript language occupies 67.7% of the share, and this is also the 8th year that JavaScript has been the most commonly used programming language [14]. As the primary language in Web development, JavaScript's widely used proved the universality and process of Web technology. Web development relies on good network interaction between the browser and the back-end server, and its essence is to build applications based on the HTTP protocol. Therefore, API design is critical in Web development. This article mainly discusses API security under the web framework.

At present, there are many security risks in API design, such as various attacks caused by out-of-date API, unauthorized users abusing the API, sensitive API calls, and version confusion. API security testing can understand and mitigate the risks. Therefore, it is necessary to implement security testing on APIs. Security testing generally collects assets and then analyzes the assets through the data flow. At present, the industry mainly relies on API fingerprints to identify API assets. For example, common API frameworks such as REST [4] and GraphQL [6] have some features that can be used to generate corresponding fingerprints. User-defined APIs can also complete matching recognition by customizing fingerprints.

In the field of digital technology, an asset refers to any object of value to an organization. Digital assets are the essential components of business systems and networks. Digital assets are also the foundation for the regular operation of business systems. In recent years, with the rapid development of computer technology, digital assets are gradually becoming an essential tool and support for the operation and management of enterprises and organizations [5]. As the business of enterprises and organizations continues to grow, a large number of unowned API assets and zombie API assets are generated in the business system. Suppose these assets are not maintained for a long time. In that case, they may cause many vulnerabilities and configuration problems, which affect the response speed to attacks and bring hidden dangers to the safety of enterprises and organizations (Table 2).

Table 1. 3 kind of critical API assets should be concerned

API Asset Type	Asset Characteristics and Threats
Unowned assets	Despite the lack of maintainers, such API assets are still part of the supporters' services due to their limited robustness. Once such API assets are exposed to vulnerabilities, problems such as difficulty in locating issues and difficulty in troubleshooting will arise. Such valuable but poorly maintained APIs should be arranged as soon as possible, and good documentation should be prepared adequately to support the development and maintenance of the team in the future.
Zombie assets	Such API assets also lack maintenance personnel. But compared with unowned assets, it no longer provides valuable services. In other words, the life cycle of this type of API asset has ended, but it has not been offline for some reason. Assets that do not produce value will naturally not be maintained, so such assets are often the target of attacks. Clearing out such assets and taking them offline will improve the security of the service system.
Critical assets	Such API assets are the core assets of Internet applications. A large number of apps integrate such assets. Therefore, the security, robustness, and maintainability of such assets are critical. Applications such as WeChat and Facebook provide APIs for cross-platform authentication and login of other apps, and these APIs appear in many third-party apps. Once such APIs have privacy leaks, there will be a massive number of victim groups.

Strengthening the management of API assets from the development of digital assets is the fundamental means to solve unowned assets. However, many enterprises or organizations have failed to manage from the development cycle's beginning, and many such assets have already existed. The API defines the interaction details between the front and back ends of the Web. Finding out the set of APIs in chaotic IT assets is the key to alleviating such management problems. However, APIs generally hide deeply, and it isn't easy to obtain a comprehensive collection by active scanning. Therefore, it is necessary to complement the asset discovery capabilities based on passive traffic analysis. The general process is first to collect and analyze HTTP/HTTPS traffic and then discover API assets with fingerprint technology. There are various methods of API asset identification. The technical basis is traffic collection. The auxiliary technologies

Table 2. API asset discovery technology: summary, pros and cons

Discovery Techs	Technical summary	Pros and Cons
Traffic capture and manual analysis	Traffic capture is the primary method of API asset discovery. Although there have been quite a few auxiliary methods, capturing traffic packets and performing manual analysis is still a fundamental and effective method.	The technical threshold is low. However, relying on manual analysis requires high technical personnel's experience, which is not conducive to automation.
API fingerprint matching	This is an auxiliary method based on traffic capture. The basic principle is to match the captured data stream according to the characteristics of some common APIs.	The technical solution is relatively mature, and commercial products have appeared. However, it can only identify some special APIs and cannot identify new APIs.
Deep learning	Before the API is officially launched, run a single API service on the test server, capture TCP/UDP sessions, and establish the correspondence between sessions and API features. According to this correspondence, a certain type of deep learning model is trained for future asset discovery.	The technology is relatively advanced, and the prospects are fairly broad. But it cannot deal with mixed API data streams. In practice, communication subjects often use multiple APIs for communication, so the data flow in this context is very different from single API communication, which brings significant challenges to deep learning algorithms.

include API feature matching, API message analysis, deep learning technology, etc. The technical summary and analysis of advantages and disadvantages are shown in Fig. 1.

In April 2021, the data of 500 million Facebook users were publicly sold on the dark web, including the user's nickname, email address, phone number, and home address information. Facebook responded that in 2019, a function of the online business API was misused, resulting in information leakage, affecting approximately 300 million users. Security assets are the most basic and vital carrier in information security management, and it is excellent to grasp secure asset information in all directions without blind spots.

Unowned assets and zombie assets will directly affect network security and even affect the emergency response to attacks. By combing API assets, administrators can quickly restore the currently hidden web architecture to help them find vulnerabilities, make a quick response the first time, and quickly locate the scope of vulnerability. Currently, three key objects of concern in API assets are shown in Table 1.

3   API Vulnerability Detection Method

3.1   API Security Audit Based on Data Flow Tracing

API was established for network communication, so the vulnerabilities in API mainly come from data flow abnormalities. The spread of sensitive data through the web requires strict data flow inspections on related APIs. Therefore, leakage detection and in-depth tracking of sensitive data is an essential issue in API security research. In the traditional data stream tracking research, the taint analysis method has strong applicability [3]. Dynamic taint propagation is widely used in three major areas: malicious code detection and defense, software vulnerability analysis and mining, and sensitive information leakage detection. Like traditional taint analysis technology, various modern web-based software with sensitive data input, such as mini apps, distributed programs, can also use taint analysis after some redesign and transformation to complete data flow analysis.

Web technology is oriented to the interaction between multiple computers based on the network. In contrast, taint analysis technology is more suitable for tests running on a single computing system because of its dependence on memory space. In this contradiction, the traditional technology migration idea is to spread the taint separately on the client and the server and then analyze them separately. However, in this separate test, the API call flow between the tested subjects is not well tracked, and the focus is on the data flow of the client or the server itself.

API-based web communication relies on TCP/IP technology. Data packaged by the sender is routed and forwarded across the network, the data will be re-read into the receiver's memory. The taint analysis technology relies on the tainted mark at the memory byte-level or bit-level [2, 7], so the tainted spot will get into invalid after transmission across a network that cannot be directly traced. In addition, the underlying protocol stack of network transmission in the operating system is generally completed by kernel-mode code, and non-system-level taint marking cannot mark kernel-state variables. Therefore, a whole-system taint analysis platform becomes a necessary condition for API data flow taint tracking. The embarrassment of taint propagation and analysis methods in API data flow analysis urges academic and industrial exploration. A significant achievement of this research is to face this problem.

It can be seen from Fig. 1 that after the client's key variable k is sent through the send key over API function, it is essentially handed over to a socket and then transmitted over the TCP/IP network. In a non-RDMA communication network, the address of the sent variable k at the receiver cannot be perceived by the client. So the separated client-side taint propagation ends here, and the sensitive memory address cannot be detected. In this process, the call stack of the function send key over API is also sensitive element because this process is closely related to some specific sensitive API. To address this, we propose a method that can mark tainted data in cross-network communication and at the same time track the API and part that initiated the cross-network contact. Under this method, the client and server can be tainted and traced synchronously on the supported system.

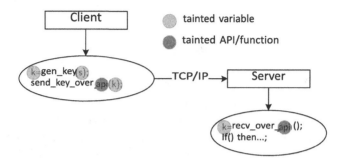

Fig. 1. Taint analysis of crossing network communication

The main idea of this method is based on the system-level emulation of the client and the server, and the communication layer of both is overhead so that the physical layer and link layer of traditional network communication is realized by software. For example, when the client sends a data packet to the server, the system-level emulator of the client will backtrack the variables that constitute this type of data packet in the memory space of the client; after the client sends, the communication layer intercepts the data, and directly It is copied to the buffer corresponding to the server. At the same time, the emulator on the server is notified that it needs to track the reading process of this buffer in advance (before the notification is completed, the reading process is not allowed to be executed); the server emulator will then track the reading process and Relevant variables, and mark these variables as tainted data. As a result, the spread of taint to communication in a set of APIs is realized.

3.2 Finite State Machine Model of Interaction by API

From a broad perspective, all interactions between the client and multiple frontend services can be boiled down to a finite state machine [12]. Finite state machine is a powerful tool used to model the behavior of an object. Its function mainly describes the state sequence that the object experiences during its lifecycle and how to respond to various events from the outside world. The wellknown finite state machine is the state machine of the TCP protocol. Before the new API is developed, FSM modeling should be performed first, and then the operation of the API should be simulated. Through FSM modeling and preliminary simulation, certain specific loopholes in the actual implementation of the entire set of API can be found. And it can also enable developers to understand complex and heavy development requirements more efficiently. As the protocol becomes more and more complex, how to accurately and comprehensively understand or even discover all the details of the entire protocol has become a very challenging problem. Although the principle is straightforward, and it is not difficult to convert API interaction logic to FSM, there are no good tools for how to efficiently and automatically execute and test FSM. Concerning the idea of automated formal verification, we designed and implemented a framework for fast FSM semi-automatic construction of APIs.

In API communication, take IoT smart home devices as an example. Device A will be placed in state S1 through the user's physical click. In S1, device A will become a WiFi access point and wait for a connection. After that, when the user's mobile phone joins this WiFi, and the device is notified of the WLAN password, device A will enter state S2, in which it will wait for the Internet connection. If getting the Internet connection successfully, device A will enter state S3.1, in which it will wait for cloud device ID registration. Otherwise, it will enter state S3.2, that is, the password is incorrect, couldn't connect to the IoT cloud, cloud refused, etc., then device A will returns to state S2 and continues to wait. In S3.1, if a successful ACK of cloud binding can be received, it will enter state S4 and running regularly. The specific process, such as user reconfiguration, will not be repeated here. It can be found that the device can transfer between S1, S2, S3.1, S3.2, and S4 due to various trigger conditions. However, a set of APIs does not only contain one device. We still take IoT as an example. There are usually three objects in the cloud, mobile app, and device [17]. It is not enough to model the state of one thing. By associating the state transitions of three objects, a directed diagram of state transitions can be formed or called an FSM. In this diagram, we define safe initialization conditions, such as the user pressing the reset button and then traversing the path according to all possible trigger conditions until all feasible paths are completed. If an event defined as dangerous is triggered in the FSM diagram, such as the device goes offline and falls into an unavailable state, the API is problematic. By constructing FSM, the model can be tested quickly, and the design flaws of API can be found, and the vulnerabilities can be found in time.

3.3 Demonstration

In the traditional formal verification of network protocols, security investigations are entirely dependent on the input which describe the whole protocol. So when the input is unreliable, the result of the formal verification is also unpredictable. The principle is straightforward. After all, all model checking and system simulation can only prove the insecurity of a protocol, but not the security of the protocol. The same reasoning is fully applicable to the API security field. According to the new API attack chain discovered by Jice Wang et al. [16], we try to replicate the experiment based on our theory. Jice's paper proposes a new attack vector: multiple APIs integrated in the same App will share the same virtual address space, so there are attacks between each other. And the attack is mainly focused on the theft of user's data, which undoubtedly poses a great threat to the current compassionate privacy data protection! However, the primary method of this work is to reverse engineer and statically analyze the Android APK file, so fewer attack instances were found.

As shown in Fig. 2, the tested Android App is constructed by us to test whether our API will be attacked. Like WeChat, an open platform that provides logins, applicants must be qualified when providing open services. Therefore, apps with WeChat login qualifications are considered won't steal WeChat user's data. In the Cross-Library API call, the caller and the caller are in the same memory space, so a library can naturally call functions in another library through specific APIs. In this case, API security becomes particularly critical. A malicious library can call our API and then reasonably get all kinds of data outside the security boundary from our server. In the narration of the first two sections of this chapter, we emphasized the importance of dynamic taint tracking. We set a certain type of Token as tainted data. When a request is sent on the App side, the caller related to the Token will appear in the tracking list. By setting up a reasonable tracking list, you can easily find illegal cases that appear in the taint mark list. Because our system overheads the network transmission layer, when the Token is sent to the receiver via TCP, it can directly find the caller's information on the server, thereby intercepting the attack. Unlike Jice's work, we focus on the security of the API instead of emphasizing the existence of the attack chain.

The above case demonstrates the importance of system-level taint tracking tools for API protection. Combined with the automata shown in Fig. 2, vulnerabilities outside the protocol can be found. This is of great positive significance for improving API protection capabilities.

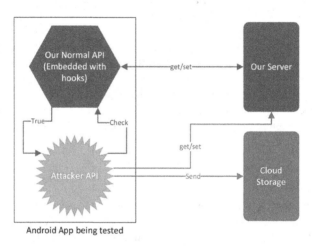

Fig. 2. API under cross library attacks

3.4   Relationship Between FSM Testing and Data Flow Taint Analysis

FSM modeling and possible simulation of the communication time sequences between network objects based on API communication can find the loopholes of the protocol at a relatively macro level. It is also conducive to simplifying and reducing some APIs in the later stage. Full system-level emulation is performed on the network entities running the entire set of APIs, and the taint analysis method that overheads TCP/IP communication can be used to discover the moving traces of sensitive data in the API. The above two methods have certain similarities, both of which have carried out different degrees of modeling, and the models need to be executed. However, the granularity of the two ideas is entirely different. The FSM-based method focuses on the macro logic of the API system. By analyzing the topology of the FSM, some hidden logical vulnerabilities can be found. For example, by using FSM to investigate the application of MQTT in IoT, Yan Jia [9] and others found that during the process of binding and unbinding intelligent home devices, the MQTT protocol will enable the former authorized person to regain control. Emulating the client and server running the API and tracking the sensitive data that the programmer cares about (after this referred to as the EMU method) operated at a more fine-grained level. Although the EMU method also needs to be abstracted, it only removes some unnecessary communication intermediate processes. The specific code is still executed in the actual runtime environment. So, the EMU method will find vulnerabilities related to the tested API more precisely. In the EMU method, whole-system simulations are required for the client and server, and some symbolic execution methods are even needed to bypass the input and output of the peripherals of the complex client. Therefore, there are many automation problems in the design.

4 API Security Audit System Based on Traffic

At present, it is not easy to manage APIs safely and effectively. Building and managing APIs quickly and easily has become an essential issue in developing web-based programs [13]. Traditional API security gateways are too expensive to deploy and maintain. They lack effective strategies to build defenses and cannot efficiently respond to the threats of emerging automated tools. The development of automated auditing API methods to improve security is still challenging. In response to the above problems, this section proposes an API security audit system based on the Internet traffic, which is designed based on intelligence asset collection to provide research ideas for the security protection of massive API assets.

4.1 Research Ideas

API exists in the form of digital data. Using API as a form of digital asset management can more effectively improve API security. From the perspective of API assets, API security audit is divided into three parts, as shown in Fig. 3.

The API asset discovery module uses various methods such as traffic analysis, docking data, and importing data to identify the data processing modes of APIs, such as RESTful and GraphQL. This module will enable the full discovering of API assets, especially for the discovery of unknown APIs. What's more, precise identification is given to prevent the access of obscure APIs from causing the unavailability of functions.

API asset portrait uses data analysis to accurately portray the API's functions and permissions, such as user login, registration, data query, and administrator permissions. According to the API profile list, we can quickly check the status of each API, such as usage, access source, exception, etc.

API safety detection and protection module use active and passive methods to audit the API security of application and business dimensions. Remote command/code execution, data leakage, unauthorized access, unauthorized access, logic defects, etc., will be detected during this part. According to the audit results, we will respond dynamically and implement protective measures to increase the difficulty of attacks.

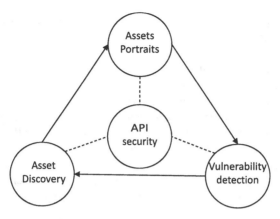

Fig. 3. Security audit process

4.2   System Framework Design

When designing the system, we should emphasize the network, data, and business APIs. On the network side, connecting the internal and external application terminals through APIs would expand network attacks, increases risk transmission paths and make the system more vulnerable to malicious. All of these could lead to server intrusion and business continuity interruption. In terms of data, once the open API has design flaws or improper permission settings, malicious attackers may illegally obtain user data. In terms of business, as the amount of API openness increases, service interfaces may be used beyond the scope, increasing the probability of business compliance risk events.

Starting from the characteristics of data processing, taking into efficient reading and writing, data conversion, transaction processing, and caching strategies, we can divide the system into four layers from bottom to top: collection layer, pre-processing layer, detection layer, and the user interfaces layer. The structure is as follows, shown in Fig. 4.

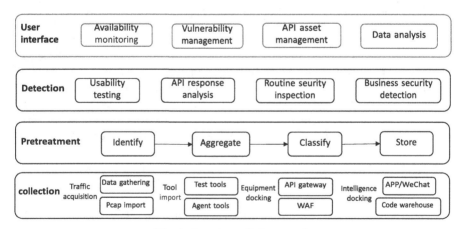

Fig. 4. Security audit framework

The collection layer is mainly used to collect data in four ways. Traffic collection takes deploying collection nodes and PCAP import, which is the essential way. Tool importing is by capturing data directly in contact with software such as testing tools and proxy tools. The API also communicates information through hardware devices and captures data from web application firewalls and API gateways utilizing device docking. Intelligence data on various platforms is also an essential component of API assets. Intelligence-based API asset collection is mainly from the following aspects: cooperation with APP security vendors to obtain API asset information in APP; obtain API asset information in applets; get API asset information leaked in well-known open code warehouses; Cooperate with Internet terminals, browsers, cloud platforms, Internet of Things, Internet of Vehicles and other companies to obtain API asset information. The above four methods can establish an API asset information system more comprehensively.

4.3   Key Techniques

The core of the API security audit system proposed in this paper is flow-based. First, collect traffic according to the underlying driver. Then, recreate an API asset library using URL, request templates, etc.; the original traffic can be directly constructed to form a traffic library that can be massively stored, quickly searched, and visualized. Last, Perform data pre-processing on the API asset library and traffic library.

Extract the assets in the API asset library for active detection, analyze the availability of the detection results, and mark if they are not available. For the available assets, conduct functional analysis and permission analysis and construct the API vulnerability library for the problems found. Analyze the traffic content in the traffic database, extract sensitive information, and write the issues into the API vulnerability database. Through a series of API audits around traffic, API security issues can be handled quickly and efficiently.

According to the OWASP API Security Top 10 2019 [11], it can be found that API security issues are more concentrated in the business security field, such as ultra vires, data leakage, and invalid identity authentication. The security of conventional applications mainly relies on the detection rules to analyze the request and response and then judge the risk. However, API business security needs to dynamically compare and analyze multiple consecutive business request data to discover hidden business security hazards such as unauthorized access and user identity authentication failure. To improve the efficiency of traffic auditing, deep learning methods can be used to detect such problems continuously.

When the API sample data is sufficient, we can continuously accumulate positive and negative samples during the API security audit and constantly train and modify the security audit model through cluster analysis, supervised learning, and other methods. Then we can use the security audit model to discover more unknown API security threats.

5   Opportunities and Challenges

With the rapid development of mobilization, openness, and IoT, API provides the impetus for today's digital transformation. With the changes in business forms, the open cooperation of business APIs has become an inevitable trend, and new security opportunities often accompany emerging businesses. Although digital transformation promotes API in various industries, malicious threats target API more than ever. There is a big gap between the current API security situation and actual needs, and the API ecosystem faces different challenges and threats.

Applications and logic transform to the cloud to provide services for more users with exposing more attack surfaces of APIs and triggering a variety of potential attacks. Attackers can use network traffic, reverse code, security vulnerabilities, and other means to carry out attacks. For example, in terms of authentication, attackers obtain API login credentials through phishing, social engineering, botnets, etc., to steal customer data or personal information. In terms of vulnerability exploitation, common attack methods such as SQL injection and XSS could be used to steal sensitive data or destroy the system. API attacks have been instrumentalized. Attackers can use tools to collect a list of domain names and APIs used for attacks and then use other means to find or delete sensitive data.

Table 3. Issues and methods of API security research.

Issues	Methods
API security framework	Service grid
Accurate recognition and portrait	Deep learning, reinforcement learning
Automatic correlation	Machine learning
Security situation prediction	Automatic perception and Self-learning
Cross-platform interconnection	Security value sharing
Monitoring and visualization	Big data
API vulnerability mining	Automated mining
API protection system	New artificial intelligence technology

The number of APIs continues to grow, and API security research needs to continue to keep pace with the times and innovate. Table 3 summarizes some complicated problems and possible solutions in API security research. Build an API security framework through the service grid, classify, share and aggregate API information, and improve the efficiency and security of API management [8]. Service grid access control has advantages and can enhance the authentication and authorization process. API security management needs to identify all aspects of API information accurately, build an API asset attribute library through deep learning and other methods, automatically sort out API asset portraits, and provide rich analysis data for API asset security analysis. The intelligent model based on machine learning solves the problem of automatic association between new API and existing assets through active scanning, passive traffic monitoring, etc., and improves automation. Security posture assessment is an essential part of network security, and API security posture plays a significant role in security decision-making. In the face of massive network attacks, it uses automatic perception to avert dangerous situations in time and improves prediction accuracy through self-learning adjustments. Interconnection is an effective means to realize the integration of data resources in various industries, enriching data and business functionality through value sharing and integration. In the process of opening to the outside world and integration in the form of API, unified security life-cycle management and fine-grained security control can help the organization to achieve effective governance inside and outside. API security needs to be monitored throughout the entire process. The data obtained by using big data visualization is convenient for managers to intuitively and accurately grasp the current security status. Excavating the vulnerabilities of the existing large-scale and complex API systems and discovering the vulnerabilities of newly launched APIs are two fundamental issues in the academic world. It will also be a hot topic of continuous attention. Currently, the API protection system is still immature. With the constant emergence of new scenarios, security solutions are not fully applicable in open service scenarios. Use a new generation of artificial intelligence technology to solve multi-level security protection and security threats and increase the intelligence level of API security.

6 Conclusion

The core functions and micro-service architecture of mobile applications, websites, applications, etc., are inseparable from the support of APIs. The scrum development model is a mainstream development mode. In improving the speed and flexibility of innovation, API risks are underestimated, and API construction security is ignored.

This work sorts out API security protection-related methods and proposes a finite state machine analysis method that can help improve the API security design and safety evaluation. An API security audit framework was proposed, the core of which is API auditing based on traffic, which provides ideas for studying the best practices for protecting APIs. Finally, it explains the existing problems in the current research and looks forward to its future development.

References

1. Corral, L., Sillitti, A., Succi, G., Garibbo, A., Ramella, P.: Evolution of mobile software development from platform-specific to web-based multiplatform paradigm. In: Proceedings of the 10th SIGPLAN Symposium on New ideas, New Paradigms, and Reflections on Programming and Software, pp. 181–183 (2012)
2. Davanian, A., Qi, Z., Qu, Y., Yin, H.: Decaf++: elastic whole-system dynamic taint analysis. In: 22nd International Symposium on Research in Attacks, Intrusions and Defenses ({RAID} 2019), pp. 31–45 (2019)
3. Ding, Y., Wei, T., Xue, H., Zhang, Y., Zhang, C., Han, X.: Accurate and efficient exploit capture and classification. Sci. China Inf. Sci. **60**(5), 1–17 (2017)
4. Fielding, R.T.: Architectural styles and the design of network-based software architectures. University of California, Irvine (2000)
5. Gandert, N., et al.: Method and system for searching for digital assets, uS Patent 9,251,172 (2016)
6. Hartig, O., Pérez, J.: An Initial Analysis of Facebook's GraphQL Language (2017)

7. Henderson, A., Yan, L.K., Hu, X., Prakash, A., Yin, H., McCamant, S.: Decaf: a platform-neutral whole-system dynamic binary analysis platform. IEEE Trans. Softw. Eng. **43**(2), 164–184 (2016)

8. Hussain, F., Li, W., Noye, B., Sharieh, S., Ferworn, A.: Intelligent service mesh framework for API security and management. In: 2019 IEEE 10th Annual Information Technology, Electronics and Mobile Communication Conference (IEMCON). pp. 0735–0742. IEEE (2019)

9. Jia, Y., et al.: Burglars' IoT paradise: understanding and mitigating security risks of general messaging protocols on IoT clouds. In: 2020 IEEE Symposium on Security and Privacy (SP). pp. 465–481. IEEE (2020)

10. Mendoza, A., Gu, G.: Mobile application web API reconnaissance: web-to-mobile inconsistencies & vulnerabilities. In: 2018 IEEE Symposium on Security and Privacy (SP), pp. 756–769. IEEE (2018)

11. OWASP Foundation (2019). https://owasp.org/www-project-api-security/

12. Ramesh, G., Menen, A.: Automated dynamic approach for detecting ransomware using finite-state machine. Decis. Supp. Syst. **138**, 113400 (2020)

13. Song, Y.: Resrach and implementation of monitoring of monitoring oriented open API service. Ph.D. thesis, Beijing University of Posts and Telecommunications (2017)

14. StackOverflow Survey (2020). https://insights.stackoverflow.com/survey/

15. Sucuri Guides (2021). https://sucuri.net/guides/owasp-top-10-security-vulnerabilities-2021/

16. Wang, J., et al.: Understanding malicious cross-library data harvesting on android. In: 30th {USENIX} Security Symposium ({USENIX} Security 21) (2021)

17. Zhou, W., et al.: Discovering and understanding the security hazards in the interactions between iot devices, mobile apps, and clouds on smart home platforms. In: 28th {USENIX} Security Symposium ({USENIX} Security 19), pp. 1133–1150 (2019)

Smart Contract Vulnerability Detection Based on Symbolic Execution Technology

Yiping Liu$^{(\boxtimes)}$, Jie Xu, and Baojiang Cui

Department of Cyberspace Security,
Beijing University of Posts and Telecommunications, Beijing, China
linkleep@bupt.edu.cn

Abstract. With the rapid development of the blockchain, smart contract technology has been widely applied. The number of smart contracts has grown at a high rate and nearly at an average of thousands per day. However, the correctness and security of the smart contract itself are facing huge problems. The well-known DAO vulnerability, and Parity multi-signature wallet' vulnerabilities have leaded to a hundreds of millions dollars loss, and they are both caused by the security problems of smart contracts. Once the smart contract vulnerability is exploited, it is very likely to bring the loss of cryptocurrencies, the disorder of the financial order and other catastrophic consequences. Therefore the security of smart contracts is imminent. This project has designed and implemented a vulnerability detection system of Ethereum smart contract. The system uses the assembly instruction sequences of the smart contract to generate the control flow graph, then performs symbolic execution and vulnerability constraint solving over the control flow. The system can detect some common types of vulnerabilities, such as the integer overflow and underflow vulnerability, reentry vulnerability and unchecked call return value vulnerability. It has a high accuracy of detection result, and gives support for export vulnerability report.

Keywords: Ethereum · Smart contract · Control flow · Symbolic execution · Vulnerability detection

1 Introduction

With the rise of Bitcoin, blockchain technology has gradually appeared in people's vision. In April 2014, Gavin published the Yellow Paper of Ethereum [1] and the concept of smart contracts began to spread widely. Ethereum is an open source decentralized blockchain platform, mainly used for the execution of smart contracts. Smart contracts are programs deployed on the Ethereum network and executed by the Ethereum virtual machine. The Ethereum consensus protocol guarantees the fairness of contract execution.

Smart contract technology is widely used in various fields such as infrastructure, commercial retail, games, social media and communications because of its

© The Author(s) 2022
W. Lu et al. (Eds.): CNCERT 2021, CCIS 1506, pp. 193–207, 2022.
https://doi.org/10.1007/978-981-16-9229-1_12

safety, reliability, fairness, and efficiency characteristics. At the same time, the security of smart contracts is also facing huge challenges.

In June 2016, the DAO security breach broke out, which caused a loss of 60 million dollars. The first vulnerability of parity multi-signature wallet resulted in a $30 million loss, and the second vulnerability led to a freezing of $100 million. So far, the losses caused by the security issues of smart contracts have ranged from 30 million to 152 million dollars, and the upper limit number is still growing.

The security issues of smart contracts have emerged rapidly in the past two years. How to judge the correctness and security of the smart contract codes effectively has become an important direction of today's blockchain security research.

This paper analyzes the characteristics of Ethereum smart contract vulnerabilities and proposes a smart contract vulnerability detection technology based on symbolic execution and constraint solving. Experimental results show that the technology can detect common vulnerabilities in 1552 different contracts with high accuracy.

This article is mainly divided into five parts. Section 1 mainly introduces the background and summary of this article; Sect. 2 introduces related work; Sect. 3 introduces the most current types of vulnerabilities in smart contracts; Sect. 4 introduces framework design and vulnerability detection details of our system; Sect. 5 introduces the experimental results of our vulnerability detection, the last section summarizes our main contributions

2   Related Work

At present, there have been a lot of related work on smart contract vulnerability detection, and the main methods adopted are fuzzing testing, symbolic execution, formal verification and other technologies. Based on the special operating environment, life cycle and program characteristics of smart contracts, these studies have improved existing program analysis techniques to achieve better automated vulnerability mining effects.

Oyente [2] is one of the earliest researches on automated smart contract vulnerability mining. It takes smart contract bytecode as input and uses four components including CFG builder, explorer, core analysis and validator to perform CFG construction, symbolic execution, constraint solving, and false alarm filtering. Oyente can detect common types of vulnerabilities such as integer overflow vulnerabilities and stack overflow vulnerabilities of smart contracts.

Osiris [3] conducts further research and development on the basis of Oyente, using symbolic execution technology to detect integer vulnerabilities in smart contracts, mainly detailed to the types of vulnerabilities such as integer overflow, symbol conversion and so on. Compared with Osiris, Oyente pays more attention to the arithmetic operation instructions in the smart contract. At the same time, it introduces the taint analysis technology to mark the source and transfer direction of the operands, filter out invalid vulnerabilities that cannot be exploited, and improve the accuracy of the vulnerability detection results.

Echidna [4] is one of the earliest open source smart contract fuzzing solutions. It uses sophisticated grammar-based fuzzing campaigns based on a contract ABI to falsify user-defined predicates or Solidity assertions. Testers need to add specific detection code to the smart contract source code in order to judge whether there is a vulnerability based on the return status of Echidna.

Another fuzzing program, ContractFuzzer [5], is mainly aimed at smart contract vulnerability detection. It can generate fuzz test inputs according to the ABI specification of smart contracts, define test oracles for detecting security vulnerabilities. And record the run-time state of the smart contract, analyze the log and report security vulnerabilities through the Ethereum Virtual Machine (EVM) instrumentation. ContractFuzzer tools include an offline EVM instrumentation tool and an online fuzzing tool. The offline EVM instrumentation tool enables the fuzzing tool to monitor the execution of smart contracts and extract execution logs for vulnerability analysis by instrumenting the EVM.

ZEUS [6] uses formal verification methods to detect smart contract vulnerabilities. It applys abstract interpretation and symbolic execution to automate the formal verification of smart contracts. And it also uses a smart contract written in a high-level language as input and user assistance to generate a standard for the correctness and fairness of the XACML template style.

It translates these contracts and specific guidelines into a low-level intermediate representation, such as LLVM bytecode, and encodes the execution semantics to correctly infer contract behavior. Then static analysis is performed on the intermediate code to determine the predicates that must be declared for verification. Finally, ZEUS puts the modified IR into the verification engine, which uses CHCs to quickly verify the security of the smart contract.

Securify [7] also uses formal verification methods to detect the vulnerabilities of smart contracts, which can analyze whether there are vulnerabilities in smart contracts with given characteristics. Securify derives the dependency graph by analyzing the bytecode of the smart contract. Then, according to the given characteristics, it analyzes whether the semantic information of the contract satisfies or violates these characteristics and judges whether there are loopholes in the contract. The input of Securify is the bytecode of the smart contract and a series of patterns, which are described in domain-specific language. The output is the location of the specific vulnerability. Users can write patterns by themselves, so Securify is extensible.

Teether [8] uses automatic injection to detect contract vulnerabilities. It looks for critical paths in the control flow diagram of the contract, and then determines the key instructions whose parameters can be controlled by the attacker. Once a path is determined, symbolic execution is used to convert this path into a series of constraints. Using the constraint solver, you can infer what transactions the attacker must perform to trigger the vulnerability.

3 Background

3.1 Reentrancy Vulnerability

Ethereum smart contracts can call and utilize the codes of other external contracts. When the contract executes the transfer operation, if the counterparty account is a contract account, the callback function in the contract account will be called. If the called contract is a contract constructed by an attacker, there is likely to be malicious code in it. The DAO attack exploited the reentrance loopholes in the contract code, causing economic losses of up to 60 million dollars.

Figure 1 is an example of an error when you forget to check the return value.

```
1  contract EtherStore
2  {
3       uint256 public withdrawLimit = 1 ether;
4       mapping(address => uint256) public balances;
5       function depositFunds() public payable
6       {
7           balances[msg.sender] += msg.value;
8       }
9       function withdrawFunds(uint256 _weiToWithdraw) public
10      {
11          require(balances[msg.sender] >= _weiToWithdraw);
12          require(_weiToWithdraw <= withdrawLimit);
13          require(msg.sender.call.value(_weiToWithdraw)());
14          balances[msg.sender] -= _weiToWithdraw;
15      }
16 }
```

Fig. 1. An error instance of forgetting to detect the return value.

The code in line 13 can be used to transfer money to the msg.sender account, but if msg.sender is a contract account, it will call the callback function in the destination contract to perform the transfer operation. The attacker can construct a special callback function to cut off the control flow. So that the contract will continue to execute lines 11–13 of code without executing 14, then the condition of line 11 will be met forever, until the attacker takes out all the balance in the contract. Figure 2 is the attack contract constructed for this EtherStore contract. Lines 15–21 are the special callback function constructed by the attacker. When the 13th line of the EtherStore code is executed, the attack's callback function will be called, and the attack contract will call the withdrawFunds function of EtherStore when the 19th line is executed. The 14th line in EtherStore is not executed, so the 11th line still meets the conditions to achieve reentry, and continuous reentry can take out all the balance in the EtherStore contract.

```
1  import "EtherStore.sol";
2  contract Attack
3  {
4      EtherStore public etherStore;
5      constructor(address _etherStoreAddress)
6      {
7          etherStore = EtherStore(_etherStoreAddress);
8      }
9      function pwnEtherStore() public payable
10     {
11         require(msg.value >= 1 ether);
12         etherStore.depositFunds.value(1 ether)();
13         etherStore.withdrawFunds(1 ether);
14     }
15     function () payable
16     {
17         if(etherStore.balance > 1 ether)
18         {
19             etherStore.withdrawFunds(1 ether);
20         }
21     }
22 }
```

Fig. 2. An attack contract target for EtherStore contract.

3.2   Integer Overflow Vulnerability

The Ethereum Virtual Machine (EVM) specifies fixed-size data types for integers. This means that an integer variable can only be represented by a certain range of numbers, respectively (u)int8/16/24/.../256. For example, a uint8 can only store numbers in the range [0,255]. Attempting to store 256 into a uint8 will become 0. Therefore, performing calculations without checking user input can easily occur the calculation result exceeds the maximum range that the variable type can represent. This situation is called integer overflow or underflow. Integer overflow vulnerabilities can be easily exploited by attackers to perform logic processes that developers did not anticipate. Figure 3 is a contract with an integer overflow vulnerability.

If an attacker maliciously calls the increaseLockTime function to cause the lockTime variable overflowed in line 12. Then the attacker can break the time limit and call the withdraw function to successfully withdraw the account balance. Figure 4 is a contract with integer underflow vulnerability.

The balance variable on lines 11 and 12 may underflow. When the attacker does not deposit money in the contract, the value of balance is 0. Then the attacker calls the transfer function and sets _value to any positive integer, the balance-value will underflow and becomes a very large positive integer.

```
1  contract TimeLock
2  {
3      mapping(address => uint) public balances;
4      mapping(address => uint) public lockTime;
5      function deposit() public payable
6      {
7          balances[msg.sender] += msg.value;
8          lockTime[msg.sender] += now + 1 weeks;
9      }
10     function increaseLockTime(uint _seconds) public
11     {
12         lockTime[msg.sender] += _seconds;
13     }
14     function withdraw() public
15     {
16         require(balances[msg.sender] > 0);
17         require(now > lockTime[msg.sender]);
18         balances[msg.sender] = 0;
19         msg.sender.transfer(balances[msg.sender]);
20     }
21 }
```

Fig. 3. A contract with an integer overflow vulnerability

```
1  contract Token
2  {
3      mapping(address => uint) balances;
4      uint public totalSupply;
5      function Token(uint _initial)
6      {
7          balances[msg.sender] = totalSupply - _initial;
8      }
9      function transfer(address _to, uint _value) public
10 returns (bool)
11     {
12         require(balances[msg.sender] - _value >= 0);
13         balances[msg.sender] -= _value;
14         balances[_to] += _value;
15         return true;
16     }
17     function balanceOf(address _owner) public constant
18 returns (uint balance)
19     {
20         return balances[_owner];
21     }
22 }
```

Fig. 4. A contract with integer underflow vulnerability

3.3   Unchecked Call Return Value Vulnerability

Some methods in solidity can send Ether to external accounts. For example, transfer() method, send() method, call method, etc. The call() and send() functions will return a boolean value after completion. The return value is true to indicate the operation is successful, and false to indicate failure. So when the send or call function fails, the contract will not terminate execution and complete the state rollback, but will simply return false. Therefore, without checking the return value of the send or call operation, it is likely that the result of inconsistent intentions of the developer may occur. Figure 5 is an example of an error when you forget to check the return value.

```
1  contract Call_Vul
2  {
3      // ... local variables definitions
4      function withdraw(uint256 _amount) public
5      {
6          require(balances[msg.sender] >= _amount);
7          balances[msg.sender] -= _amount;
8          etherLeft -= _amount;
9          msg.sender.send(_amount);
10     }
11 }
```

Fig. 5. An error when you forget to check the return value

If the call is used to send ether to a smart contract that does not accept them (for example, because it does not have a fallback function) or a callback occurs during the call to an external smart contract, the send operation may run out of gas and cause the send to fail and return false. Since the return value is not checked in our example, even though msg.sender has not received the money, the balance in the account has decreased.

4   Vulnerability Detection Methods

In this section, we will introduce our vulnerability detection system in detail. Our system is designed to detect common types of vulnerabilities such as reentrancy vulnerability, integer overflow vulnerability, and unchecked call return value vulnerability in smart contracts. Our system uses bytecode, the address or the source code of a smart contract as input, and outputs the vulnerability detection result, including specific information such as the type and the location of the vulnerability. Figure 6 depicts the workflow of our vulnerability detection system. It mainly includes the following five modules.

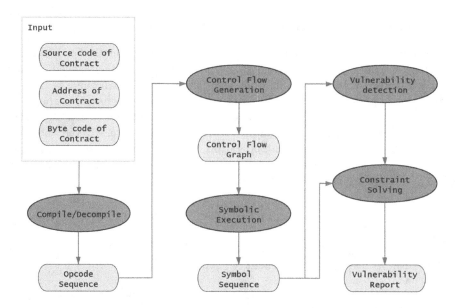

Fig. 6. Workflow of our vulnerability detection system.

Compile and Decompile. The input of the system may be solidity code or EVM bytecode, so it needs to be compiled or decompiled to generate the opcode sequence. The generated instruction sequence includes instruction offset, instruction name and instruction parameters.

Control Flow Generation. The control flow graph is composed of the basic block and the edge between them. The basic block is analyzed and constructed from the first instruction, and it is ended when *JUMP* instruction is encountered and the next basic block is generated. The basic block is ended when the *JUMPI* instruction is encountered and it will generate two basic blocks with different conditions then record the rules that the jump conditions need to meet.

Symbolic Execution. Our system constructs a virtual machine executed by the EVM bytecode and use the control flow graph in the control flow generation module to traverse all possible paths and record the possible results of each step according to Depth-First-Search principle. At the same time, the constraint conditions of each step and the operand will be transformed into the variable type of constraint solving.

Vulnerability Detection. Vulnerability detection is synchronized with the execution of the contract in the virtual machine. If a sensitive operation that may trigger the vulnerability condition is encountered during the execution, it will jump into the vulnerability detection module. The vulnerability detection module will solve the jump conditions and vulnerability status. The existence of possible explanations indicates the vulnerability may exist.

Constraint Solving. The constraint solving module provides assistance for the virtual executor module and the vulnerability detection module. It is mainly used to convert variables into z3 type variables and to solve various conditional constraints.

4.1   Control Flow Generation

The control flow generation module is used to determine all possible path conditions during program execution. The edges of the control flow graph represent each basic block in the process of program execution, and the edges between nodes represent the jump conditions between nodes. The generation of control flow graphs is not necessary in the process of symbolic execution, but generating control flow graphs can help better understand the calling relationship between programs or perform the next step of analysis. The detailed of control flow generation process is as follows:

1. After generating the opcode sequence, fetch an instruction from it.
2. Determine whether this instruction is *JUMP* or *JUMPI*.
3. If it is *JUMP*, take out the parameter which is the target address of this instruction.
4. If it is *JUMPI*, take out the parameters which include jump conditions and jump addresses.
5. If it is *CALL/CALLCODE/DELEGATECALL/STATICCALL*, you first need to set this address as the end of current node.
6. If it is *RETURN* instruction, record the offset of this instruction as the end of current node. Check whether the next instruction is the last instruction or *JUMPDST*, if not, throw an error.
7. If the instruction is *JUMPDST*, traverse all nodes to find the starting address of this *JUMPDST* instruction, and set the currently executing NodeID as the ID of this node.

4.2   Symbolic Execution

Based on the control flow graph, the symbolic execution module uses Depth-First-Search principle to execute each node in the graph, and updates the global state at the same time. When encountering a conditional jump instruction or an operand operation instruction, converted it into a variable type for constraint solving, so that the vulnerability detection module can solve the constraint for the vulnerability. The symbolic execution module is divided into three parts: the state design of the virtual machine, the instruction realization of the virtual machine and the path call of the symbolic execution.

1. State design of the virtual machine. Virtual machine of the system is modeled on the Ethereum virtual machine(EVM). After each transaction is executed, the state of the EVM, including the program counter, the stack, and account balance may change. Figure 7 is an example of the internal state transition of the virtual machine after a transaction is completed. The transition

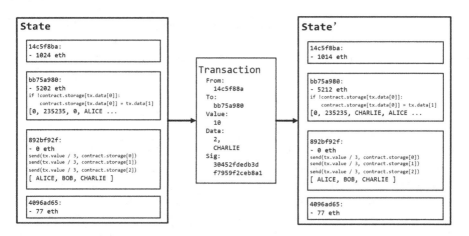

Fig. 7. An example of the EVM internal state transition after a transaction is completed.

models of these three states are implemented separately in the virtual machine we built.

2. Implementation of virtual machine instructions. The current EVM instructions have implemented a total of 142 instructions. According to the instructions of the EVM, our system has implemented 117 commonly used instructions.

3. The principle of path calling. Before symbolic execution of control flow graph, the calling principle of the path must be determined first. Here we use the Depth-First-Search principle. Differ from the general graph traversal progress, we need to save the state of this path when it is ended.

4.3 Vulnerability Detection

We will introduce the details of reentrancy vulnerability, integer overflow vulnerability and unchecked call return value vulnerability detection method separately.

Reentrancy Vulnerability Detection. The main reasons of why reentrancy vulnerabilities exist are as follows:

1. When using the *call* instruction to transfer money to a contract account, the contract's callback function will be called.
2. The *call* instruction does not restrict the use of Gas by default
3. Complete the transfer operation before reducing the user account balance.

The *call* instruction has 7 parameters, the meaning of each parameter is shown in Table 1. Considering the gas limit of the other two transfer operations *transfer* and *send* are both 2300, if the gas can be greater than 2300, it is equal

Table 1. Parameters of call instruction.

Parameter	Meaning
Gas	Gas limit
Address	Target address of the transfer operation
Value	Transfer amount
In	Input data address of the call instruction in EVM memory
Insize	Length of input data
Out	Output data address of the call instruction in EVM memory
Outsize	Length of output data

to no restriction. So we use $gas > 2300$ as a vulnerability constraint. And if the address can be equal to the malicious contract address, there may be a reentrancy vulnerability.

Integer Overflow Vulnerability Detection. Integer vulnerabilities has been widespreaded and brought a lot of loss. In EVM, there may be integer overflow operations such as *add*, *sub*, *mul*, and *div*. The detection for these four operations are shown in Table 2.

Table 2. Vulnerability detection methods for integer operation.

Op	Detection
ADD	Under the constraints of entering this node, if the sum of two operands is less than one of the operands is solved, there may be an overflow error
MUL	Under the constraints of entering this node, if the multiplication of two operands is greater than 2^{256}, there may be an overflow error
SUB	Under the constraints of entering this node, if the minuend number is greater than the subtracted one, there may be an underflow error
DIV	Under the constraints of entering this node, if the divisor can be equal to 0, there may be an underflow error

When encountering with these four instructions, *add/sub/mul/div*, enter the integer overflow detection module to perform overflow detection. Perform different functions for different operations, and if the solution result exists, add the vulnerability information to the issue.

Unchecked Call Return Value Vulnerability Detection. The correct way to write the *call* or *send* function should be:

```
1 require(msg.sender.send(value))
```

Due to the existence of require statement, if the return value of *send* is false, it will directly revert and exit. When calling *CALL/CALLCODE/ DELEGATECALL/STATICCALL* or other commands, the return value of the command is recorded and stored in a variable of z3 format. If this block is normal ended by *RETURN* or *STOP*, take out the return value of the previous *CALL/CALLCODE/DELEGATECALL/STATICCALL* instruction. If the value can be equal to 0, it means that the *send/call* operation can be failed. In addition to other operations, there may be a vulnerability that does not check the return value of *call* at this time.

4.4 Constraint Solving

The z3 solver supports all theoretical solution classifications, so we use the z3 solver here to solve the constraints of the path state. According to the parameter types in EVM, use z3 solver to realize two types of variables, they are: *Bool* and *BitVec*. *Bool* represents the Boolean type, *BitVec* is a bit array type. Generally the length is 256 bits, because EVM does not have a series of data types such as int8/int16/int24/.../int256 like *Solidity*. When this data type is converted to bytecode, it will be stored as a 256bit variable. Aiming at these two data types and using the z3 solving library function, the realization of the data operation rules is redesigned.

5   Evalution

We did a vulnerability detection experiment on 1552 contracts from awesome-buggy-erc20-tokens [9] data set, which shows 1320 contracts are detected as vulnerabilities, and the accuracy rate of the vulnerability detection is 85.1%. Figure 8 shows the vulnerability detection results.

We manually checked twenty contracts which are reported as vulnerable by our system and we think all of them have vulnerabilities. For example, the contract in 0x0b76544F6C413a555F309Bf76260d1E02377c02A[1] has no-Approval, owner-control-sell-price-for-overflow, owner-decrease-balance-by-mint-by- overflow, totalsupply-overflow and transfer-no-return issues defined by awesome-buggy-erc20-tokens. Our tool has detected an integer overflow vulnerability in this contract. Check the contract code snippets in Fig. 9, and we found line 5 does have an integer overflow problem.

---

[1] https://etherscan.io/address/0x0b76544F6C413a555F309Bf76260d1E02377c02A.

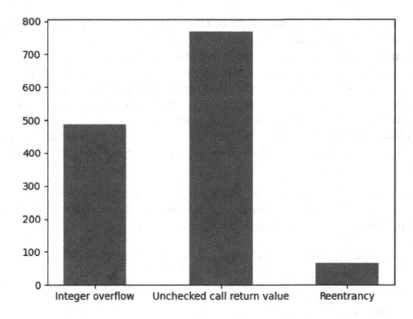

Fig. 8. Vulnerability detection results of awesome-buggy-erc20-tokens.

```
1  contract INTToken is owned, token
2  {
3      //....
4      function sell(uint256 amount) {
5          require(this.balance >= amount * sellPrice);        //
       checks if the contract has enough ether to buy
6          _transfer(msg.sender, this, amount);                //
       makes the transfers
7          msg.sender.transfer(amount * sellPrice);            //
       sends ether to the seller. It's important to do this last
       to avoid recursion attacks
8      }
9      //...
10 }
```

Fig. 9. Code snippets of 0x0b76544F6C413a555F309Bf76260d1E02377c02A

6   Conclusion

We investigate the most common contract security issues and the most widely
used smart contract vulnerability detection methods currently. Then we design
and implement a smart contract detection system. The main functions covered
by the system are as follows:

(1) **Disassembly of EVM bytecode.** Disassemble the EVM bytecode to generate an opcode sequence for specific instruction analysis in the next step.

(2) **Generation control flow graph.** Generate control flow graph of the contract to provide a basis for symbolic execution.

(3) **symbolic execution implementation.** Implementation a simple Ethereum virtual machine according to the Ethereum EVM instructions and the EVM design principle. Perform path depth-first traversal on the control flow graph, store each data as a variable in the form of z3, and use symbolic variables to represent path constraints.

(4) **Vulnerability detection.** Detect integer overflow vulnerabilities, reentrance vulnerabilities, and unchecked call return value vulnerabilities of smart contracts.

We tested the vulnerability detection system on awesome-buggy-erc20-tokens data set and analyzed the experimental results which shows our system has a good performance on the vulnerability detection accuracy.

Acknowledgments. This work is supported by CNKLSTISS and the National Natural Science Foundation of China (Grant No. 61802025).

References

1. https://ethereum.github.io/yellowpaper/paper.pdf
2. Luu, L., Chu, D.H., Olickel, H., et al.: Making smart contracts smarter. In: Proceedings of the ACM SIGSAC Conference on Computer and Communications Security, pp. 254–269 (2016). https://doi.org/10.1145/2976749.2978309
3. Torres, C.F., Schütte, J., State, R.: Osiris: hunting for integer bugs in Ethereum smart contracts. In: Proceedings of the 34th Annual Computer Security Applications Conference, pp. 664–676 (2018). https://doi.org/10.1145/3274694.3274737
4. Grieco, G., Song, W., Cygan, A., et al.: Echidna: effective, usable, and fast fuzzing for smart contracts. In: Proceedings of the 29th ACM SIGSOFT International Symposium on Software Testing and Analysis, pp. 557–560 (2018). https://doi.org/10.1145/3395363.3404366
5. Jiang, B., Liu, Y., Chan, W.K.: ContractFuzzer: fuzzing smart contracts for vulnerability detection. In: 2018 33rd IEEE/ACM International Conference on Automated Software Engineering (ASE), pp. 259–269. IEEE (2018). https://doi.org/10.1145/3238147.3238177
6. Kalra, S., Goel, S., Dhawan, M., et al.: Zeus: analyzing safety of smart contracts. In: NDSS, pp. 1–12 (2018). https://doi.org/10.14722/ndss.2018.23082
7. Tsankov, P., Dan, A., Drachsler-Cohen, D., et al.: Securify: practical security analysis of smart contracts. In: Proceedings of the ACM SIGSAC Conference on Computer and Communications Security, pp. 67–82 (2018). https://doi.org/10.1145/3243734.3243780
8. Krupp, J., Rossow, C.: teether: Gnawing at Ethereum to automatically exploit smart contracts. In: 27th USENIX Security Symposium (USENIX Security 2018), pp. 1317–1333 (2018)
9. https://github.com/search?q=awesome-buggy-erc20-tokens

Text Classification

A Multi-task Text Classification Model Based on Label Embedding Learning

Yuemei Xu[1(✉)], Zuwei Fan[2,3], and Han Cao[1]

[1] School of Information Science and Technology, Beijing Foreign Studies University,
Beijing, China
xuyuemei@bfsu.edu.cn
[2] Institute of Information Engineering, Chinese Academy of Science, Beijing, China
[3] School of Cyber Security, University of Chinese Academy of Sciences,
Beijing, China

Abstract. Different text classification tasks have specific task features and the performance of text classification algorithm is highly affected by these task-specific features. It is crucial for text classification algorithms to extract task-specific features and thus improve the performance of text classification in different text classification tasks. The existing text classification algorithms use the attention-based neural network models to capture contextualized semantic features while ignores the task-specific features. In this paper, a text classification algorithm based on label-improved attention mechanism is proposed by integrating both contextualized semantic and task-specific features. Through label embedding to learn both word vector and modified-TF-IDF matrix, the task-specific features can be extracted and then attention weights are assigned to different words according to the extracted features, so as to improve the effectiveness of the attention-based neural network models on text classification. Experiments are carried on three text classification task data sets to verify the performance of the proposed method, including a six-category question classification data set, a two-category user comment data set, and a five-category sentiment data set. Results show that the proposed method has an average increase of 3.02% and 5.85% in F1 value compared with the existing LSTMAtt and SelfAtt models.

Keywords: Text classification · Label embedding · Attention mechanism · Multi-task

1 Introduction

Thanks to the rapid development of Internet technology, text information on the Internet are explosively increased and has raised higher requirement for data

This work is supported by the Fundamental Research Funds for the Central Universities (No. 2022JJ006).

W. Lu et al. (Eds.): CNCERT 2021, CCIS 1506, pp. 211–225, 2022.
https://doi.org/10.1007/978-981-16-9229-1_13

organization and management. Text classification algorithm is one of the efficient ways to manage such huge volumes of text information, and has been applied on different scenarios, such as question classification, sentiment classification, spam detection, topic classification. Different text classification tasks own specific features. It is crucial for text classification algorithms to extract these task-specific features and to guarantee its performance on different classification tasks.

Traditional text classification mainly uses machine learning algorithms, such as logistic regression [7], decision tree [4], support vector machine [5] and naive Bayes [8]. These algorithms have achieved good performance on text classification tasks, but they require manual text features extraction, which is cumbersome and costly. What's more, the manual extraction of text feature cannot be adjusted dynamically when the text classification task changes.

Recently, with the rapid development of deep learning algorithms and models, text classification has gradually shifted from models based on machine learning to deep learning models based on neural network. The neural network models support automatic feature extraction. Therefore, it exhibits better potential in multi-task text classification than the traditional machine learning based models. For example, Kalchbrenner et al. [14] proposed a Dynamic Convolutional Neural Network (DCNN) model in 2014. It was for the first time that Convolutional Neural Networks (CNN) was applied to the field of text classification. Later, Kim proposed a simpler TextCNN model [21]. Subsequently, other neural network models, such as RNN [17], BiGRU [15], and LSTM [6], were proposed to solve the problem of CNN model, which only captures the local semantic features of the text while ignores the relationship between text sequence.

In order to extract features that are more relevant to the text classification task, attention mechanism is introduced on the basis of deep learning models [2]. The attention mechanism enables the deep learning models to focus on the words that are more relevant to the classification task through assigning more weights to the important words. It has been proved that the attention-based text classification algorithms (e.g., LSTMAtt [22], SelfAtt [9]) have achieved better performance than BiGRU and LSTM on text classification tasks. However, these attention-based text classification algorithms assign weights to different words mainly according to the text semantics, without considering the impact of task-specific features. For example, for the sentence "the food quality is decent, but the price is very steep", the objective words "decent", "steep" should be assigned more attention weight in sentiment classification task, whereas words of "food" and "price" should be assigned more weight in topic classification task. If the attention weight assignment can be dynamically adaptive to different text classification tasks, the effectiveness of text classification can be greatly improved [19].

Therefore, for the purpose of exploiting both text semantic features and task-specific features, label embedding is introduced to the existing attention-based text classification algorithm in this paper. By considering task-specific features, words and their category labels to which they belong are embedded to a joint space for attention weight learning, so that the attention weight of each word incorporates its importance according to different classification labels. In specific, a modified TF-IDF matrix generated in a supervised manner for multi-task text classification is used to incorporate category label information for text classification. Then the words having important impact on text classification are found and given greater weight, which helps greatly improve the efficiency of text classification. In order to verify the adaptive of the proposed model on different text classification tasks, experiments are conducted on 3 different data sets, including a TREC data set with six-category question classification, a CR data set with two-category customer review classification and a Stanford SST-1 data set with five-category sentiment classification. The results show that text classification performance of the proposed model is better than the existing LSTMAtt and SelfAtt methods, and the F1 value is improved by 3.02% and 5.85% on average compared with that of LSTMAtt and SelfAtt respectively. Among the three data sets, the proposed model performs in the TREC data set, improving respectively F1 values of 6.18% and 10.86% on average compared with LSTMAtt and SelfAtt.

The rest of this paper is organized as follows. Section 2 reviews a survey of the related work. Section 3 presents the proposed label embedding-based text classification model. Section 4 shows the experiment settings and the experimental results for verifying the effectiveness of our model. Finally, Sect. 5 concludes the paper.

2   Related Work and Background

2.1   Text Classification

The existing text classification research can be divided into two categories: one is traditional text classification methods based on machine learning and the other is deep learning classification methods based on neural network models.

Traditional machine learning based text classification methods need to define feature calculation rules, such as Bag-of-words model (BOW) [11], TF-IDF model [18], topic model [3] and etc., to construct text representations. The BOW model considers the text as a collection of words and constructs text representation in terms of the words that appear in the text. Therefore, the BOW model only reflects the frequency of words but cannot reflect the importance of words. Joachims et al. proposed the TF-IDF model [18]. In specific, TF refers to term frequency and if a term appears in a document more times, its TF value is higher. IDF refers to inverse document frequency and if there are fewer documents containing the term, its IDF is higher. TF-IDF model believes that when a term's TF and IDF are higher, the term is more important and has better classification ability. However, the word representations constructed in BOW or TF-IDF models are independent of each other and the contextual relationship between words and semantic information cannot be well represented. Subsequently, topic model Latent Dirichlet Allocation (LDA) was proposed [3]. LDA constructs the text representation from the perspective of the probabilistic generative model, and obtains the text-topic probability distribution and the word-topic probability distribution. The topic model solves the problem caused in the BOW and TF-IDF models, but still has the problems of high dimension and high sparseness.

After constructing the text representation, the early text classification methods used machine learning algorithms, such as logistic regression [7], decision tree [4], support vector machine [5] and naive Bayes [8] as text classifiers to classify text. These traditional classification methods achieved good results but required to construct text features manually. What's more, the text features constructed by manual extraction cannot adapt to the dynamic adjustment of text classification tasks.

The text classification methods based on deep learning methods do not need to construct the text features manually. They obtain word representations of semantic information by using word embedding models, such as static word embedding models (Word2Vec [13] and Glove [10]) and dynamic word embedding models (ELMO [16]). Then the vector representation of the text is obtained through word representations and is taken as input of neural network models, such as CNN and RNN, to predict the text category. Kalchbrenner [14] applied CNN to the field of text classification for the first time in 2014, which achieved good results. Subsequently, other neural network models, such as RNN [17], BiGRU [15], and LSTM [6], were successively proposed to solve the problem that CNN can only capture the local semantic features of text, but cannot learn sequence correlation. Among these neutral network models, LSTM has outstanding performance in text classification tasks and solves the problem of gradient vanishing and gradient explosion. LSTM adopts a gate structure to selectively let information through, therefore, it can effectively capture long-distance information and better express the contextual semantic information of the text.

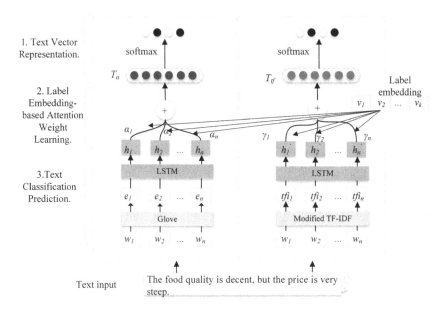

Fig. 1. Framework of the label embedding-based attention model for text classification.

2.2 Attention Mechanism

Attention mechanism was first proposed in the field of computer vision and then was introduced to deal with the machine translation task [2]. Recently, attention mechanism has been widely used in various natural language processing tasks, such as sentiment analysis, dialogue systems and text classification.

The exiting works mainly used the attention mechanism to help neural network models such as CNN and RNN select more important features For instance, the ATAE-LSTM model [20] proposed to combine the attention mechanism with LSTM model, where the attention weight was computed over the hidden layers of the LSTM by combining the aspect information. The attention mechanism in ATAE-LSTM model could concentrate on different parts of a sentence if different aspects are taken as input. Lin et al. proposed a sentence-level SelfAtt model [9], which extracted different aspects of the sentence into multiple vector representations and learned the hidden state information between these vector representations through the attention mechanism. Thus, it can extract different key information of the sentence. These existing studies show that the combination of attention mechanism and neural network model can successfully improve the effectiveness of text representation.

However, these existing text classification models mainly use the attention mechanism to learn the implicit relationship between the input and output, for the purpose of further improving the text representation. But the impact of the classification goals of different tasks, namely task categories, on the attention weight is largely ignored.

3 Methodology of Text Classification Model

3.1 Framework Overview

Figure 1 is the flowchart of the proposed label embedding-based attention model (termed as LabelAtt model). The establishment process includes 3 steps: (1) The first step is text vector representation. It is designed to obtain word embedding representation of each word in the text through both the Golve(or word2vector) model and the modified TF-IDF method. Then word vector representation of text document is generated and taken as input of LSTM model to generate the initial text vector representation. (2) The second step is jointly learning of label embedding and attention weight. This step takes the initial text vector representation and label embedding as input. The neural network model then is used to learn the attention weight of each word and output label-aware text representation. (3) The third step is text classification prediction. It takes the label-aware text representation as input and uses a fully connected layer with sigmoid activation function to predict the category of text. These 3 steps will be discussed in the following sections in detail.

3.2   Problem Statement

Let $\mathbf{s} = \{s_1, s_2, ..., s_N\}$ be a set of text documents, where s_j represents a text j and N is the total number of texts. Let y_j be the text category of s_j. s_j contains a sequence of words $\{w_1, w_2, ..., w_n\}$, where n is the number of words in s_j. The importance of words in the text classification task is learned through the attention weight mechanism. Words are assigned with different weight values according to their importance relevant to the text classification task. The greater the importance is, the more the weight value is assigned.

$\mathbf{l} = \{l_1, l_2, ..., l_K\}$ is defined as a set of category labels and K is the total number of categories in text classification tasks. The value of K is different in different text classification tasks. For instance, K equals to 6 in the six-category text classification tasks and the set of category labels can be represented as $\mathbf{l} = \{0, 1, 2, 3, 4, 5\}$. Corresponding to the category set $\mathbf{l}$, we define the category label tensor as $\mathbf{v} = \{v_1, v_2, ..., v_K\}$, where $\mathbf{v} \in \mathcal{R}^{K \times D}$ and D is the dimension of word embedding vector. $\mathbf{v}$ is initialized randomly and will be iteratively updated during model training.

3.3   Attention Learning on Word Embedding

Text documents are pre-trained by using Golve model and then the word embedding vector of each text, denoted as $\mathbf{e} = \{e_1, e_2, ..., e_n\}$, is obtained, where $e_i \in \mathcal{R}^D$ is the word embedding of word w_i and D is the dimension of word embedding vector. Furthermore, LSTM is used to pre-encode the vector representation of each text. LSTM is a special recurrent neural network and is capable to capture the long-distance information in the text sequence through the Gates structure. Therefore, the text vector obtained by LSTM encoding can better represent the sequence information and context semantics of the text. The pre-encoded vector representation is defined as the initial text vector representation $H, H \in \mathcal{R}^{n \times D}$.

Given $\mathbf{l}$ as the set of category labels, and we define $B = \{b_1, b_2, ..., b_n\}$ as the semantic attention weight matrix of $\{w_1, w_2, ..., w_n\}$, where b_i represents the attention weight of word w_i over K labels, $b_i \in \mathcal{R}^K$. Then the attention weight matrix is calculated based on the label embedding, as showed in Eq. (1).

$$B = [(\mathbf{v} \otimes H^T) \odot \hat{B}]^T \tag{1}$$

where $\hat{B}$ is the normalized matrix of B. The symbol $\odot$ represents the division of each corresponding element in the two matrices.

The max pooling operation is performed over each element b_i in B and then the maximum weight value of each words over all labels is obtained, which is considered to be the attention weight of each word w_i, calculated as:

$$\beta = \text{max\_pooling}(b_i) \tag{2}$$

Finally, $\beta = \{\beta_1, \beta_2, ..., \beta_n\}$ is normalized by a softmax function to ensure that the sum of the attention weights of all words is equal to 1, which is defined as label attention weight vector $\alpha = \{\alpha_1, \alpha_2, ..., \alpha_n\}$. The calculation is shown in Eq. (3).

$$\alpha = \text{softmax}(\beta) \tag{3}$$

Let T_α be the weighted average of α and the initial text vector representation H, calculated in Eq. (4).

$$T_\alpha = \sum_{i=1}^{n} \alpha_i \times h_i \tag{4}$$

Where α_i is the label attention weight of w_i and h_i is the initial text vector representation of w_i, $T_\alpha \in \mathcal{R}^D$.

We feed T_α into our model to predict the text classification distribution of the input text.

$$\tilde{y}_j^\alpha = \text{softmax}(T_\alpha) \tag{5}$$

where $\tilde{y}_j^\alpha$ is the text classification label of s_j predicted by our model.

The cost function is defined as the average cross entropy that measures the difference between the category label predicted by our model and the classification annotation of text s_j, calculated as:

$$f_{loss(\alpha)} = -\sum_{j=1}^{N} y_j \log \tilde{y}_j^\alpha \tag{6}$$

Where N is the number of texts in training set and y_j is the classification annotation of text s_j.

3.4 Attention Learning on Modified TF-IDF Matrix

A modified TF-IDF matrix is used to learn the importance of words for classification task and the generated TF-IDF matrix can be used to supervise the attention weight learning of each word.

TF-IDF is one of the most commonly used weighting metrics to measure the relationship of words to documents. The modified TF-IDF method proposed by Jin et al. [23] uses the known classification information of training data set to compute the weights of each word term in different text classification tasks. Each word appears in the training data set corresponds to K TF-IDF values and each value corresponds to the texts associated to one category label.

Let $\mathbf{tfi} = \{tfi_1, tfi_2, ..., tfi_n\}$ be the TF-IDF matrix of word sequence $\{w_1, w_2, ..., w_n\}$ of text s_j, $\mathbf{tfi} \in \mathcal{R}^{n \times K}$, where $tfi_i = \{tfi_{i,1}, tfi_{i,2}, ..., tfi_{i,n}\}$ represents the TF-IDF weight vector of word w_i over K category labels. Let $tf(w_i, l_k)$ be the frequency of word w_i in text category l_k, which is calculated as:

$$tf(w_i, l_k) = \frac{nw_{i,k}}{\sum_q nw_{q,k}} \tag{7}$$

where $nw_{i,k}$ is the number of word w_i occurrences in the text category l_k, and $\sum_q nw_{q,k}$ is the number of all words in the text category l_k.

Inverse document frequency is defined to eliminate the influence of common words, denoted as $idf(w_i, l_k)$ intuitively, if a word w_i has less other text category containing it, its representativeness of category l_k should be given higher value. $idf(w_i, l_k)$ is calculated as follows.

$$idf(w_i, l_k) = \log \frac{|j : s_j \in l_k|}{|k : w_i \in l_k| + 1} \tag{8}$$

where $|j : s_j \in l_k|$ is the number of texts in category l_k and $|k : w_i \in l_k|$ is the number of categories containing the word w_i. If a word doesn't appear in the training data set, the value of $|k : w_i \in l_k|$ is zero and 1 will be added to avoid zero division.

By integrating Eq. (7) and Eq. (8), we can get the TF-IDF weight vector of word w_i in category l_k as:

$$tfi_{i,k} = tf(w_i, l_k) \times idf(w_i, l_k) \tag{9}$$

For each category l_k, we repeat the above calculations as shown in Eq. (7)–Eq. (9) and then obtain the modified TF-IDF matrix. Similar with the operations in the attention learning on word embedding vector, LSTM is used to pre-encode the TF-IDF matrix and the output of LSTM is considered as the text vector representation under modified TF-IDF, denoted as TFI.

Then the initial text vector representation H in Eq. (1)–Eq. (3) is replaced by TFI. After attention weight matrix calculation, maximum pooling operation and softmax normalization, TF-IDF attention weight vector is obtained and denoted as $\gamma = \{\gamma_1, \gamma_2, ..., \gamma_n\}$.

Let T_{tf} be the weighted average of γ and TFI, which is calculated in Eq. (10).

$$T_{tf} = \sum_{i=1}^{n} \gamma_i \times tfi_i \tag{10}$$

We feed T_{tf} into our model to predict the text classification distribution of the input text.

$$\tilde{y}_j^{tf} = \text{softmax}(T_{tf}) \tag{11}$$

where $\tilde{y}_j^{tf}$ is the text classification label of s_j predicted according to T_{tf}.

Similarly, the cost function is defined as the average cross entropy that measures the difference between the category label predicted by our model and the classification annotation of text s_j, calculated as:

$$f_{loss(tf)} = -\sum_{j=1}^{N} y_j \log \tilde{y}_j^{tf} \tag{12}$$

Where N is the number of texts in training set and y_j is the classification annotation of text s_j.

In order to learn the label-aware text vector representation according to both contextual semantic and the task-specific features, the final cost function is defined as follows:

$$\text{loss} = \lambda \times f_{loss(\alpha)} + (1 - \lambda) \times f_{loss(tf)} \tag{13}$$

where λ is a tradeoff parameter ($0 \leq \lambda \leq 1$). The weight of $f_{loss(\alpha)}$ can be increased by choosing a lager value of λ.

4   Experiment Evaluation

In this section, in order to evaluate the performance of the proposed model (termed as LabelAtt) on different text classification tasks, three different datasets are selected. On each dataset, LabelAtt model is compared with two existing models, namely LSTMAtt [20] and SelfAtt [1] models, which are based on attention mechanism but without label embedding. LSTMAtt [20] and SelfAtt [1] are regarded as the baseline models to verify the effectiveness of LabelAtt on improvement of attention mechanism.

4.1   Dataset and Parameter Settings

The experiment datasets are TREC [22], Customer Review (CR) [23], and SST-1 [24]. Detailed information on these datasets is shown in Table 1.

Table 1. Information of the datasets TREC, CR and SST-1.

Dataset	Number of labels	Numbers of samples	Training set	Test set
TREC	6	5952	5452	500
CR	2	3769	2638	1131
SST-1	5	10754	8544	2210

The TREC data set is a 6-category question classification data set containing 6 labels: definition, entity, person, place, data, and abbreviation. The CR data set is a 2-category user comment data set. All the comments in this data set have been labeled either positive or negative. The SST-1 is Stanford Sentiment Treebank, a 5-category sentiment data set. The data set includes five categories of text of different levels of emotion score, and divides the score from 0 to 1:0–0.2, 0.2–0.4, 0.4–0.6, 0.6–0.8, and 0.8–1, which respectively representing very negative, negative, neutral, positive, and very positive.

The dimension of the hidden layer is 100. The dimension of the word embedding vector needs to be identical with the hidden layer, which is also equal to 100; batch size is 16; epoch is 100; The learning rate of training on TREC and CR datasets is set to 1×10^{-3}, and that of training on SST-1 dataset is set to 2×10^{-5}. The penalty term coefficient of LabelAtt and SelfAtt is 0.1, and LSTMAtt does not introduce the penalty term coefficient. In the experiment, we used Accuracy, Precision, Recall, and F1 to evaluate the performance of the classification model.

4.2 Experiment Result

The prediction accuracy of each text classification model on TREC, CR and SST-1datasets is shown in Table 2.

Table 2. Comparison of accuracy of each model on TREC, CR and SST-1 %.

	TREC	CR	SST-1
LSTMAtt	88.8	79.92	41.13
SelfAtt	86.00	78.16	35.02
LabelAtt	**92.2**	**81.96**	**43.17**

It is clear that the prediction accuracy of LabelAtt model on TREC dataset reaches 92.2%, which is much better than that of LSTMAtt model (88.8%) and SelfAtt model (86%). The performance is improved by 2.49% and 3.4% respectively. The prediction accuracy of LabelAtt model on CR dataset is 81.96%, which is about 4.9% higher than that of SelfAtt model (78.16%). The prediction accuracy of LabelAtt model on SST-1 dataset is 43.17%, which is about 23.3% higher than that of SelfAtt model (35.02%).

Table 3. Comparison of Recall, Precision and F1 of each model on three datasets (%).

	Recal			Precision			F1		
	TREC	CR	SST-1	TREC	CR	SST-1	TREC	CR	SST-1
LSTMAtt	85.46	81.97	36.42	56.16	**85.9**	13.64	65.11	83.89	19.74
SelfAtt	82.71	81.14	33.49	50.47	84.05	11.82	60.43	82.57	17.26
LabelAtt	**86.43**	**86.55**	**37.51**	**63.06**	85.36	**14.23**	**71.29**	**85.95**	**20.57**

Recall, Precision, and F1 of each text classification model on TREC, CR and SST-1 dataset are shown in Table 3 respectively. F1 is used as the comprehensive evaluation index of Recall and Precision. LabelAtt model obtained the highest F1 on the three datasets, followed by LSTMAtt model, and SelfAtt model performed the worst. Compared with LSTMAtt model, our model improves F1 by 3.02% on average on the three datasets, and the highest improvement is 6.18% on TREC dataset. Compared with SelfAtt model, F1 of our model on the three datasets has been improved by 5.85% on average, and that on TREC dataset has been improved by 10.86% at the highest. The results indicate that our model can improve the attention mechanism through label embedding, obtain text representation closer to the text classification goal, and improve the effect of text classification. Meanwhile, the applicability of our model for different classification tasks is proved by experiments on datasets of different classification tasks.

4.3   Text Classification Visualization Analysis

Visualization analysis is adopted to verify the effectiveness of LabelAtt model on text classification tasks and demonstrate the characteristics of task classification in attention weight assignment. Considering that the performance of LSTMAtt is better than that of SelfAtt, the visual analysis in this section only shows the comparison between LabelAtt model and LSTMAtt model.

In this paper, the t-SNE [12] dimension reduction method is applied to reduce the high-dimensional text representation learned by the model to two-dimensional vectors, and then a scatter plot is drawn for visualization.

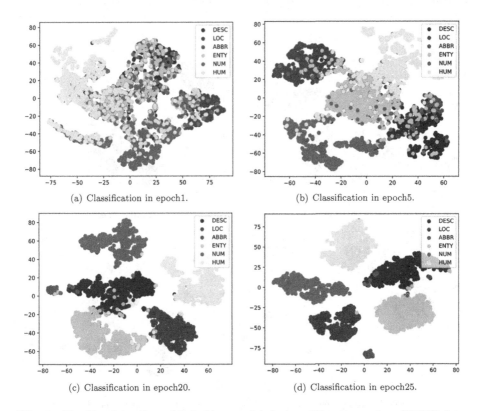

(a) Classification in epoch1.　　　　　　　(b) Classification in epoch5.

(c) Classification in epoch20.　　　　　　(d) Classification in epoch25.

Fig. 2. Classification effect of LabelAtt model during different epoches (TREC data set). (Color figure online)

Table 4. Comparison of accuracy of LabelAtt model and LSTMAtt model on TREC data set %.

	Epoch 1	Epoch 5	Epoch 20	Epoch 25
LabelAtt	0.766	0.866	0.912	0.918
LSTMAtt	0.726	0.834	0.880	0.882

Figure 2 shows the effect of LabelAtt model on text classification in TREC data set as the training times increase. For comparison, Fig. 3 shows the classification effect of LSTMAtt model in the same data set and the same training stage. As shown in Fig. 2, when the epoch is equal to 1, the text representation of LabelAtt model is in a chaotic state. With the increase of training times, when the epoch is equal to 5, the edge of each label becomes clear and clustered by color. When the epoch is equal to 20 and 25, the effect of text classification of LabelAtt model has reached a good state with relatively clear edges and few scattered points.

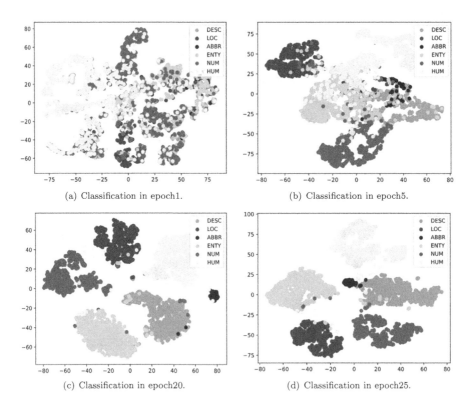

(a) Classification in epoch1.

(b) Classification in epoch5.

(c) Classification in epoch20.

(d) Classification in epoch25.

Fig. 3. Classification effect of LSTMAtt model during different epoches (TREC data set). (Color figure online)

As shown in Fig. 3, when the Epoch is equal to 1, the text representation of the LSTMAtt model is also in a chaotic state. With the increase of training times, when the Epoch is equal to 5, the edge of each label become clearer and clustered by color. When the Epoch is equal to 20, compared with LabelAtt model in Fig. 2 which the text classification effect has reached a better state, there are still more points scattered in LSTMAtt model. In order to examine the visual text classification results as shown in Fig. 2 and Fig. 3, the text classification accuracy of LabelAtt model and LSTMAtt model on the TERC data set when the Epoch is equal to 1, 5, 20 and 25 are shown in Table 4. It can be found that the accuracy of LabelAtt model is significantly higher than that of LSTMAtt model at the beginning of training. When Epoch = 1, the accuracy of LabelAtt model is 0.714 whereas the accuracy of LSTMAtt model is 0.298. With the increase of training times, t he accuracy of both LabelAtt model and LSTMAtt model gradually improves, while LabelAtt model converges faster and has higher accuracy.

The result indicates that with the increase of training times, the convergence rate of LabelAtt model is faster and the classification accuracy is higher.

5   Conclusion

In this paper, we exploit the problem of multi-task text classification and introduce a novel label embedding based model to solve the problem. With the proposed model, we could effectively (1) extract the semantic features of context and the task-specific features (2) adapt to different text classification datasets (3) improve the convergence rate of text classification. We evaluate our model on three different datasets with different classification tasks. The results show that the proposed model is effective for text classification, revealing more in-depth information and more accuracy text classification results than the state-of-the-art methods.

References

1. Akata, Z., Perronnin, F., Harchaoui, Z., Schmid, C.: Label-embedding for image classification. IEEE Trans. Pattern Anal. Mach. Intell. **38**(7), 1425–1438 (2016)
2. Bahdanau, D., Cho, K., Bengio, Y.: Neural machine translation by jointly learning to align and translate. Comput. Sci. **9**(8), 835–841 (2014)
3. Blei, D.M., Ng, A.Y., Jordan, M.I.: Latent Dirichlet allocation. J. Mach. Learn. **3**(8), 993–1022 (2012)
4. Breiman, L., Friedman, J., Olshen, R., Stone, C.: Classification and regression trees. Wadsworth. Biometrics **40**(3), 358–367 (1984)
5. Burges, C.J.: A tutorial on support vector machines for pattern recognition. Data Min. Knowl. Discov. **2**(2), 121–167 (1998)
6. Hochreiter, S., Schmidhuber, J.: Long short-term memory. Neural Comput. **9**(8), 1735–1780 (1997)
7. Ifrim, G., Bakir, G., Weikum, G.: Fast logistic regression for text categorization with variable-length n-grams. In: ACM SIGKDD, pp. 354–362. ACM (2008)

8. Kim, S.B., Han, K.S., Rim, H.C., Myaeng, S.H.: Some effective techniques for Naive Bayes text classification. IEEE Trans. Knowl. Data Eng. **18**(1), 1457–1466 (2006)
9. Lin, Z., et al.: A structured self-attentive sentence embedding. arXiv Preprint arXiv:1703.03130 (2018)
10. Liu, Y., Liu, Z., Chua, T.S., Sun, M.: Topical word embeddings. In: AAAI Conference on Artificial Intelligence, pp. 2418–2424. ACM (2015)
11. Wallach, H.M.: Topic modeling: beyond bag-of-words. In: International Conference on Machine Learning, pp. 977–984. ACM (2006)
12. Van der Maaten, L., Hinton, G.: Visualizing data using t-SNE. J. Mach. Learn. Res. **9**(11), 2579–2605 (2008)
13. Mikolov, T., Chen, K., Corrado, G., Dean, J.: Efficient estimation of word representations in vector space. arXiv Preprint, arXiv:1301.3781 (2017)
14. Kalchbrenner, N., Grefenstette, E., Blunsom, P.: A convolutional neural network for modelling sentences. In: Proceedings of the Conference 52nd Annual Meeting of the Association for Computational Linguistics, pp. 1252–1262. ACM (2014)
15. Nair, V., Hinton, G.E.: Rectified linear units improve restricted Boltzmann machines Vinod Nair. In: Proceedings of the 27th International Conference on Machine Learning, pp. 807–814. ACM (2010)
16. Peters, M.E., et al.: Deep contextualized word representations. In: Proceedings of the 2018 Conference of the North American Chapter of the Association for Computational Linguistic, vol. 3, pp. 567–577. ACM (2018)
17. Socher, R., Lin, C.C.Y., Ng, A.Y., Manning, C.D.: Parsing natural scenes and natural language with recursive neural networks. In: Proceedings of the 28th International Conference on Machine Learning (ICML), pp. 129–136. ACM (2011)
18. Joachims, T.: A probabilistic analysis of the Rocchio algorithm with Tfidf for text categorization. Computer Science Technical Report, CMU-CS-96-118 (1996)
19. Wang, G., et al.: Joint embedding of words and labels for text classification. arXiv preprint arXiv: 1805.04174 (2018)
20. Wang, Y., Huang, M., Zhu, X., Zhao, L.: Attention-based LSTM for aspect-level sentiment classification. In: Conference on Empirical Methods in Natural Language Processing, pp. 606–615. ACM (2016)
21. Chen, Y.: Convolutional neural networks for sentence classification. arXiv Preprint arXiv: 1408.5882 (2015)
22. Wang, Y., Huang, M., Zhu, X., Zhao, L.: Attention-based LSTM for aspect-level sentiment classification. In: Proceedings of the 2016 Conference on Empirical Methods in Natural Language Processing, pp. 606–615. IEEE (2016)
23. Jin, Z., Lai, X., Cao, J.: Multi-label sentiment analysis base on BERT with modified TD-IDF. In: International Symposium on Product Compliance Engineering-Asia, pp. 865–871. IEEE (2020)
24. Richard, S., Alex, P., Jean, Y.W., et al.: Stanford Sentiment Treebank dataset. http://nlp.stanford.edu/sentiment

A Review of Machine Learning Algorithms for Text Classification

Ruiguang Li[1,2(✉)], Ming Liu[2], Dawei Xu[1,3], Jiaqi Gao[3], Fudong Wu[3], and Liehuang Zhu[1]

[1] School of Cyberspace Science and Technology, Beijing Institute of Technology, Beijing, China
lrg@cert.org.cn
[2] National Computer Network Emergency Response
Technical Team/Coordination Center of China, Beijing, China
[3] Changchun University, Changchun, China

Abstract. Text classification is a basic task in the field of natural language processing, and it is a basic technology for information retrieval, questioning and answering system, emotion analysis and other advanced tasks. It is one of the earliest application of machine learning algorithm, and has achieved good results. In this paper, we made a review of the traditional and state-of-the-art machine learning algorithms for text classification, such as Naive Bayes, Supporting Vector Machine, Decision Tree, K Nearest Neighbor, Random Forest and neural networks. Then, we discussed the advantages and disadvantages of all kinds of machine learning algorithms in depth. Finally, we made a summary that neural networks and deep learning will become the main research topic in the future.

Keywords: Natural language processing · Text classification · Machine learning · Neural network

Text classification is a basic task in the field of natural language processing. It is a process of extracting the key elements of sentences, judging the authors' views, intentions and emotions of the sentences. It is the basis of information retrieval, questioning and answering system, emotion analysis and other advanced tasks. It can be said that text classification technology is the basic technology of natural language processing and social network analyzing, which will be beneficial to information discovery, public opinion analysis in the web space.

Text classification is the earliest application of machine learning algorithm, and has achieved good results. In addition to the traditional methods based on statistical analysis such as Naive Bayes, Supporting Vector Machine and so on, neural networks and deep learning algorithms have also been widely used in the field of text analysis in recent years. Therefore, a comprehensive study and review of machine learning algorithms in the field of text classification is very valuable for academic research and engineering development.

W. Lu et al. (Eds.): CNCERT 2021, CCIS 1506, pp. 226–234, 2022.
https://doi.org/10.1007/978-981-16-9229-1_14

1 Introduction

Machine learning mainly studies how to learn unknown rules from given data, that is, to find some objective rules from observed data (samples), and use the learned rules (models) to analyze and predict irregular data or unknown events. The following figure illustrates the application principle of machine learning algorithm in text classification (Fig. 1).

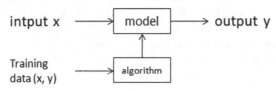

Fig. 1. Principle of text classification

As is shown in the above figure, the input is "x", and the output is "y". Through the model's processing, we got expected results from the irregular data. The "model" is previously trained by the "data (x, y)". That is the basic procedure of processing text content by machine learning algorithms.

At present, the main machine learning method is to conduct statistical analysis on the existing marked data, by which we can find laws and obtain models. Using these trained models, we can make prediction and analysis on unknown data to obtain classification results. Text classification algorithm based on machine learning is usually divided into four steps:

1) Features extracting and document modeling. Feature extracting is a very important task in machine learning. The traditional feature extraction method is usually manual extraction, the manual feature engineering is time-consuming, and the feature dimension is too large and the efficiency is low. In order to solve these problems, features extracted by traditional methods are usually dimensionality reduced, and a subset of features that can best represent text information and achieve the best classification effect are selected among all features.

2) Training the model. The machine learning model is trained by training data sets, and the labeling quality of training data sets has a great influence on the actual classification effect. Compared with the traditional machine learning algorithm based on statistics, deep learning has excellent feature learning ability, and the features acquired by learning have more essential characterization ability on data, which is conducive to visualization and classification.

3) Classifying the test text. Input the text data to be classified to the model, the classifier will judge the text data according to the learned rules, and give the classification result.

4) Evaluating the classification effect. After the completion of text classification, it is necessary to verify the quality of the classifier with some quantitative indicators, such as accuracy, recall rate and F measurement. The accuracy rate refers to the proportion

of samples with positive classification results that are truly positive; the recall rate refers to how many samples of all positive classes can be correctly classified by the classifier; the measurement value of F is the geometric average of the accuracy rate and recall rate.

2 Principles of Machine Learning Algorithms

We made a review of the traditional and state-of-the-art machine learning algorithms for text classification including Naive Bayes, Supporting Vector Machine, Decision Tree, K Nearest Neighbor, Random Forest and neural networks, and so on. We introduce the principles of various machine learning algorithms, and discuss the advantages and disadvantages in depth.

2.1 Naive Bayes

Naive Bayes Classifier is a common statistical classification algorithm, which classifies input samples based on Bayes' theorem and the independence of the eigenvector elements.

Its working principle is as follows [1]: First, text vector is generated from the text to be classified, that is, text vector of document x is constructed based on a given dictionary, where n is the number of elements in dictionary set W, and represents the number of occurrences in document d.

$$W = \{w_1, w_2, \cdots, w_n\}$$

$$X = \{x_1, x_2, \cdots, x_n\}$$

Given the training data, the classification vector indicates that the text can be divided into m classes.

$$D = \{d_1, d_2, \cdots, d_m\}$$

$$Y = \{y_1, y_2, \cdots, y_m\}$$

D is used to train the naive bayesian algorithm. On this basis, the classification with the maximum probability is to solve argmaxP:

$$\text{argmax}P(y_j|X)$$

According to bayes' theorem,

$$P(y_j|X) = \frac{P(y_j)P(X|y_j)}{P(X)} = \frac{P(y_j)\prod_{i=1}^{n}P(x_i|y_j)}{\prod_{i=1}^{n}P(x_i)}$$

From the given training data $D = \{d_1, d_2, \cdots, d_m\}$, we can calculate $P(y_j)$, and each $P(x_i)$. So, for the new input data X, we can calculate all $P(y_j|X)$, in which the highest probability value is the classification result of document X.

The naive bayes algorithm assumes that the attributes of the data set are independent from each other, so the logic of the algorithm is very simple. And the algorithm is relatively stable. When the data show different characteristics, the classification performance of the naive bayes will not have much difference. In other words, the simplicity bayes algorithm is relatively robust and will not show too much difference for different types of data sets.

2.2 Supporting Vector Machine (SVM)

Supporting Vector Machine is a new statistical classification algorithm proposed by Vapnik and his team at Bell Labs in 1995, which is mainly used to solve binary classification problems. The basic idea is to find a hyper-plane in the sample feature space, which can divide all the sample data well and make the distance between the sample point and the hyper-plane maximum.

Its working principle is as follows [2]: Text vector is also generated from the text to be classified, that is, the text vector of document x is constructed based on the given dictionary, where n is the number of elements in the dictionary set W, and x_i represents the number of x_i occurrences in document d.

$$W = \{w_1, w_2, \cdots, w_n\}$$

$$X = \{x_1, x_2, \cdots, x_n\}$$

The classification vector $Y = \{y_1, y_2, \cdots, y_m\}$, where $y_i \in \{-1, 1\}$ respectively represents the negative class and the positive class in the dichotomy.

$$Y = \{y_1, y_2, \cdots, y_m\} \, y_i \in \{-1, 1\}$$

Assuming that there is a decision boundary in the characteristic space of the input sample data, all sample points can be separated by a hyper-plane according to positive class and negative class, and the distance between any sample point and the plane is greater than 1, then the classification problem is said to be linearly separable.

The Decision boundary:

$$w^T X + b = 0$$

Point to plane short:

$$y_i \left(w^T X_i + b \right) \geq 1$$

In the following figure, the solid line in the figure is the hyper-plane $w^T X + b = 0$, and w and b are the normal vector and intercept of the hyper-plane respectively. The solid red dot constructs the upper interval boundary $(w^T X_i + b) \geq 1$, the hollow red dot constructs the lower interval boundary $(w^T X_i + b) \leq -1$, the distance between the two interval boundaries $d = \frac{2}{\|w\|}$. The positive class and the negative class samples on the interval boundary are the support vectors (Fig. 2).

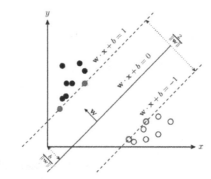

Fig. 2. Principle of supporting vector machine

The Supporting Vector Machine classification algorithm has good generalization ability and learning ability [3]. It aims at minimizing structural risk, and the solution obtained is the global optimal solution. This algorithm overcomes the problem of "dimension disaster". It is widely used in text automatic classification, face recognition, gene expression, handwriting recognition and other fields.

2.3 Decision Tree

Decision tree is a method to classify texts by constructing a tree-like decision system on the basis of known probabilities. Because the branch of the decision system is drawn like the branches of a tree, it is called Decision Tree. The processing of decision tree algorithm can be divided into three steps: Feature selection, Decision tree generation and Pruning:

1) Feature selection: Feature selection refers to the selection of some features from text vectors as the decision basis. These features will affect the branch shape of the decision tree and have an important impact on the classification results.
2) Decision tree generation: This step is the main decision process. The root node is a specific word sequence, that is, there is only one word, which has the best classification error rate among all words and the highest probability for a certain category. The subsequent child nodes are divided into left and right sub-trees according to the above decision. If the coefficient is not zero or the word sequence has no child sequence, the decision will stop; if it is not zero and not unique, the decision will continue in the possible category.
3) Pruning: The decision tree will form a very large tree-like system according to all the training samples, which has a high accuracy in the training samples and a poor accuracy in the test samples, forming a phenomenon of over fitting. The solution of the over-fitting phenomenon requires manual observation and debugging, observation and control of the size of the decision tree at each layer, setting the number of samples of the smallest leaf node, adjusting the minimum weight of the leaf node, etc.

2.4   KNN (K-Nearest Neighbor)

KNN is one of the simplest classification algorithms, but it is also one of the most commonly used classification algorithms [4]. KNN algorithm is a supervised classification algorithm, which is similar to another machine learning algorithm "K-means". KNN (K-nearest neighbor) algorithm is to find K texts in the training set that are most similar to the target text according to the known data category and the text to be tested, and then score the candidate category according to K samples.

The advantage of KNN algorithm is that it is simple and easy to use. Compared with other algorithms, KNN is a relatively simple and clear algorithm. Even without a high mathematical foundation, we can find out its principle. The model has fast training time and good prediction effect. The disadvantage of KNN algorithm is that it requires high memory, because it stores all training data, the prediction stage may be very slow, and it is sensitive to irrelevant functions and data scale.

2.5   Random Forest

Random forest is a classifier that contains multiple decision trees, and the classification results of its output are determined by the number of votes of all the output results of the tree. By means of integration, the random forest integrates multiple trees together. Its basic unit is the decision tree, and each decision tree is a classifier. For an input sample, N trees will have N classification results. The random forest integrates all the classification voting results and specifies the category with the most votes as the final output. This is the simplest Bagging idea. The principle of random forest is:

1) N is used to represent the number of training cases (samples), and M is used to represent the number of features.
2) The number of input features m is used to determine the decision result of a node in the decision tree; Where m should be much less than m.
3) A training set (i.e., bootstrap sampling) was formed by sampling N times from N training cases (samples), and the prediction was made with the unselected use cases (samples) to evaluate the error.
4) For each node, m features are randomly selected, and the decision of each node in the decision tree is determined based on these features. According to these m characteristics, the optimal splitting mode is calculated.
5) Each tree will grow intact without pruning, which may be adopted after the construction of a normal tree classifier.

2.6   Neural Network

Neural network is an adaptive nonlinear dynamic network system composed of a large number of neurons connected with each other. The classifier establishes a neural network for each category document, inputs feature word vector, and finally outputs text category after repeated learning.

At present, CNN (Convolutional Neural Network) and RNN (Recursive Neural Network) are two important components of deep learning [5]. CNN based on convolution is good at identifying the structure of the target task, while RNN has advantages in sequence recognition modeling due to its memory function. For natural language processing tasks, CNN and RNN have their own advantages. In 2014, Kim proposed the Text CNN algorithm for text classification based on CNN, applied the convolutional neural network to the text classification task, used the convolution kernel with different channel number and different size to extract the key information in the sentence (similar to n-gram with multi-window size), and could better capture the local correlation. However, Text CNN can only extract sentence features in a limited window, and cannot consider the long distance dependence on information and word order information, so it will lose some semantic information. RNN is characterized by automatic learning and memory of text sequence features, and has achieved great success in text processing in natural language processing.

Both short-term and long-term memory network (LSTM) is a kind of special used for time series data of network [6], the traditional RNN neural networks of neurons is after applying input function to calculate the output of the unit, and LSTM will neurons into the memory unit, each memory unit door to door, forgotten by the input and output, the LSTM this one design solved the RNN gradient disappeared and gradient explosion problems of the network. Bidirectional LSTM (BiLSTM) USES two LSTM networks to process the sequence from front to back, which can extract the context information of the sequence more comprehensively, thus making the classification effect better.

3 Comparative Study of the Machine Learning Algorithms

The Naive Bayesian algorithm assumes that attributes are independent from each other, which is often not true in practical applications, which has some influence on the correct classification of NBC model. When the relation between attributes of data set is relatively independent, the Naive Bayesian classification algorithm will have better effect. However, when the independence of attributes of data sets is difficult to satisfy in many cases, because the attributes of data sets are often correlated with each other, the classification effect will be greatly reduced.

Support vector machine (SVM) in tackling small sample, nonlinear and high dimension data is a great advantage, but it also has disadvantages: limited to small cluster sample, can only handle the second class classification problem, for many classification problem to solve the effect is not good, and in dealing with a specific classification problem to select the correct effective kernel function, in turn, affects the efficiency of classifier.

The Decision Tree classifier has the following disadvantages: it is difficult to predict the continuous fields; For the data with time sequence, it needs a lot of preprocessing. Errors may increase more quickly when there are too many categories; General algorithm classification, just according to a field to classify, accuracy is not enough.

The main shortcomings of KNN algorithm are as follows: first, when the samples are unbalanced, for example, the samples of one class are large, while the samples of other classes are small. As the samples of K neighbors of the new sample are large in size, it may lead to classification errors. Second, the algorithm is computationally intensive, because for each text to be classified, the distance from it to all known samples must be calculated to obtain its K nearest neighbor points.

The advantage of random forest algorithm is high accuracy. Because the integrated algorithm is adopted, its accuracy is better than most single algorithms, so it has high accuracy, especially in the test set. Due to the introduction of two random elements, the random forest is not easy to fall into over fitting. The disadvantage of random forest algorithm is that when there are many decision trees in random forest, the space and time required for training will be large. In addition, there are many unexplainable places in the random forest, which is a bit of a black box model. On some noisy sample sets, the random forest model is easy to fall into over fitting.

The neural network classifier has a high prediction accuracy and certain parallel processing and learning capabilities. It also has strong robustness and fault tolerance against noise. But the neural network requires a large number of parameters, long learning time, large runtime resource consumption, and low interpretability of output results.

4 Conclusion

This paper discusses various machine learning algorithms, including Naive Bayes, Support Vector Machines, KNN algorithm, Decision Tree algorithm, Random Forest, Neural Network model and Deep Learning model. In general, these methods have been widely studied and applied, and have achieved good practical results. In practice, the suitable algorithm can be selected flexibly according to the advantages and disadvantages of various algorithms and the actual situation of the text data to be classified.

In general, the machine learning algorithm based on neural network is the main research direction in the future due to the traditional machine learning algorithm based on statistical theory in the aspects of feature automatic learning, classification accuracy, operation robustness and fault tolerance.

Acknowledgement. This work was supported by the National Natural Science Foundation of China under Grant U2003206 and 62106060.

References

1. Liu, Y.: The application of naive bayes in text classification preprocessing. Comput. Inf. Technol. (2010)
2. Zhang, X.: The summary of text classification based on support vector machines. Sci. Technol. Inf. (2008)
3. Zhao, D.: Research on the vector space model based text automatic classification system. Int. J. Digit. Content Technol. Appl. **7**(3), 381–388 (2013)
4. Zhou, Y., Li, Y., Xia, S.: An improved KNN text classification algorithm based on clustering. J. Comput. **4**(3) (2009)
5. Zhou, Y., Chen, S., Wang, Y., et al.: Review of research on lightweight convolutional neural networks. In: 2020 IEEE 5th Information Technology and Mechatronics Engineering Conference (ITOEC). IEEE (2020)
6. Niu, S., Chai, X., Deqi, L.I., et al.: A text classification algorithm based on neural network and LDA. Comput. Eng. (2019)

Author Index

Printed in the United States
by Baker & Taylor Publisher Services